THE STONES THAT GROUND THE CORN

The
Stones that Ground
the Corn

The story of an
Irish country grain mill
1850–2000

TONY DEESON
et al

EDITED BY RICHARD SCOTT

ULSTER HISTORICAL
FOUNDATION

Dedicated to our customers
during 150 years a-milling,
without whom
there would be no story to tell

The title of this book is inspired by W.F. Marshall's poem,
'The Centenarian', which he wrote in 1950 to celebrate the centenary of
Scotts' foundation. The poem is reproduced in full on pages 76–77;
the relevant verse is as follows:

But I think no shame of my wooden wheel,
　　Or the past I've long outgrown,
For the wheel went round and the corn was ground,
　　And so I served Tyrone:
And I made the meal, good oaten meal
　　From the day that I was born,
With a wooden wheel and the wheen of wheels
　　And the stones that ground the corn.

Published 2002
by the Ulster Historical Foundation
12 College Square East, Belfast, BT1 6DD
www.ancestryireland.com

Printed by Betaprint
Design and production, Dunbar Design

HARDBACK ISBN 1-903688-29-9
SOFTBACK ISBN 1-903688-27-2

Contents

Acknowledgements

AS THIS IS A HISTORY OF A FAMILY'S six-generation involvement in W & C Scott's milling enterprise, it is not surprising that today's members of the family should be first and foremost in my mind. In pride of place I must state my particular gratitude to Richard Scott. The phrase, 'without whose help this book could never have been written', has become somewhat trite through overuse, but in this case it is very near the truth – at any rate it would have taken years rather than months to complete. He was tireless in producing documents and records from the company's archives as well as giving explicit information about the many years of his active association with the company and particularly of the period when he was chairman and managing director. I wish to thank him, too, for his organisation of my visit to Northern Ireland when he saw to it that I obtained a great deal of information in a very short time. It would be ungracious to say the least if I did not also thank his wife, Shirley, who did so much to ensure that I was well fed and looked after during my visit, even inviting me to smoke my smelly old pipe in her new and pristine house!

My grateful thanks are also due to Robert and David Scott and William McAusland for their information about the mill as it is today and their plans for its future. And to Rosemary Duncan (née Scott) for her very clear memories of the mill as it was nearly 60 years ago.

Then there are the past generations of Scotts who have made significant contributions to my knowledge of the business as it was many years ago: Margaret Scott, the wife of Charles Scott; Lewis Scott, who wrote a very full description of the mill in the early part of the last century; Maddin Scott, who took over from Lewis at very short notice at the beginning of the 1920s; and Walford Scott Green, who was chairman for so many years. Their recollections are contained in *A Hundred Years A-Milling*, which was edited by Maddin Scott, and *From Country Mill to County Millers* by Walford Scott Green. I have also made use of material by Professor R.L. Marshall, the Reverend W.F. Marshall, Florence Irwin, W.K. Ellis, E.O. Byrne, David McClelland, Mat Mulcaghey (pen-name of Wilson Guy) and Felicity Walton, all of whose contributions appeared in the first of these books.

Then I am greatly indebted to the present directors for their help. I have already mentioned Robert and David Scott and William McAusland, but I should also like to thank Fred Charters, Siobhan Kelly, David Garrett and Desmond Given, who all contributed information relating to their various areas of expertise within the company. Roy Howard retired from the board a few years ago but I am most grateful to him for his information about technical developments within the mill over the past 30 years.

Members of the 'family round the mill' have also made their contributions by describing life as it was in the mill when they were young. I am grateful to Willie Graham, Jim Orr, Anna Orr (née Jamieson), Roisín Orr, Herbie Cockburn, Paddy McBride, Tommy Ewing, Noel Mitchell, Andy Monteith and Eddie McAleer for their reminiscences.

Richard Scott would wish me also to acknowledge the assistance of Jim Reed, of UKASTA, Doris Leeman, of NIGTA, and Diane Montague, author of *Farming, Food and Politics – The Merchant's Tale*, (IAWS Group, Dublin, 2000) for refreshing and correcting his recollection of trade events over the past quarter-century or so. He hastens to add that the interpretation of such material is his responsibility alone.

Dr Haldane Mitchell, local historian, has generously provided images of people and events in the mill's history.

In the course of my research I have consulted the following newspapers and journals: *Northern Whig, Tyrone Constitution, Parliamentary Gazetteer of 1846, Economic Journal, Ulster Herald, The Times Literary Supplement, Milling* and *Feed Compounder*, as well as a variety of bulletins issued by UKASTA and history leaflets and general information from Omagh District Council.

The following books provided background information:

- L. M. Cullen, *An Economic History of Ireland since 1660* (Cork, 1978).
- L. Kennedy and P. Ollerenshaw (eds), *An Economic History of Ulster 1820–1939* (Manchester, 1985), especially D. S. Johnson, 'The Northern Ireland Economy 1914–1939'
- *The History of Ireland* (Mann)
- J. Mokyr, *Why Ireland Starved: a quantitative and analytical history of the Irish economy 1800–1850* (London, 1983)
- J. O'Connor, *History of Ireland, 1798–1924* (London, 1925)
- C. Ó Gráda, *Ireland: A New Economic History 1780–1937* (Oxford, 1994)
- *Irish Population, Economy and Society: essays in honour of the late K.H. Connell* (Oxford, 1981)
- H. Shearman, *Ulster* (London, 1949)
- *Encyclopaedia Britannica* 1911, 1956 and 1999 editions, the last being on CD.

I also place on record my gratitude to the librarians of the University of Kent, who directed me to most of the books mentioned in this paragraph.

TONY DEESON

Foreword

BENEDICT KIELY

Thrice happy and blest were the days of my childhood,
And happy the hours I wandered from school,
By Mountjoy's green forest, our dear native wildwood,
And the green flowery banks of the serpentine Strule ...

I COULD SING THAT IF I HAD THE MUSIC with me. Yet the music is in my ears and in my memory, if not, any longer, in my aged mouth. One part of the music is the sound of the running water of young streams surfacing and mingling in the lovely land below Pigeon Top Mountain and Porter's Bridge and Cavanacaw and Clanabogan, and aiming their combined force at the town of Omagh, the Virgin Plain. Clanabogan lies between Omagh and the village of Dromore, close to which I came into the world at a place called Drumskinney. It was all my world, as the great town was to become. I bow before it. And quote with reverence the words of the Reverend W. F. Marshall of Sixmilecross:

There's many a river I have found enchanting,
  There's many a stream where I have joyed to be:
The tuneful Mourne with melody so haunting,
  The gracious Strule that is so fair to see:
Camowen in its loveliness at Cranny,

The wee Glenelly rushing after rain,
  Yet still for me the loveliest of any
    Is that bright burn that flows in Ballintrain.

Resounding and musical and moving, even if other men might have other preferences in streams or burns or laughing waters. Myself I might think first and before all others of the Killyclogher Burn that comes down from Glenhordial in the mountains to meet the Camowen and mingle ultimately into the mighty Strule. A famous answer to questions as to where you had been and what you had been doing was: 'Catching minnows in the Killyclogher Burn'.

Which you will find in a song, written and composed by a most remarkable man, Frank McCrory, related to me through my sister Eileen, both of them now gone into eternity. Frank was renowned as a man of music, on violin and piano and cello and clarinet and, perhaps also, on the ocarina: and, also, as the man who kept St Eugene's Brass and Reed band going for years. He had also been a famous footballer in the days of Omagh Wanderers. He was a senior postal official, and a man with a fine library who loaned generously and wisely to a bookish young relative. It is always possible for me to switch back the clock and sit with him among his books in his fine house on the hill where the road rises out of Omagh and heads on for Lough Muck and Clanabogan and Dromore:

Sealion and sharks, alligators and whales
  With mouths that would swallow a truck.
Oh the sights that we saw as we waited for death
  On the treacherous waves of Lough Muck.

A comic song about what, in spite of the odd name which comes, without translation, from the Irish, is a handsome and sunny sheet of water: where, in my time, I have swum and caught good fish.

But come with me now back to the town and the noble name of Scott. Walk up the High Street, climb up the Courthouse Hill and up the Courthouse steps, and swing around and survey the splendid town all the way over Campsie Bridge to the Swinging Bars and the lands beyond.

To quote from the writings of local historian W. K. Ellis:

The Courthouse built on the site of the Old Gaol, between 1814 and 1822 (of stones from the quarries of Kirlish, eight miles distant), with its Doric columns and the royal arms above the architrave, on the top of the hill facing down the High Street, is the most imposing building in the town and lends an air of dignity which would otherwise be lacking … It was in this gaol on the 26th of August, 1873, that Thomas Hartley Montgomery was executed on the morning after a wild and stormy night for the murder of Mr Glass at Newtownstewart.

With the help of a careful record kept by the Scotts to commemorate and bring back to life a hundred years spent a-milling, I walk again in the town that made me: turning one of two corners of the great Courthouse where the road widened into an open space once called the Diamond, but later changed to George Street. It led on to the Derry Road passing down Castle Street and Abbey Street, 'but in those days known as Dry Bridge Street, which would lead one to suppose that the Brook, so clearly marked on the old maps, had become a mere drain'.

It is hard to walk around these ancient and, you could say, hallowed places without being moved and gratified by memories of ancient customs. To recall for instance that the hostler who placed the skid under the wheel of the judge's carriage going down the Courthouse Hill received a half-sovereign for his pains.

But looking down from the top of those Courthouse steps the good true Omey Boy always felt that he owned the world. And still feels that way. The descent must be slow and careful and dignified. Here to my left are the RUC. What names do I remember: Gilroy and Cox and Muirhead. And here is the Munster and Leinster Bank where my father worked and loved it with its long and lovely garden that stepped down to the handsome Strule. My father, who had in his time walked round South Africa, always thought that the walk down that garden brought him halfways to Heaven.

And here is the place where I once stood out on a stage and recited to a Townhall, full of people, the many many verses of that fine narrative poem: 'The Man From God Knows Where':

> Into our townland on a night of snow
>   Rode a man from God Knows Where.
> None of us bade him stay or go,
>   Or deemed him friend or damned him foe,
> But we stabled his big roan mare.
>   For in our townland we're decent folk,
> And if he didn't speak, why none of us spoke,
>   And we sat 'til the fire burned low.

And on and on and on. Did I have it right there, so far?

That great effort was undertaken under the suasion of a Christian Brother, J.D. Hamill, a Belfastman who had been to China and who pronounced Hong Kong as if bells were ringing. His brother in the flesh was Mickey Hamill who had a pub in Belfast called The Centrehalf and who had been himself a centrehalf for Belfast Celtic. That good and great centrehalf visited his brother's pupils on one splendid sunny day and shook hands with every one of us.

Then one became positively part of the Townhall by being asked to join the Omagh Players under the leadership and guidance of F.J. Nugent, Gerry

Mullen, Paddy McAlinney and others; and in several plays. The one that stays most in my memory is *The Coming of the Magi*, a play in verse by the poet, Padraic Gregory. He came down from Belfast to talk to us, and I can still see his sharp and sensitive face, his mane of snow-white hair, his Chestertonian outer garment; and as I was pretending to be one of the Magi I was privileged to sit close to him at our meetings. That was the only time I was ever privileged to utter words of wisdom, which gave rise to gentle mockery among my contemporaries of a character called Benny the Magi. But the nickname like the wisdom did not last.

Slowly, and in the most gentle fashion, I continue my dignified descent of this portion of the High Street. And here is the Post Office where I was employed for a while under the title of Sorting Clerk and Telegraphist. Wasn't there long enough to acquire the skill to telegraph anything. But in the great sorting-office I did work among friendly and lovable people and acquired there a vast and musical repertoire of the placenames of the surrounding countryside: Aghee-Dunwish, Aughanamerigan, and on and on. My friend and fellow-worker, Elwood Grier, used to sing them and some years later W.F. Marshall committed townland names to verse in 'Tyrone Jigs', from which poem here is a couple of stanzas:

> There's CAVANAMARA and dark DERRYMEEN,
>   There's CARRICKATANE and MUNDERRYDOE,
> With STRAWLETTERDALLAN and CAVANKILGREEN
>   All dancing a jig with CREGGANCONROE.
> Oh there's CURRAGHMACALL and BOMACATALL
>   And MULLAGHSHANTULLAGH and bright GORTICRUM,
> While merrily tripping and up and down dipping
>   Are SANAGHANROE and FERNAGHANDRUM.
>
> SANAGHANROE and FERNAGHANDRUM,
>   Where is the like from the MOY to the PLUM?
> A fiddler could play it, a lilter could hum
>   SANAGHANROE and FERNAGHANDRUM!

But here my gentle descent has ended. I am turning Bridge Street corner and stepping towards Scotts' Mills. Every house I pass has its memories of people who were important to me and became a vivid part of my life and memories. Over there now in the house of McSorleys lived Anthony Shannon, one of the great men who did their best to educate me in secondary school. He married a beautiful Miss Minjoe McSorley and became as much a part of Omagh as he had ever been of Derry. Around him gather, as I walk, the impressive spirit-figures of other teachers and their pupils, my friends and companions.

Shannon's memories of his student days in Dublin were vivid. His senior, the great M.J. Curry, was a Clareman to begin with, but had been to university in England and could talk most eloquently on all authors from Cicero to Bret Harte. Frank McLaughlin came from Cork and Leo Sullivan from Wexford. But both of them, one a classicist, the other a scientist, were totally devoted to the Tyrone countryside. And there were other notables. In the pulpit of the Sacred Heart Church was Dr John McShane who studied in Rome and talked in friendship with Gabriele D'Annunzio. There was Father Lagan who was related to the famous family, in the town of Dr Barney Lagan, another Chestertonian figure of a man with fine sons: Aidan, Hassan, John, all eventually to become doctors also.

There was the Reverend Dr Gallagher, and Father MacBride and Father McGilligan. And in Killyclogher parish on the Camowen River there was Father Paul McKenna who could forever, and copiously and accurately, quote Robert Burns and who brought me one day out to Mountfield to meet the aged poetess, Alice Milligan.

Alice lived in a fine old house that had once been the Mountfield Rectory. Where the Rector now reposed I never found out but his former residence stood up, solid and dignified and Paul and myself respectfully advanced, and eager I was to meet the great lady-poet who had mingled with the best: Yeats and all. We hammered on the door. No bells here, and Paul shouted so as to be heard at the top of Mullaghcarn: 'Alice, where art thou?' And the door opened and peat-smelling smoke came out like an ocean. No poetess to be seen. What had simply happened was that the jackdaws had got to the old chimney before we got to the old Rectory and had made in their clattering to settle to build up the old chimney and keep the dear poetess in the warm gloom. Perhaps it was a fondness for her poetry that made them keep her in that heavenly corner. For it was heavenly and is there not smoke in Heaven?

While Paul and herself talked I was quoting to myself until Paul, who knew my tricks, asked me to come it out loud. And I obeyed:

> To hear of a night in March,
>   And loyal folk waiting,
> To see a great army of men
>   Come devastating –
>
> An army of papists grim,
>   With a green flag o'er them,
> Red coats and black police
>   Flying before them.
>
> But God (who our nurse declared
>   Guards British dominions)
> Sent down a deep fall of snow
>   And scattered the Fenians …

But one little rebel there,
   Watching all with laughter,
Thought, 'When the Fenians come,
   I'll rise and go after.'

A few verses from the dear lady that Paul and myself rescued from the smoke. It is still an encounter that remains in my memory among many happy memories of Omagh Town.

That great gathering of memories in Bridge Street has sent me for a brief while running around all over the place; but has not taken me away from the main purpose of my journey. And here is Bell's Bridge bravely leaping the smiling Strule, and downstream I can glimpse the radiant smiles of my father's garden, and send all happiness to those who now walk in it. Here to the left is the Model (Primary) School where I had many good friends, including Elwood Grier from Seskinore who used to cycle the miles into school. And a little further on is the Orange Hall, solid and handsome and with a beflowered lawn in front.

And here, at the corner of what becomes the road to Derry City, all the way along that splendid river, is the side of the Orange Hall and almost opposite is the War Memorial, which now stands for two monstrous and monumental wars. One must recall tenderly friends who went down in the last horror: Gerry Cassidy, Michael Mossey and others who are beside us, not visible beings yet not insubstantial wraiths, and one must bow the knee. It always staggers me how, over the years, you can see the faces and hear the voices of those who have gone a long way from us and on a mysterious journey.

Now to our left are many fine houses and one of them a Murnaghan house that belonged to the great Murnaghan family: lawyers and, also, doctors. The voice of the great George Murnaghan is still in my ears and well do I remember the occasions on which I did sneak into the Courthouse to hear and see the unconquerable George at his best. But now here is another voice, softer than that of George Murnaghan but no less authoritative. It is that of Captain William Maddin Scott welcoming us to ground sacred to the Scotts and to any Omagh person who ever stepped a foot on it. Every senior person that I looked up to spoke with reverence and respect of the Captain. He was more than a person, he was an institution. My father and my elder brother Gerald, to begin with. My father had his memories of the Boer War and the Captain had his memories of other military moments. They were quite happy exchanging such memories and, in doing so, could be walking on wide plains far away from the Strule. My brother had his stories about the expert use of the dry fly on the Strule and Drumragh and Camowen and other rivers, and on lakes, and the great Captain listened and added his stories from here, there and everywhere. He had been around.

Young fellows like myself walked with a certain awe near Lisnamallard or on the Scott country, but we felt at home there and always welcome. And in our ears we carried with us everywhere the sound of the working of the great mill. Not by any means a loud or raucous sound but a low, musical, continuous murmur as if the contented earth were breathing.

> The shades of night were falling fast
> As through an Alpine village passed
> A youth, who bore mid storm and ice
> A banner with the strange device:
> Excelsior, Excelsior …

Which was the first piece of poetry that any and every Omey boy knew by heart and could sing or recite. For there, in coloured style, was the picture of the young boy on the package of Scotts Excelsior Flaked Oatmeal. That image built us all up and we all loved our porridge. My father said you could walk through wars and maintain yourself in sprightly fashion on Excelsior porridge and I learned easily to believe him. Why, after that breakfast I found I could run up Church Hill on the way to school and that, by God, was a very steep hill. It still is.

The great story of the mill and what it has done for the people is well told here, all around us. For to serve the people was the first and basic motivation. To that great book one should add one of the most treasured books, the same story told more succinctly in the one bound volume: *A Hundred Years A-Milling: Commemorating an Ulster Mill Centenary*, edited by William Maddin Scott. My brother was then part of the working-staff for James Campbell of Knocknamoe Castle. And the Captain and James were two large and powerful and kindly men whose very existence bestowed benison on the town and countryside.

And let the final words I have to offer be spoken by Maddin Scott in that same centenary volume and under the title of 'Jottings from a Miller's Notebook – 1950'. This is Authority speaking from his own ground:

> The reader may well ask what is the idea behind this centenary volume published by one small, independent unit in an industry that must vie with farming for the distinction of being the oldest in the world?
>
> H.P. Swan, himself a miller and antiquarian of great industry and fame, tells us in *The Ancient Art of Milling* that the milling of grain (by hand) began six thousand years ago. So the journey our business has travelled

could be represented, in time, as only a day in a progress of two months; but much can happen in twenty-four hours … I am sure, too, that centenaries, even in the more stable trades, don't 'just happen', they have to be earned … we have received so much kindness from all and sundry, should we not try to pay back a little by leaving here behind us a record of a number of things in the old craft of milling and something of the old days and customs of the countryside that otherwise are in danger of being buried by the erupting lava of remorseless time?

A family business such as ours, like hundreds more in the country, grows to the semblance of a family itself as it gets older, a family with the mill as its home, the mill its breadwinner, the mill its child, aye, the mill its mother who inculcates the family feeling in us all, from the youngest apprentice to the oldest director … We have achieved much in a small way, but there is no commercial empire to extol in these pages … if any merit is thought to have accrued to us by just sticking to our job, one generation after another, let it be awarded not to us or even to the mill but to the river that gave us the incentive to stay where we belong and discouraged us from seeking our fortune along the deep water wharves of some city by the sea.

Also, the truth is, we have all been extremely fond of Omagh and its surrounding countryside, where our friends live and work.

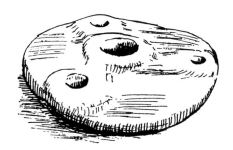

Quern – turning stone.
This stone was presented to the mill on its centenary
by Joseph Sheppard of Derry

Introduction

RICHARD SCOTT

On Friday 2 June 2000 Scotts organised a dinner at the Silverbirch Hotel, Omagh to celebrate 150 years a-milling. Richard Scott, for many years chairman and managing director of the family firm and a member of the fifth generation of millers, responded to the toast to the company. His speech, reproduced below, is a fitting introduction to this book.

THIS IS AN OCCASION FOR CELEBRATION, for entertainment and perhaps just a little for mutual congratulation and justified pride. When we are very young, our parents and our schoolteachers are inclined to remind us of the old proverb, which tells us that pride comes before a fall. That refers, of course, to personal, hubristic pride; not, I feel confident, to the sort of collective pride that can justifiably be felt by everyone here this evening at the survival and cautious, steady growth of this fine old business for 150 years. Such a long history is unusual in itself, but even more unusual is the fact that the company is owned and still to a large extent directed by the sixth generation of the family.

I know how proud my father, Maddin Scott, would be to know he now has four grandsons, William McAusland, Charles, Robert and David Scott, as directors of the business. And even more proud to see how it has developed and how well the present management team, which of course for the past 30 years has included many people not called Scott or McAusland, is evidently running the show. How lucky we are that in the early 1960s two young Turks, Fred Charters and Roy Howard, after their training elsewhere, decided that Omagh was the place for them and that Scotts was a company within which they could realise their personal ambitions.

Apart from the Scotts and McAuslands, other families, too, go back into

the second and third generations. Herbie Cockburn and Anna Orr represent the third generations of their respective families to have been involved in the business; as does George Orr, whose grandfather, father Louis and uncle Jim used to draw goods by horse and cart from the railway station to the Newtownstewart mill many years ago; Victor Anderson's father, Jack, in his later years used to delight in reminding me that his first job – on joining the mill as a carpenter in 1940 – was to construct a gate at the Millbank entrance to the yard, so as to restrain the young Richard Scott, then two years old and totally unbiddable, from dashing out of the kitchen door and under the wheels of a lorry or cart. Many of us remember with affection Ned Martin, father of Raymond. Paddy McBride, now a hale and hearty 81-year-old, is the son of Charlie McBride, who was with us longer ago than I can remember; and Davy Kinnear, whose father Jimmy's many years of employment started in my great-grandfather Charlie's time.

Charlie Scott died before 1900, but Jimmy Kinnear remembered him clearly in 1950 when my father and I visited him at home at the time of the centenary celebrations. My father recorded in *A Hundred Years A-Milling* Jimmy's commentary on the entire Scott family: 'Och, sure I worked for the whole lot of yiz and the only one worth a damn was Masther Charlie!' and I well remember the shared laughter of Maddin Scott and Jimmy Kinnear as this was said.

So, these are just a few examples of how this old business is a family concern, and to many more families than the Scotts. Among our customers, too, there are many examples of families who have chosen to buy their feed

Fred Charters, Robert Scott, David Scott, Charles Scott, William McAusland. The board of W&C Scott, 2001.

requirements from us for two or three generations.

Quite a few of us, who are young in spirit of course, but do not move quite as fast as some of the others or perhaps do not understand some of the dances these days, remember the centenary celebrations that took place in 1950. So much has happened since then.

In 1950 the company had emerged from a busy time during the Second World War when, with somewhat antiquated machinery but many ingenious and willing hands working long hours, we did our bit to convert locally grown oats into valuable breakfast food as a healthy part of the meagre wartime rations of the nation. Two years on from the end of the war, the 1947 Agriculture Act opened a window of opportunity for the farming com-

munity and the directors of the time, Maddin Scott, Walford Scott Green and Bobby Scott – soon to be joined by John McAusland – saw that there must be immediate and substantial investment so as to meet the opportunities that would present themselves to us in the production of 'Excelsior Feeds for all the Needs of Cattle, Pigs and Poultry', as the slogan of the time ran.

This was an ambitious undertaking for a company that had never had a tradition of spending very much money on anything, let alone on expensive new milling machinery and a huge concrete silo. I think that my father, in particular, believed that after the expensive reconstruction, which had the aim of providing a mill that could produce 200 tons of compound feed in a 45-hour week, no more money would need to be spent for the foreseeable future. Certainly it meant borrowing heavily at the bank to finance both fixed and working capital, an experience to which the company has become accustomed over the years.

The 1950 directors' vision was optimistic and forward-looking but events have certainly proved it to be unduly conservative. The mill's total production during the calendar year 1999 was over 100,000 tonnes, the highest ever and surely a significant milestone. Perhaps the most remarkable fact is that these 100,000 tonnes were produced by many fewer production staff than there were in 1950, when sales probably did not exceed five or six thousand tons (1 tonne – 0.984 ton). This not only says a good deal for those who have been responsible for selling our products and those who designed the expansion of the plant during the years between 1950 and 1999, it also says much that is complimentary about those in the mill itself, who have developed their skills over the years to keep the wheels turning and to control the flow of ingredients as they are converted into finished feeds.

It says a great deal, too, for the shareholders, the owners of the company, some living as far away as New Zealand, who for so many years were content with extremely modest dividends, as profits were reinvested in the modernisation and expansion of the business.

The amazing rise in productivity has much to do with our early enthusiasm for computers, originally to organise feed formulation and office paperwork, but soon to find their way into plant and machinery control. Our fathers' and grandfathers' eyes would bubble in disbelief if they could come back today and see one man pressing computer controls to route ingredients from the bulk lorry into the blending bins, another working at a keyboard to operate the entire blending, grinding and mixing process, and a third controlling the output of three gigantic pelleting presses by the same means.

Transport of feed to the farm has also been revolutionised by the use of bulk delivery lorries; these are so expensive to buy that most large mills use hauliers to deliver all their feed to farm. We have never found that to be necessary or desirable, and still believe that this link with our customers is a particularly important one.

So, the small but proud company of 50 years ago has been transformed into the sophisticated marketing, production and delivery service of year 2000. Northern Ireland's total mill production of feed has not grown appreciably since around 1970, but our share of the total market has risen in that time from around 3 per cent to almost 10 per cent today. We also ventured with others into grain trading and still have a share in the port services company through which the greater part of our grain supplies are imported. Livestock farming operations at Aughentaine, Inisclan and Glenpark have consolidated into the success and growth of Erne Eggs at Lisnaskea.

Yes, we have much to be proud of and much to celebrate. But the world is changing around us more rapidly than ever and we must not only observe the changes but be ready to respond, even to anticipate them. I so well remember my father, in 1955, remarking that the huge investment by Unilever companies in a mill in Belfast was bound to make life very tough for us. He used to refer somewhat wryly to 'millionaire millers' and their economic power: the likes of BOCM, Silcocks, ET Green (later Dalgety), Thompsons, Andrews, Bibbys, Whites, and there were many more.

Technology from the 1970s.
Top: Chronos Richardson production control panel
Below: Richard Scott seated at the console of the Qeleq Mark II feed formulation computer

John McAusland, my brother-in-law, friend and mentor for so many years, a shrewd Scotsman and in the 1950s and 1960s having the natural aggression and confidence of the younger man, was less fearful of the 'big boys', as he called them; and, in one favourite and disrespectful phrase, which I shall slightly paraphrase, was inclined to remark, 'the bigger the elephant, the bigger the vulnerable bits!'

Well, many of the elephants did become vulnerable and have staggered off the scene to perish in the elephants' graveyard. But the competitive threat is still there, as the surviving competitors have become hungry tigers and are possibly more dangerous to us than ever before. Even more critically, the economics of livestock farming seem now to be more precarious than at any time since the 1930s. I know this must be a worry to the present directors of the company as they contemplate the need to reinvest massively yet again, to meet the food safety and traceability standards of the 21st century. Today's challenges are every bit as daunting as those which faced William Scott when as a sole trader he started his mill on the present site in 1850, and those that faced a later generation in 1950 as we celebrated the conclusion of our first century.

But now we celebrate our 150th anniversary. We look back with pride but we also look forward to the future, with confidence in ourselves and in our capability to tackle further challenges.

William Scott

1

The Irish Famine
of 1845–50

TONY DEESON

WILLIAM SCOTT (1805–1890), the founder of the present-day W & C Scott Ltd of Excelsior Mills, Omagh, began his business career as an apprentice to William Cooke of Londonderry, to whom he was bound by indentures dated 21 July 1821. The Cookes came to Ulster sometime in the 18th century, originally as tenant farmers, but by the time William Scott joined them they were ship-owners, although they also owned a timber yard and at some time in the 19th century were engaged in milling.

As a result of the Irish potato famine of 1845–50 William Scott saw room for a milling enterprise in Omagh, where he had settled in 1831. He was 26 at the time of his arrival in Omagh and quickly became known as a building contractor and manufacturer of farm gates. In autumn 1847 he set up Cranny Mills and in 1850, emboldened by success, opened a larger mill on the site of the present business, which for many years has been known as

Excelsior Mills. It is the latter year that W & C Scott Ltd prefers to regard as its foundation, giving it 150 years of unbroken trading, under six generations of Scotts, in the first year of the third millennium.

When William Scott went into the milling business on his own account, Ireland was in a desperate state. There had previously been famines because of the failure of the potato crop, but none as severe and far-reaching as that of 1845–50. Potatoes had been the staple diet of the Irish poor since the 18th century. They were nutritious, especially when complemented with milk or buttermilk, which supplied the essential fats and vitamin A. In 1845 there was a partial failure of the crop, which caused much suffering, but in 1846 the failure was complete and within weeks starvation stalked the whole country, with disease hard on its heels. In five years Ireland lost a third of its population by death and emigration. Emigration was mostly to America, Canada, England and Australia. The fare to America was £5 and to Canada, £3. For many these were impossible sums to find and they were forced to stay behind, often to meet death.

When the partial blight arrived in 1845, Robert Peel and his Cabinet decided that whatever else happened, the export of corn from Ireland must continue. This was the country's trade and the sale of corn the only way the people could pay their rents and remain in possession of their land. It was unfortunately often true that the English absentee landlords did not care whether or not their tenants starved, provided their rents were paid. Thus the corn grown on the spot was not fed to the starving people, but was traded as usual. Ships laden with grain left a starving land. In its place Peel's government did what it could to introduce foreign food. The Corn Laws, which placed a duty on foreign grain, were repealed with the principal object of reducing the price of grain imported from America.

These measures were only moderately successful in 1845; when the crop failed totally in 1846 a different government held power and Lord John Russell and his Cabinet were faced with a far more serious situation, which developed with alarming rapidity. Lord John held firm to his predecessor's decision that locally grown grain should not be used to alleviate the desperate situation. Instead, a special commission was set up to find food that could be imported. Irish dealers scoured the world. Indian corn (maize) was brought to 34 large depots in the west of Ireland. By early 1847 over three million people were entirely supported by the rations issued by special commissions and government agencies. This helped to tide them over until the improved potato harvest of 1847 had been gathered, but for many it was too little and too late, and they turned their faces to the wall and quietly died. The government was slow to provide funds from the UK revenue to relieve the famine, insisting that the local poor rates should provide the funds to aid the Irish people. In 1845 the population of Ireland was eight million; by 1851 it had fallen to 5.5 million and the drain by emigration continued on a large scale for the next 50 years. One of the officials who had been commissioned by parliament to visit and report on the different districts wrote to the Northern Whig: 'There is not any necessity that I should point out

individual cases of abject want, though in my visitations I have seen many of those whose extreme destitution I could not have possibly have formed a true estimate had I not seen them.' He asserted that the harrowing details which he appended to his report were not over-drawn.

The General Relief Committee for all Ireland was formed and soup kitchens were set up all over the country. The daily ration consisted of $1\frac{1}{2}$ pounds of bread or one pound of biscuit, or one pound of meal or flour, or any grain, or one quart of soup thickened with a portion of meal, or if the meal was not available a quarter ration of bread or biscuit. Children below the age of nine were allotted half rations.

William Scott chose Omagh, Co. Tyrone to set up his venture, which has been nurtured for 150 years by successive generations of Scotts. How did Omagh and Tyrone fare in the famine?

In Omagh from January to June 1847, an average of over 2,000 people received rations at a cost of 5d (2p) per head per week. In February the number fed each week averaged 2,900 and the total cost for four weeks was £236. The quantity per person (including children) per week was 5 pounds 2 ounces of oats and Indian meal in equal quantities.

At the beginning of the 1840s the population density in Tyrone was more than 400 to the square mile, but between 1841 and 1851 it declined by 19 per cent. However, this was less than in other counties, where there was a greater dependence on potatoes – although in 1800 it was remarked that even in Tyrone small potato patches were edging 'upwards almost to the summits of the mountains'. But relatively more grain, area by area, was farmed in Tyrone than in the other counties. Perhaps the local landlords were kindlier, too, because it is recorded that some of them provided employment by setting the poor to work draining and reclaiming land and making roads. They also supplied turnip, carrot and cabbage seeds, and beans and peas. Rents were abated for some tenants. A number of landlords, according to the *Tyrone Constitution*, were 'unceasingly employed administering to the wants of the poor'. William Scott, though by no means a landlord, was one of a large number of local worthies who formed a committee for the relief of the famine. Nevertheless, the crowded workhouses, in the words of the *Tyrone Constitution*, 'the last resource of the suffering poor, afford a true test of the destitution and show the rapid strides with which the famine approaches the North'. There were 1,293 inmates in the Omagh Union Workhouse on 4 February 1847, a number which the Poor Law

Commissioners ordered should be reduced to 800.

The famine has to be seen as a disaster overlying the normal grinding poverty of many Ulster inhabitants of that era. In the first half of the 19th century the main issue was not, as some historians have suggested, Catholic Emancipation or the repeal of the Act of Union. It was poverty, lived day by day and experienced on a massive scale. Ultimately this spilled over into the harrowing scenes of hunger, disease, and death in the famine years. According to *An Economic History of Ulster*:

> Population pressure, subdivision of holdings, narrowing economic opportunities in agriculture and rural industry, and increasing reliance on the potato were the crucial elements in the build-up to the famine crisis at mid-century ... the famine claimed possibly in excess of one million lives, over and above those that would normally have been expected to die in this period. Relatively few actually starved to death. Most were the victims of fever and dysentery, diseases which flourished under conditions of malnutrition, poor hygiene and inadequate public health measures.

It is said that the famine had one positive effect: it broke down English apathy towards Irish conditions, and to deal with the problem of poverty heavy poor rates were levied on the English landowners. But this caused more difficulty because in most cases the landowners could not, or did not want to, afford the levies, so they ousted their tenants and turned the land to pasture. As cattle grazing increased, crop growing decreased and there was a call for the greater milling of imported grains to feed the cattle and to wean the people away from their dependence on potatoes; indeed, thus encouraged they developed a taste for maize mixed with oatmeal.

The first responsibility of the Irish mills was to grind corn for export but when this need was satisfied it was found that most of the small grist mills, equipped with only a few pairs of mill stones and run by water, were totally unable to deal with large quantities of coarse Indian corn. When the immediate crisis was over the lack of power of the majority of the Irish mills brought about the construction of larger units. Such was the idea of William Scott when he started milling at Cranny Mills in 1847.

The Great Famine was the last major subsistence crisis in Ireland, and indeed in western Europe generally. Now we switch on our televisions to see similar harrowing scenes in other parts of the world. Many were lost in the Irish famine, many left their native country and never returned, but others stuck it out as best they could. This poem, 'Unconquered' by R.L. Marshall (published in *A Hundred Years A-Milling*, which celebrated the centenary of the foundation of W & C Scott Ltd), pays tribute to one Ulster farmer who stayed:

I'm only a mountain farmer,
With forty acres there;
I nivir slept below a slate,
An' my thatch was often bare.

In cowl' Spring days I ploughed,
In sleet I dug the spuds,
I snedded frosted thurnips
In beggars' cast-off duds.

I nivir married Annie
For money she had noan,
I thought of rid-haired Fanny
But I'd sooner live my lone.

Without a ben-weed's shelther
I raired a power of sheep,
I niver needed lamp oil,
I spent the dark in sleep.

I went ta Meetin' little,
For habit's hard ta kill,
But I dhrained the Mossy Meadow,
An' stubbed the Whinny Hill.

Now stiff an' sore, I'm headin'
For the grave-yard over by,
An' few ther'll be ta miss me,
An' fewer still to cry.

An' when I'm dead and buried,
An' the Judgment Cock has crowed,
I'll not have much ta offer
For all the seed was sowed.

But this I'll say at last
When of sins they've talked their fill,
'I dhrained the Mossy Meadow,
An' stubbed the Whinny Hill.'

2

Cranny, Excelsior and Omagh

TONY DEESON

A S WE HAVE SEEN, William Scott began milling at Cranny, 'fed by the waters of Camowen in its loveliness at Cranny', in the autumn of 1847.

He took the buildings on a three-year lease and also leased a store in Omagh to supply the grain milled at Cranny. After three years he used his experience to move to what became known as Excelsior Mills. ('Excelsior' was first used by William Scott as a trademark in 1859.)

His first milling advertisement appeared in the *Tyrone Constitution* on 1 September 1847:

CRANNY MILL

The Subscriber takes leave to inform the Public that he is now
prepared for grinding Oats, Wheat, Indian Corn, Beans, Peas etc at
his new Mill in Cranny, all of which can be ground in a superior
manner, on moderate terms.
He will be supplied at his store in Omagh, at all times, with the
following fresh from the Mill, viz., Oatmeal, Wheatmeal, Indian Meal
and Bran which will be sold to wholesale purchasers at lowest prices.

William Scott

The mill with kiln behind was of quite substantial construction but tucked away out of sight of the road. It was driven by water power from the Ballinamullan burn. The dam was about an acre in size and was sometimes known as Leg of Mutton Pond. From there the water flowed for 250 yards through a leat, or lade, to the mill and drove two 20ft waterwheels, developing a total power of 40hp at full water. There was no auxiliary power.

After William Scott set up his new mill in 1850 he leased Cranny to John Carson from Enniskillen at £20 a year; Carson's nephews, John and Robert Waterson, succeeded him. In 1911 another Robert Waterson, son and nephew of John and Robert respectively, took over the management of the mill. During his management three-quarters of the production was in

farmers' oats. In the First World War Cranny was worked for six days and nights a week. Flathead kilns for drying oats were situated in a separate building behind the mill, adjacent to the storage accommodation.

Robert Waterson finally closed the mill in 1947 because the cost of repair and modernisation could not be justified by the amount of trade he could secure. A photograph taken in June 1949 shows the buildings to be much the same as they were in William Scott's day. The year before, Cranny had been sold to Omagh Mental Hospital, together with the surrounding land. By September 1955 another photograph shows the mill deserted and in an advanced state of ruin, although the waterwheels and some shafting with bevel wheels were still in place. The mill was later demolished and the new mental hospital buildings were built on the site.

Excelsior Mill on the Mountjoy Road was a larger and grander affair. There was probably an earlier mill on or near the site, as indicated on a 17th-century map of Omagh. An extract from the deeds of Mr Hawkes Ellis, dated July 1754, states:

> They the said William Blythe and Andrew Menagh, their heirs, administrators or assigns shall grind or cause to be ground at the miln of Lisnamallagh all such grindable grain as shall grow on the hereby devised premises [part of the old Omagh Academy, on the High Street] and shall pay the accustomed toll or moulter for grinding the same (royalties of all kinds excepted to the present landlord) as far as the said Thomas Blythe in his grand lease is set out.

About 1820 a brewery was built on the site and it seems likely that the mill lade, a man-made cut from the river Camowen, pre-dated the brewery because the supply of water far exceeded a brewer's needs. When the mill yard was dug up in 1950 quantities of sawdust were found at a depth of 3–5 feet below the surface. If indeed the mill lade was cut before the brewery it may have served an earlier mill and possibly a sawmill on the same site.

In 1850 William Scott set about adapting the existing buildings. An oat mill was equipped and in production by 13 April 1852, and a few days earlier work had started on a flour mill. In the same year a steam engine was installed to supplement the water-power, and early letter headings proudly proclaim: 'Steam Mills, Omagh'.

William Scott made Omagh his home from 1831 until his death in 1890. The town of Omagh derives its name from the Irish 'Oigh Maigh', meaning 'virgin plain'; it is also called the 'seat of the chiefs'. It was later known as 'Omey', a name that still lingers. It originated as a tiny settlement at a point where the River Strule flows shallow and wide from the conjunction of the rivers Camowen and Drumragh. The high ground near by offered security from the highest winter floods – and unwelcome visitors of a different kind.

The earliest known map of Omagh dates back to the first decade of the 17th century and shows a settlement of some 20 houses. It appears that a mill of the Ladle or Danish type was at work in this small village; in 1950, when Scotts celebrated its centenary, the number of houses had grown to 1,477 within the town boundary. As already noted, in 1754 a mill leased to William Blythe and Andrew Menagh existed at Lisnamallagh. It would seem that the Ladle Mill of 1610 was on the Strule just below the 'meeting of the waters' and above an island that has long since disappeared. In an 1846 bill

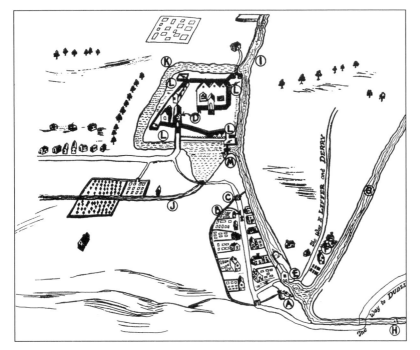

Seventeenth century map of Omagh showing a mill on the river and a fort erected by the English commanding the approaches to the town.

of sale prepared for land which Lord Blessington was selling, there is reference to 'a good corn mill and about 1¹/₂ acres of land. Yearly rent £38 15s 4d [£38.77]. Mill, Mill Pond and Winnowing Ground.' This seems to have been a description of Cranny Mill, which William Scott acquired shortly afterwards.

Omagh's early history was turbulent. Fire and battle have destroyed most of the ancient documents and records, but legends have waxed (and never waned) over the years. The town is said to owe its origin to an abbey founded in 792. In 1464 the abbey was converted into a house for the Third Order of Franciscans and flourished until its dissolution in 1600, when its site and possessions were granted to Sir Henry Piers. However, the religious foundation had little effect on 'the warring O'Neills' who ruled from a castle at the top of what is now High Street. In 1471 or thereabouts it was occupied by one Art O'Neill, but Henry O'Neill, king of Ulster, captured the castle and handed it over to Conn, his eldest son and heir. Seeking a bride for Conn, he decided it should be the beautiful Elinor FitzGerald, sister of Garret, the 8th Earl of Kildare. Conn wooed and won Elinor and brought her back to his castle at Omagh. The match had far-reaching effects on the history of Ulster, for on at least three occasions when the interests of her husband or family were menaced Elinor called south and her brother the Earl, with his powerful clan backed by English cannon, sped to Tyrone to the rescue.

At the beginning of the 17th century Chichester, writing about Omagh, or 'St Omey' said: 'Round about this place there is great desolation, by reason of which it happeneth that merchants and other passengers weakly guarded travelling from Derrie or Liffer to the Pale are usually in their passage cut off and murdered.' With the Plantation of Ulster in 1609 Omagh was granted to Lord Castlehaven but he failed to erect a castle or settle a sufficient number of English on the land, and the town and district were given to Captain Edmund Leigh and his brothers. In 1611 Lord Carew reported:

> The Fort of Omye. Here is a good fort walled with lime and stone about thirty feet high above the ground with a parapet, the river on one side and a large ditch about the rest; in which is built a fair house of timber after the English manner. Begun by Captain Edmund Leigh and finished by his brothers at their own charge upon the lands of the Abbey of Omye, at which place are many families of English and Irish, who have built them good dwelling houses, which is a safety and comfort for passengers between Dungannon and the Liffer. The fort is a place of good import upon all occasions of service and fit to be maintained.

James II was a noted visitor in April 1689, but an unwelcome one. Thomas Babington Macaulay writes in his *History of England*:

> On 14th of April, 1689, King James II and his train proceeded to Omagh.

The rain fell, the wind blew, the horses could scarcely make their way through the mud, and in the face of the storm the road was frequently intersected by torrents which might almost be called rivers. The travellers had to pass several fords where the water was breast high. Some of the party fainted from fatigue and hunger. All around lay a frightful wilderness. In a journey of forty miles Avaux counted only three miserable cabins. Everything else was rock and bog and moor. When at length the travellers reached Omagh they found it in ruins. The Protestants, who were the majority of inhabitants, had abandoned it leaving not a wisp of straw nor a cask of liquor. The windows had been broken, the chimneys had been broken in: the very locks and bolts of the doors had been carried away.

Later, on his retreat from Londonderry, James left a garrison at Omagh. The occupation did not last long. The men of Omagh drove out the garrison 'with great slaughter' but before the soldiers left they set the town ablaze.

Disaster again befell Omagh in May 1742. A fire broke out and the town was destroyed, only the church and two houses escaping the flames. Rebuilding started on a new plan, so that the layout of the town today has no relationship to what was destroyed 260 years ago.

When William Scott settled in Omagh in 1831 it was a very small town with a population said to number 2,211; ten years later this had increased to 2,947 before suffering the post-famine decline, which affected almost all Irish centres. Today Omagh has the largest population of towns in Tyrone, with over 20,000 inhabitants. It is the county town and was so in William Scott's time, having taken the title from Dungannon about 1768. The *Parliamentary Gazetteer* of 1846 waxes lyrical over Omagh:

The site of the town is a declivity or rapid slope upon the side of one of a numerous series of tortuous vales and sinuous dells, which cut all the circumjacent country into a labyrinth of hillocks, ridges, hills and hollows; yet it is both sufficiently low in itself, and sufficiently uncommanded by surrounding swells and eminences, to be fully and very pictorially seen from the Dublin and Londonderry mail-road – at a considerable distance – lying like a bright and variegated gem upon a rich ground-work of green and gold colouring.

A century and more later, the local guidebook says:

The sheltered and generally fertile basin in which the town nestles has a colourful backcloth of heath-clad hills on almost every side. Mullaghcarn rising 1,800 ft to the northeast and Bessy Bell to the northwest are the most prominent. Easily visible on the broad ridges of Mullaghcarn is the green cloak of Gortin Forest.

But a glimpse of the town at the beginning of the 19th century was not encouraging. J. Gamble found the streets dirty and irregular, and while there were some good houses they were by no means so numerous as the others to which by no stretch of the imagination this description could be applied. He stayed at the Abercorn Arms Hotel, familiarly known as 'Harkins'. When he asked the landlord about the history of the town he was told he was the only traveller who had ever made enquiries about it. Gamble concludes by saying: 'there is a degree of gloom about the town which is more easy to feel than to describe – if I were confined to a county town I would not choose Omagh.' That was in 1810. When he revisited the town in 1819 he saw a great improvement, and spoke in high terms of the cleanliness of the inn.

William Scott would have known the Abercorn Arms Hotel. It stood on the southwest side of the road where High Street and Market Street meet. It is said that with its mahogany doors and stucco ceilings it was one of the best houses in the town. After its time as an inn it had a varied life – as a private residence, as Omagh's Post Office, the Omagh Academy, and then, in 1938, it was demolished to make way for the County Cinema, which in turn gave way to a supermarket in the last quarter of the century. Two other hostelries that Scott would have known were the Royal Arms Hotel, which was founded in 1787 and had been described as 'one of the best hotels in the County', and the White Hart Hotel, a great feature of the town in the nineteenth century, on the site of the present Post Office in High Street. Above its porch was a beautiful sculpture of a white stag.

Later generations of the Waterson family, who had leased and later owned the Cranny mills after William Scott had moved to Excelsior Mills, became the proprietors of the Royal Arms Hotel after the Second World War, and ran it as a successful and well-respected family business until its sale in 1999.

Nine years before young Scott arrived in Omagh, Thomas Reid visited the town. He found the road good but the country 'exceedingly dreary' and the cabins he passed, shocking. 'The roofs were often covered with green sward which at a little distance resembled neglected dung heaps.' In the town he saw the beginning of progress in the public buildings but condemned the management of the gaol. When Queen Victoria came to the throne the population was 2,211 and there were 715 houses in the town, of which 585 were 'of respectable appearance' and slated. The streets were paved but not lighted. By 1862 the population had increased to 3,485 and 'the footpaths of the principal streets had been paved recently with best Caithness Flags, which has vastly improved the appearance of the town'. In 1850 the streets were gas-lit by a private company of which William Scott was a director. Water was very scarce throughout the town and there were no public fountains or wells. There was, of course, the river, but the water fit for drinking in dry weather must have been very limited. Is it any wonder that in 1832, the year after William Scott moved to Omagh, 41 people died of cholera?

He found a very compact town, the houses shoulder to shoulder 'like soldiers on parade'. Some of the houses in the High Street were thatched and

Omagh Courthouse,
a distant view painted *c.* 1850

remained so until the beginning of the 20th century. Where the houses ended the country began at once. The houses were huddled together mainly for protection but also because the site of the town was very cramped, the river hemming it on one side and the other side was wet swampy ground unfit for building. The construction of Campsie Bridge in 1836 aided access to the other side of the Drumragh river, where it joins the Camowen close to that point to form the Strule.

In 1847, when William Scott started Cranny mills, trade and industry were developing very slowly in the area. There was, however, a thriving brewery in the town with a product 'that has gained some celebrity'. This brewery was established in the town about 1820 and the premises it vacated in 1850 were leased by William Scott and converted into what was to become Excelsior Mills. The only other industries of any note were tobacco manufacturing, which was carried on at 17 Market Street, a house built by William Scott, and rope-making, carried out by Ann Collin in Gortmore. The town did not possess a bank until the Provincial Bank opened a branch on 13 October 1834, following a petition got up by Scott.

Being built around the confluence of the Camowen and Drumragh rivers, forming the river Strule, Omagh has always depended on its bridges to facilitate trade. A number of these were in place when William Scott started in business: notably the King James Bridge over the Drumragh river at Crevenagh, which was erected in the 17th century; Bell's Bridge, built in the early 19th century; the bridge at Campsie, built in 1836; and Donnelly's Bridge on the Cookstown road, in 1840. (Abbey Bridge followed in 1900 and Strule Bridge in 1966.)

As it was the county town the assizes were held at the Omagh Courthouse, built in 1814, and the building with a fine portico added in 1823 still dominates the High Street. A gaol was erected in 1804, enlarged in 1823, and closed towards the end of the 19th century.

North of the gaol was the old military barracks, which Scott would have remembered. It had accommodation for a field officer, seven other officers, 110 private soldiers and 60 horses. When the new barracks was built in 1881 it became the headquarters of the Tyrone Militia, previously the 2nd Tyrone Regiment and later known as the 4th Battalion Royal Inniskilling Fusiliers. Here it was that the country folk who had walked in barefoot with their boots hung around their necks stopped to put them on before entering the town.

By 1838 Omagh could boast a reading room 'furnished with newspapers but not with periodicals or other literary works'.

When William Scott started up there was no rail line at Omagh but shortly afterwards, in September 1852, the Omagh–Dungannon line was opened by the Dundalk, Enniskillen and Londonderry Railway, with a station on the Dublin Road near the livestock mart. Later the Londonderry–Enniskillen line was opened by the Portadown, Dungannon and Omagh Junction Railway with a station at James Street. Later again the separate companies merged to form the Great Northern Railway, the Portadown–Omagh connection was opened and the Belfast line reached Omagh. The merger necessitated the building of a stretch of line to connect the two stations and from that time onwards the stagecoach on its way to or from Dublin and Derry was heard no more.

W.K. Ellis in his article, 'Bits and Pieces of Omagh History', writes:

> The coaches had well and truly served their generation and in spite of bad weather and worse roads seldom failed to reach their destination, unless the way was blocked by drifts of snow. They were wonderfully punctual and the sound of their horn was regarded as the time signal of the period. In 1824 the Royal Mail left Derry each day at 7.30 in the morning and reached Omagh at 12.30 arriving in Dublin at 6 o'clock the following morning. The down coach left Dublin from Gosson's Hotel in Bolton Street at 7.30 in the evening and was in Omagh at 1 pm the next day, finally drawing up in Society Street, Londonderry at six in the evening, when the stiff and weary travellers were only too glad to clamber down from their seats.

William Scott's early business was very local, grain being brought to the mill by wagon and returned, milled, in the same way, but as business expanded the railway was of increasing service, to bring imported grain from the deepwater docks at Londonderry and Belfast and to distribute the finished products throughout Ireland and to Scotland.

Throughout his life, Omagh was a very quiet town and except on market and fair days there was little traffic; cocks and hens scratched contentedly in the High Street. As Omagh was situated in the centre of a large agricultural district its chief trade was in farm produce sold in several markets. There was the potato market off the High Street; the butter market near Campsie Bridge; near by was the flax market, which on Thursdays became the pork market, and on fair days the horse market; near the railway station at the other end of the town was the corn market. The cattle fair was held on the first Saturday of each month on the Fair Green and fat cattle were sold in Church Street. In 1834 'a very convenient range of shambles was opened', but these fell into disuse and unnecessarily cruel slaughter was carried out wherever the slaughterman thought convenient.

Half-yearly hiring fairs were held on the Saturday after 12 May and at Hallowday, and there were also quarterly fairs at Lammas and Candlemas. All the 'boys and girls' from far and near gathered on these days in the High Street to hire themselves out for the following year. Often a large contingent from Donegal, attracted by the higher wages obtainable in Tyrone, helped to swell the throng.

When William Scott came to Omagh there was some still linen trade in the town but it was declining fast. There was a market held on alternate Saturdays for brown linen and a bleach green mill in Mullaghmore nearby, but the linen trade was always centred on Strabane and Dungannon. Many of the Omagh weavers sold their web of cloth in Strabane, starting off at four in the morning and getting home before nightfall, having made a round trip of 40 miles.

In 1844 the *Tyrone Constitution* started publication and was (and still is) an important feature in the life of Omagh and other Tyrone townships. With its interest in all Tyrone matters it has been important reading for generations of Scotts and, long before the days of radio and television, it would have been an essential source of information for William Scott. In 1944 the affectionately nicknamed 'Con' celebrated its centenary and this congratulatory message by Maddin Scott, who in that year was the High Sheriff of the County (and obviously a cricket enthusiast) provides another picture of Omagh and Tyrone:

> Congratulations on reaching your century! When you first faced the bowling one hundred years ago, there was no wireless, telephone, telegraph or even railway to supply you with up-to-the-minute news, and you had, perforce, to get all your 'scoops' of the outside world and even 'Our Representatives' shorthand notes by the Penny Post, Royal Mail Coach or Carrier, for the nearest railway was then far away.
>
> I hope you didn't find yourselves batting on a 'sticky wicket' when the famine came along, a catastrophe from which we suffered badly enough; it reduced the population of Tyrone by 19 per cent, from 312,956 in 1841 to 255,374 in 1851 – just when you thought you were 'getting set' after

your first few overs. Very probably the 3,000 or so inhabitants of Omagh, most of them warm and well-doing in their neatly thatched houses dominated by the Church Spire, and Court-house, with the Infantry and Cavalry Barracks and the castellated County Gaol, had by then become 'Con-conscious'. So had the 1,500 of Newtownstewart ... and so had the 4,700 of Strabane, the 3,800 of Dungannon, the 3,000 of Cookstown, the grand wee towns and the good country folk around them.

You hadn't long, but you were always good businessmen, to whom nothing is impossible. Mind you, they didn't need to buy their 'Con' in those days for a public reading room was maintained in Omagh and also probably in other towns; although the people then didn't move about as fast as we do, perhaps they knew better how to use their leisure! If one wanted an overdraft, you had the choice of two good bankers and true – the Provincial (since 1834) and the Ulster – to approach (and what can man ask more?) While if you felt flush there were no less than five 'Attorneys' and one 'Resident Barrister' ready and eager to execute your commands, to say nothing of 25 public houses!

By 1894, when your 50 went up, you must have been far too busy to celebrate; a most unwise proceeding anyway in the middle of an innings; but you looked around you perhaps? Still some thatched houses in the High Street of our County Town, giving us a nice old-world appearance in keeping with the jaunting cars and broughams spanking along the wide dusty roads in our short Tyrone summer; no change much there yet, and none at all where Bessie Bell peeped down still, over the lovely woods towards the three lakes of Baronscourt, thanks be to God.

So you go on, chronicling the passing years in Tyrone among the Bushes, a privilege to do so, you may say. Right well you have done it all the same, watching things improve whiles, gradually under the old regime, a wee thing speedier as we work out our own salvation in the last 25 years. [A reference to the parliament at Stormont, established in 1922 but an early casualty of the troubles that re-erupted in 1969.]

And now you're 100 not out. Well, good luck to the 'Con' is what every Tyrone man and woman will say heartily and also respectfully, for by good service and sound precept the 'Constitution' has become an Institution.

Half a century on from its centenary, the *Tyrone Constitution* was awarded the accolade 'UK Weekly Newspaper of the Year' in 1998 for its reporting of the Omagh bombing and its aftermath.

This is just a brief sketch of Omagh as it was in William Scott's time, Omagh as he knew it. And all around the town were (and still are) the beauties of 'Tyrone among the Bushes' – the green county – the hills and mountains, the heather and the rivers, the rain, the wind and the sun. This is how Lord Blessington's agent described it in 1846 when attempting to sell the landlord's encumbered estate:

The County of Tyrone, placed in the heart of the Province of Ulster, has long been famous for the beauty, fertility and cultivation of the soil; the peacefulness, good order and industry of its population; and the number, rank and wealth of its resident gentry; ever ready by their example and influence and money to promote and co-operate in any plan of usefulness or improvement. As a natural, or rather a necessary consequence, Agriculture in this County has advanced with a rapidity unequalled in many other counties and excelled in none, and in every district are to be seen crops of all kinds, of the very best quality; the culture of wheat so little known in the North of Ireland some years since, is now almost universal in this county, except in the mountainous districts.

In no other part of Ireland has there been a greater improvement in the breed of cattle than in Tyrone, as for years past the Landlords have been bringing over cattle of the best description from England and Scotland, and have thus been giving every encouragement to the farmers to improve their stock.

But the poet, David McClelland, does even better when he sings the praises of 'Sweet Omey':

> Sweet Omey town with all around
> Your sights of beauty rare,
> Go where you may in Summertime,
> With you none can compare.
> Why should we spend our hard-earned gold
> Some far-off land to see
> When we have here Dame Nature's hand
> Displayed so lavishly?
>
> Although the broad Atlantic
> Breaks not upon our shore,
> Our inland scenes are beautiful,
> We ask for nothing more.
> The hand of man is here unseen –
> All this the Almighty made,
> And our fond memories linger round
> The beauty here displayed.
>
> Seek Lisanelly's wooded grounds,
> And then look down and see
> The silver Strule flow racing past
> And dancing in its glee,
> The giant oaks and beeches tall
> Stand pointing to the sky,

A lovely place 'tis said to be
By every passer by.

There's Lisnamallard and Glencree
And lovely Riverdale*.
A murmuring breeze springs through the trees
And whispers in the vale.
Cool winding walks and avenues,
Demesnes broad spread and fair,
Plantations on the western side
Skirt Omey, over there.

Glenhordial's lofty peak we reach
And view the landscape o'er,
A sight most grand, our view commands,
Far reaching to Dromore
And woods of Rash. If I could sing,
Old Omey! You'd see how I adore
Our friendly hills around her spires –
Once the Abbey of Gortmore.

Sweet Edenfel, no tongue can tell
The beauty you possess,
And Crevenagh's kindly, haunting bower
Her charms are nothing less;
The old Leap Bridge, its waterfall
With rippling music sweet;
And last we turn our steps toward
The Lovers' loved Retreat.

These verses were composed at the company's kil'logie (the gathering of men at dinner hour round the kiln furnace) in 1908. The author, who was a storeman at the mill, died in 1912 and the manuscript was lost. His verses, which he set to music, were much loved by his friends and were handed down by word of mouth from one millman to another. Versions have been combined in this rendering, which was printed for the first time in *A Hundred Years A-Milling*, published to celebrate Scotts' centenary.

*Now known as Arleston

3

Milling in Ulster

TONY DEESON

THE ART OR CRAFT OF MILLING, which has occupied William Scott and the following five generations of his family, is one of the oldest in the world – almost as old as the cultivation of corn. At first grain was ground by hand by pestle and mortar, but by 1500 BC there is evidence that it was crushed between two stones. It used to be the work of women to sit at these 'querns'. They would turn the top stone round by passing its handle from one to another to crush the corn beneath.

The first watermills, which consisted of a water-propelled wheel turning an axle on which the two stones were placed, are thought to date back to about 100 BC. Felicity Walton, in *A Hundred Years A-Milling*, provides a translation of a text by Antipater of Syria, writing in 85 BC:

> Ye maids who toiled so faithfully at the mill
> Now cease from work and from your toils be still.
> For what your hands performed so long and true,
> Ceres* has charged the water nymphs to do.
> They come, the limpid sisters to her call
> And on the wheel with dashing fury fall
> Impel the wheel and with a whirling sound
> They make the massy millstone turn around
> And bring the floury heaps luxuriant to the ground.

The Romans brought watermills to Britain, but Ireland had to rely on its own resources. Traditionally the first watermill was set up by King Cormac Mac Art in the third century to relieve the toils of a beautiful slave maiden. Not surprisingly, the attention he is said to have paid to this girl did not meet with the approval of his wife, the queen, and each day the girl was set to grind nine pecks of corn, perhaps on the principle that she would have little energy left for more seductive pursuits.

With the introduction of Christianity to Ireland in the fifth century, watermills, set up by monastic foundations, became more common. In

Grinding corn in a quern on the island of Inishmurry, Co. Sligo, 1900
Courtesy of the Ulster Museum

*In Greek mythology Ceres was the goddess both of corn and of milling

St Patrick's time there were many such mills and the poor depended on meal ground from the oat crop. In the 15th and 16th centuries, an attempt was made to introduce the English feudal system into Ireland. It did not work very well but had its greatest effect on milling. By the terms of his lease a man was bound to have his own corn ground at the manor mill and to pay a toll to the landlord or his miller. This was called 'mill soccage'. The miller obtained his profit from the 'mulcture' laid on his customers, which was usually about one-sixteenth of the meal ground.

Between 1600 and 1800 there was little development in milling techniques. The corn was usually threshed on the highways, or by the old custom of burning the ears of corn, which continued despite a prohibition enacted during the reign of Charles I. The drying of the corn before grinding was not always done at the mill. Where the mills were small or ill-equipped, as most of them were, it was left to a more prosperous farmer to provide a kiln for the drying of his own and his neighbours' grain. The earliest method of drying was by plaiting straw together and stretching it on a frame of wooden ribs. The corn was spread on the straw and dried by a fire maintained underneath. In the autumn, when the drying was on, the mill would become a great centre of local gossip, the men gathering round the fire in the evening. In the latter part of the 18th century the wood ribs were supplanted by iron ribs, leading to great complaints that the corn was not as sweet.

After passing through the millstones the first time, the grain was carried to the shillin' (shelling) hill where it was held in sieves to catch the wind so that the husks were sifted and blown away. When the meal was finally ground and the miller had received his mulcture, the farmer would take it away for his own use. Any surplus corn or oatmeal might be sold at his door to travelling merchants, or taken to the local market. To grow corn with the purpose of selling it was not usual in the 17th and 18th centuries, particularly as a heavy toll had to be paid at the markets.

In 1802 there were 124 small grist-mills in Tyrone; they were often badly constructed and poorly maintained, and usually worked only during the autumn and winter. They were capable only of producing a coarse meal (called graden) and were incapable of handling the Indian corn, which was first imported at the time of the famine and gave William Scott the opportunity to open his mill. However, before that the corn trade in Ireland was given a definite uplift by Foster's Corn Laws, passed in 1784. Bounties on the export of corn were granted and the import of oats, rye and oatmeal or flour meal was prohibited. During the Napoleonic wars, Britain was blockaded from the continent and was glad to take Irish meal and oats, flour and wheat, which greatly benefited development in the north of Ireland.

Until 1800, wheat was seldom grown in Ulster and in 1812 there were only two flourmills in Tyrone, at Dungannon and Strabane. Often the new flourmills, which relied on water-power, grew up beside the oatmeal mills and most of the wheat grown was exported, since the people had no taste for it. The growth in wheat growing and export stimulated the development of the ports of Belfast and Londonderry, which in turn encouraged the development of the mills. The first mill to use a steam engine to supplement water-power was built in Derry; by 1853 William Scott had installed his own engine, in Omagh. Besides wheat, bran and pollard were exported, going to the Lancashire cotton mills at 5d (2p) a stone. As a business, flour and oatmeal milling was definitely expanding in Ulster, aided by technological advances. Iron kilns were substituted for wooden ribs and winnowing machines replaced the 'shillin' hill'. Steam engines were more and more frequently employed, and the larger ones could turn 15 pairs of stones simultaneously.

This brings this brief history of milling up to 1850 or thereabouts. The rest of the story will be told in the development of W & C Scott Ltd. But the little old watermills are not quite forgotten. Felicity Walton, writing in *Ulster Milling through the Years* some 50 or more years ago, laments the old ways thus:

One of the saddest sights of this our modern age is that of a disused mill. The small building that is little more than an empty shell, with its motionless wheel that served so faithfully the generations of the past, can all too frequently be found. The building may have been renewed through the centuries, but the site will be the same as was used by men for years unknown. Now, in the whirl of mechanisation, these little old watermills are useless indeed. Undeveloped and now silent they might be called the last surviving antiquities of agriculture; yet they now serve to remind us how very ancient is the art of milling, and how relatively unchanged it remained through the centuries. To tell the history of this art in Ireland, and of the mills which have housed it, is to tell the story of the men of our land and of how they lived.

And this is how the famous Ulster poet, W.F. Marshall – a man who knew and felt about milling as a simple, imperishable, priceless activity of man – celebrated the attraction of one of these old mills:

> There's a green glen hidden in the middle of Tyrone,
> There's a grey house sheltered by a hill
> And the glen runs along to a little bridge of stone,
> And the grey house stands beside a mill.
> Now the mills are merry from the Lagan to the Foyle,
> As the millstones triumph o'er the grain,
> But you'll hear the sweetest as you travel to Dunmoyle,
> Humming near the bridge at Shane.

Oh! The whins are covered with the gold of May again,
And the whitethorn blossom has begun;
There are blackbirds calling in the middle of the glen,
And a wee burn singing in the sun.
But the best lies yonder in the shadow of the hill
Where a wheel makes showers like rain;
For I am the miller, and my sweetheart is the mill
Humming near the bridge at Shane.

When my days are over, there's a boon I hope to win,
– The good Lord will never say me nay –
I will hie me often to the valley in Cloghfin
Where the breeze blows down from Cavanreagh.
I shall fling no shadow, though the sun may shine above,
I shall leave no footprint in the lane,
But I'll miss no greeting if I hear the mill I love
Humming near the bridge at Shane.

4

William Scott
the Man who Began it All

TONY DEESON, MADDIN SCOTT

MARGARET SCOTT, OF WHOM THERE WILL BE MORE LATER, traced the genealogy of the Scott family back to the early 11th century, although as one might expect some of the connections verge on the speculative because the Scotts in the border counties of Scotland were numerous.

Perhaps it is sufficient to begin with John Scott, who bought Woll in 1660 and married a daughter of Robert Scott of Harwood. Their first son, Walter of Woll, married Eliza, a daughter of Robert Scott of Horsleyhill. One of their sons, Robert Scott (1698–1771), was the first to bring the family to Ulster and settled at Tamnymore in Co. Londonderry. He was the great-grandfather of William Scott of Lisanelly – our William Scott – whose father and grandfather were also known as William.

The following is an extract, reproduced almost verbatim from a memoir, 'Jottings from a Miller's Notebook' by Maddin Scott, William Scott's great-grandson, which appeared in *A Hundred Years A-Milling*.

> The millmen, members of the family-round-the-mill in his day, called my great-grandfather not 'the boss' or 'the governor' but, more affectionately, 'the oul' gineral.' For he used to stand in the mill yard in his frock coat and topper directing and urging on the traffic. This must have been necessary for on many a Saturday the red farm carts would be waiting to unload oats in a long line all the way from Bell's Bridge, and there must have been considerable congestion in the mill yard, congestion I'm afraid we 'tholed' right up to 1949, when a new bridge was built over one of the head-races.
>
> He was greatly interested in the improvement of the lands at Lisanelly. He bought this property of about 100 acres in 1855, and found it very neglected. The land was drained, small houses and his own residence were built. When he began to work the mills he had gone to reside at Millbank, where he lived until 1867, when his son Charles married. In that year he removed to Lisanelly.
>
> On 10 November 1870 he retired from active participation in the mills, which were thereafter carried on by his two elder sons, but he still led a

busy life giving personal supervision to his various properties and directing the work of his steward at Lisanelly. He was now 65; it was remarkable that he still had new ideas which he was anxious to put into practice.

A few incidents may be mentioned as throwing light on the circumstances of the period and the character and personality of William Scott. He was a man whose word was his bond, and he carried out most of his important transactions by word of mouth without any documents whatever. If he was not met with equal straightforwardness he resented it very greatly. A case in point was when, having let a certain property, some conditions agreed to were not observed by the tenant. The defence of the latter was that the stipulations were not in writing; those who heard the scorn with which William Scott received this explanation long remembered it.

In his day oatmeal was shipped to Scotland regularly and oats to France. As regards the Scottish business there was a curious incident. The agent at Glasgow left the country, being in debt to the firm. Long years afterwards, when William Scott had retired and was in ill-health, his son Charles, then proprietor of the business, received a subpoena to give evidence at a case tried in London. It turned out that one of the parties in this action was the long-lost agent. William Scott was very unwilling that Charles should go, and spoke of paying the fine. However, in the end he consented; and since Charles Scott brought back valuable presents for everyone it is to be presumed the meeting with the former agent had not been wholly unsatisfactory – certainly Charles Scott took with him full particulars of the debt.

William Scott and his sons had a long business friendship with the Barry McCorkells, father and son, of Londonderry, whose firm was later carried on by William McCorkell & Co. Ltd; McCorkells imported maize (in those days in sailing ships) for the north-west of Ireland. Records give us a picture of William Scott walking from the GNR station in a stock and silk hat, accommodating his pace to that of a small grandson (W. R. Scott) he brought with him. He went to Barry McCorkell's private office – a small dark room with a dusty window. When the door was safely closed the two men unbent, and they seemed to the listening boy to discuss many things, and not without a good deal of dry humour.

My grandfather was much impressed by the clear brain and immense capacity for work of a young chartered accountant, Hugh Smylie, while he was auditing the mill books. When the latter wanted to set up for himself, the mill audit was one of the first he was assured of. For 50 years three generations of Scotts were well guided on the financial side by Mr Smylie, succeeded in the 1930s by two of his sons, and their staffs. [In a sense, the shade of Hugh Smylie is still with the company in its sixth generation, for the firm of Hugh Smylie and Sons was merged, merged again, and yet again – at least four times in the past 50 years. Its latest incarnation is as PricewaterhouseCoopers, who remain Scotts' auditors.]

Our founder was a strong and forceful personality, but withal a kindly one to his friends and employees. He helped many make a start for themselves, and his interest in the well being of his people was shown half a

Hugh Smylie, auditor

century before welfare schemes began to interest bureaucrats. This was manifested in an interesting way after he purchased the Lisanelly property. Before he built Lisanelly for himself he set to work to provide cottages for his workers.

Unlike many persons of good intentions, he had technical knowledge and an understanding of human nature. He showed both in his housing scheme. Instead of placing the workers' houses in one corner in a long, dull row (which can become depressing even in country surroundings) he separated them, sometimes two together, in other cases only one; at one point he had a group of about six.

Mrs Hugh Smylie, mother of Sydney and Cecil V. Smylie, the latter of whom was a director of W & C Scott Ltd for a time in the 1940s and 1950s.

His idea was that some of the men and their wives would be more individualistic and would be better apart. The area was large enough for the detached cottages to be out of sight of each other. In building construction he evolved a type of cottage for which there is a good deal to be said with regard to the comfort of the tenants. It was square, a fireplace with a chimney was placed in the centre. The chimney also supported the rafters of the roof.

The interior was divided first into two rectangles, the one with the fireplace being the living room. The other was divided again into two bedrooms, both of which were partially heated by the constant peat fire. This type of cottage was somewhat more expensive to construct, and certainly more expensive to maintain. Almost all of them have now disappeared.

There is an entry in his household accounts, 1872–7, which throws a pleasant light on his methods – '1873, July 5. Pd Dr Thompson by cheque £5, which was all he asked for, but I said it was too little and would give it on account.' Then follows the further entry – 'Pd Dr Thompson £20.'

William Scott's first wife was Ellen Jeffers, daughter of Charles Jeffers of Enniskillen, and a sister of James Jeffers, governor of the gaol there. They had four sons and no daughters. The two eldest, William and Charles, joined him in the business. The third, Robert John, was a surgeon in the Army and the youngest, James, was a solicitor. After the death of Ellen, William Scott married Elizabeth Noble, a widow, who was one of the Collums of Enniskillen. They had no children.

Another anecdote of William Scott may be recorded as showing the affection of his people for him. He had an old coachman, Lanty Starrs, who spent his life in his service. At the time of the first Home Rule agitation there was a secret and wholly informal 'sale' of properties owned by prominent Protestants, the Catholic 'buyers' to obtain possession when the 'English' were driven out of the country. Lanty thought it would be a terrible thing if the 'oul' masther' was deprived of the house he had built. So at the auction he bought Lisanelly – it is said for five shillings [25p] – with the intention of returning it to the owner. Later Lanty was pensioned off. He tried America but came back to the cottage reserved for him at Lisanelly.

There was a curious incident about him and one of the horses he drove, 'Captain'. In the later years my great grandfather chiefly used a 'covered car', which had the door at the back. Driving home to Lisanelly one evening the horse shied and Lanty was thrown off the box. Captain went on as usual and stopped at the hall door as he had been in the habit of doing. William Scott did not notice anything till he spoke to the coachman on the box who he found had disappeared. He was relieved to see his faithful Lanty approaching, none the worse. Captain lived to a very great age, said to be about 57, and was for a long time a pensioner in the Lisanelly fields.

William Scott retired from the business in 1870 in favour of his sons, William (1837–1880) and Charles (1841–1897) who were then 33 and 29. [William the younger never married.] When he assigned the lease of the Mill to his two sons it was made quite a formal occasion. He told them it was a good business if they worked hard at it and yet didn't let themselves become entirely dependent on it as the be-all and end-all of their lives. Also, 'Try to work out some means of treating your oatmeal before you sell it so as to reduce the housewife's time in cooking.'

The brothers may not have thought much about this at the time. They were making good-quality oatmeal, milled into the number of cuts of fineness which were in demand 'across the water' and in Ireland. But their father's words were to bear fruit about 20 years later. In the meantime their flour milling trade must have been of more concern to them.

That is the end of Maddin Scott's memoir on William Scott, but before leaving the founder of the business it may be relevant to mention briefly his contributions to Omagh and Tyrone outside of the milling trade.

He was a prodigious builder. His exertions in this direction included houses on the east side of Dublin Road before it joins Market Street; parts of Market Street itself; 15 shops on the north side of John Street and houses in Church Hill; and, in partnership with the Market Committee, the pork market. In partnership with James Greer and Samuel Galbraith he built the Bond Store in Campsie. He was also involved with Greer, Galbraith and Hans Fleming in the building of Termon and Drumnakilly churches; Trinity Presbyterian Church; the old Model School in Omagh; the Courthouse at Monaghan; Downhill House; and Lisanelly and the workers' cottages in the park land.

As already noted, he was a director of Omagh Gas Light Company, and supplied all its fittings when it started which, according to a contemporary account, gave 'extreme satisfaction as well from the superior style in which they have been put up, as from their tasteful appearance and modest price'; he also directed or managed saw mills at Lisnamallard and in Mountjoy Forest, including the Ballylucas Steam Saw Mill; and the Bond Store and the pork, flax and hide markets in Omagh. He was instrumental in planning the public water services in various places and was chairman of the Omagh Town Commissioners in 1865.

5

William and Charles Scott
Building amid Adversity

TONY DEESON

WILLIAM AND CHARLES (known to the family-round-the-mill as 'Master Willie' and 'Master Charlie') started to work for their father when they were 17. They came into their inheritance at the start of a difficult period for the mills of Ireland. Their father had correctly predicted that following the famine new lines of milling business would be stimulated. Also, at this time the cattle trade was increasing in Ireland. The turnip root had been introduced as a source of winter feedstuff so that it became possible to select and breed cattle, instead of killing them off annually, which had been the practice since time immemorial. All feedstuffs were in increased demand; the provender trade had begun.

When maize became common after 1850 the mills could supply cattle with more variety in feedstuffs, and this kept them busy after they had ground the past year's home-grown grain. Moreover, the milling of flour left a good 30 per cent of bran and pollards which could be used in the new trade. In addition, of course, oats were milled. So the business of milling waxed fat and expanded, and a vigorous industry came into being in Ulster.

However, by 1870, when William and Charles took over the business from their father, the full effect of the repeal of the corn laws 25 years earlier was beginning to be felt. Foreign flour, and American flour in particular, which could be milled so cheaply, provided steadily increasing competition, encouraged by the development of larger and faster cross-Atlantic ships, which were also cheaper to run. Overseas, new roller-mill methods were introduced for the grinding of corn. The system in the old steam and water-power mills was abandoned, and a series of iron rollers for grinding replaced the flat stones. This method produced a greater variety of grades of flour and meant that a much finer quality could be ground much faster. So cheap and so plentiful was the American flour that it made both the growing of wheat and the grinding of flour unprofitable in Ireland, particularly because the Irish wheat was so soft that it needed expensive drying before milling.

In *A Hundred Years A-Milling*, Felicity Walton remarks that 'These 30 years make a tale of sorrow.' Many of the Ulster mills could not afford the new roller-mill process, and when they could developments took place so quickly that investments were often made in obsolescent models, which were slow and cumbersome. In 1872 new stores were constructed at the mill and later in the decade young William made a journey to the USA to see the new roller-mill process and to decide which of the many variations would best replace the old millstones, but no decision was made until 1884, after his death, when Charles converted to the roller process, purchasing the plant from one Henry Simon. The decision might have been made sooner but for the ill health that dogged the brothers. Neither of them had their father's physical strength, and William was a partner for only 10 years before he died, unmarried, in 1880 when he was only 43.

In *A Hundred Years A-Milling* there is a description by Mat Mulcaghey of a corn mill of that time operated by one, possibly pseudonymous, Dan Reilly. It cannot be so very different from the Scotts' mill in the 1880s. Mat Mulcaghey writes:

> In common with all other corn mills there was a kiln for the drying of oats. Probably you know the arrangement. In a large room on the ground floor there was a big fire within an arch called the kil'logie. The fire extended far back on bars placed horizontally. Leading from this upwards was a funnel shaped opening arranged in such a way that the heat of the kiln fire impinged on the perforated metal plates of the kiln floor above. On the bars below a huge fire burned brightly, while immediately in front and reclining on one elbow old Pat McDade the kiln man lay and kept the fire replenished with fuel. This fuel consisted of dry shillen seeds, which Pat, with a dexterous twist of the wrist scattered over the flame. It was on the iron floor above that the corn was dried prior to being shilled and ground into meal.

The situation in which Charles found himself did not quickly improve. Locally grown oats were shipped as oatmeal to Scotland and it can be inferred that the quality and price were sufficiently attractive to impress the canny and pernickety Scottish buyers. But evidence given to the Commission on Irish Industries in 1887 showed the enormous force of competition from Chicago, whence flour was simply dumped on Ireland. In the 10 years prior to 1887 one-third of the mills in Ulster disappeared, and within seven miles of Newry nine lay idle. In 1885 Charles Scott petitioned the Committee on Irish Industries for a restriction on imports:

> I need scarcely remark to you that flour milling was at one time one of the principal industries of Ireland, but owing to the excessive importation of foreign flour of late years, this trade has been almost annihilated through the country. For this flour when landed must be sold at any price, irrespective of cost, and owing to being so much less bulk than wheat,

which the home miller has to purchase, can be landed at less cost.

The large importations of flour which prevent the grinding of wheat here, have increased the price of bran and other milling offals very much; and as bran is becoming more of a necessity with our farmers, they are obliged to pay an extra price for it and other offals, as being of a bulky nature, they cannot be imported at low freights from abroad.

The loss to the labouring classes by so many mills being stopped is very considerable, as many mills, from their situations, employed a large staff of carters, attendants, etc. You are aware very many large mills are stopped, and many smaller ones, in fact almost all are crushed out. Were the quantity of flour or a greater proportion of what is imported, manufactured in the country a large number of hands would be employed, and much money in wages circulated, and benefit given to the farmer in the lower price of offal. Also to the shipowner, as it would require more ships to carry the increased quantity of wheat, and to labourers to discharge cargoes, not to speak of dues which vessels would pay to the harbour trusts etc.

A small duty of say two shillings [10p] to half-a-crown [12^{1}/2p] per sack would not be felt by the customer, as it would not increase the price of bread to any extent, would perhaps, enable the milling trade to regain its former place in the industries of the country.

You are aware a number of mills through the various districts of the country have lately adopted the most improved roller machinery, so that the finest flour is now produced at home, which shows that nothing has been left undone by the milling trade to meet the foreign competition.

Charles Scott (1841–1897)

But Charles Scott's and no doubt many others' special pleading went unregarded; no duties were imposed and the Irish millers were left to fend for themselves. Times continued to be far from easy. A letter of Charles's father survives, written in 1885: 'Charles has a great deal of trouble striving to keep pace with the times, which are very much altered for the worse.' (It must have been about this time, or perhaps a little later, that the mill was connected to the telephone system. One assumes that its number – Omagh 20 – indicated that it was the 20th concern locally to make use of this amenity.)

Only very gradually did the situation improve. Those concerns that survived the initial onrush of foreign flour, having set about improving their machinery and methods, could breathe again. By 1900 the number of Irish mills had been greatly reduced but those that survived, Excelsior Mills at Omagh among them, were improved and hardened to new standards of efficiency.

In 1881, in the midst of the depression and the year after his brother William's death, it is a tribute to Charles's courage and commitment that he purchased the fee simple of the mills. At the same time he acquired the house and lands of Lisnamallard; within a few years he bought some fields that completed the area in which he was interested. This purchase gave him complete control of all the land on one side of the watercourses from the weir until they rejoined the river, a distance of about 1,350 yards. He also owned the other side except one field at each end. When he bought Lisnamallard House it had been empty for many years and required a great deal of work to make it habitable.

In 1889 Charles Scott purchased the Mullaghmore Mills, where he established his brother-in-law Edward Arnold as manager. This branch was carried on for a number of years as Arnold & Co. A year later William Scott, his father and founder of the mills at Omagh, died at the good age of 85, leaving Charles as sole proprietor.

Sadly, Charles's own life had only another seven years to run and he died in 1897 when he was 55. Nevertheless, to some degree he carried on the tradition of public service begun by his father. He was Chairman of the Omagh Gas Light Company and a director of the Bond Store and pork, flax and hide markets. He was also active in laying out the additions to Omagh in the Campsie direction as trustee of the estate of his father's friend, James Greer, and was involved in the planning and fund-raising for the First Omagh Presbyterian Church.

A garden party at Lisnamallard on 8 June 1896. The occasion was a summer meeting of the Royal Society of Antiquaries of Ireland invited by Margaret Scott. They are posed in front of the new greenhouse which later fell into disrepair and was demolished in 1982. W.R. Scott is seated front left of the picture (without a hat).

Towards the end of Charles's life he had the help of his son, Lewis Irwin Scott, who after graduating in engineering at Trinity College, Dublin was considering his career and in the meantime experimenting with the production of rolled oats or flaked oatmeal. In the early 1890s the first experimental work in flaking oatmeal had been done by Charles Scott and he brought the rolled oats into production with selling agents in London, Dublin, Glasgow and Belfast. Lewis himself ran some of the trial millings. The big problem was how to get the groats (the kernels of oats, dried, shelled and polished) sufficiently dried down again, after steaming and rolling, to ensure the keeping qualities of the flake.

Garden Party
AT
LISNAMALLARD,
JUNE 8th, 1896.

Summer Meeting of the Royal Society
of Antiquaries of Ireland.

Now William Scott had brought a head miller from Scotland, Sam Cockburn, known as 'Old Sam'. He was eventually succeeded by his son, 'Young Sam'. One afternoon Charles sent his son out on an errand and Lewis had to leave a milling to be dried over a series of trays in the charge of 'Old Sam'. Lewis came home from the mill that evening, very disconsolate, saying, 'Old Sam must be beginning to dote. When I got back he had ruined my trial by interfering with the drier and met me rubbing his silly hands saying, "Oh, Master Lewie, this is the best wheeze we ever got on to! Selling them Glenhordial water at 3d [1^{1}/4p] a pound." I'll have to run another lot through tomorrow. But please send Old Sam to the flour mill.' However, it is on record that his father did not accede to his request to remove his head miller from these interesting experiments to the straight-run monotony of the flourmill. Indeed, the flourmill was closed in 1897, although the firm continued with packeted flour and wheatmeal until the 1960s.

Charles may have had his father's words in mind, namely that the mill should not be the be-all and end-all of his life; this remark coupled with the cut-back in business encouraged him to participate in public affairs, partly through a desire to be of assistance to the community and partly as a relaxation from the strain of business worries, although the family felt that he shortened his life by his devotion to his varied interests. He was nominated a grand juror and gave much time to his duties, which were often onerous and included the work of 'Presentment Sessions', where most of the functions now discharged by district councils were at that time performed.

For the 'mill family' it was something of a disaster when Charles died. As a flour miller all his days he saw that wheat-growing was declining in Tyrone and felt there were poor prospects for a mill so far inland. Thus he intended that his eldest son, William Robert Scott, should be a barrister and Lewis, his second son, a solicitor, while he carried on the business, training a manager to run it after his day. But, as we shall see, things fell out otherwise.

Charles's widow, Margaret, was a remarkable woman, who outlived her husband by over 30 years. She was the sixth child of the Reverend John Arnold, who was appointed Minister of the First Omagh Congregational

Church in 1835. For all her long life (she died in 1930 at the age of 87) she lived within two miles of Omagh. She married when she was 24 and became successively a miller's wife, a miller's mother, a miller's grandmother, and a miller's great-grandmother. As such she became an anchor-point of the Scott family. Throughout her life she interested herself in local works of charity for the welfare of her community, and her sympathy and understanding embraced wider issues too. For example, she started a minor national health service in the Omagh rural district when she was President (1908–1930) of the Omagh Branch of the Women's National Health Association. This was founded and for many years directed by the Marchioness of Aberdeen and Temair to combat the ravages of tuberculosis. Free milk and school meals were arranged for a great number of country schools at a cost to the parents of 1d (^{1}/2p) per week per child. Shelters for the open-air treatment of patients were also provided.

Margaret Scott always firmly asserted that her education cost her father exactly 35 shillings (£1.75). Presumably this figure was expended on books. She notes among her papers that at eight years she 'was making work for herself' in Latin grammar and history, ancient and modern, and at 21 she was studying astronomy with her father. She was also a talented musician. At the age of 80 she began to write books, thus finding an outlet for a mind that was still active when advancing years compelled her to forgo physical pursuits. Her writings give a vivid account of life in the household of an Ulster minister 150 years ago, and were published privately. Some of them also appeared in *A Hundred Years A-Milling*. They form a valuable record of life in Ulster in bygone times, which can hardly be imagined today. Two extracts from her writings that have a relevance to our story are reproduced as the next two chapters.

Margaret Scott

6

Rus in Urbe

MARGARET SCOTT

IN THIS EXTRACT FROM HER WRITINGS Margaret Scott describes her coming to Millbank as the wife of Charles Scott and thus the mistress of the house where she had previously stayed as a guest following a disastrous fire which gutted her father's home. Of that time she wrote: 'The Scotts were very kind to me, but I was lonely and sad beyond words, having lost my home.' 'Rus in urbe' refers to the fact that Margaret Scott was 'a country-woman in town' for most of her days, and she often used these words as a pseudonym.

After the fire my father was offered a small house in the heart of the town, free of rent for a year, by a very kind friend. It was from this house I was married and went, as a bride, to Millbank, where I had been a visitor in 1864, whereas I was now the mistress. I was still well pleased with myself; in fact, I thought I was very clever and competent at the time of my marriage. I meant to work as I had done at home, but I soon made the discovery that there I had been one of many, whereas I was now one only, with a man and a maid. The latter was much older than I was and a highly competent person. However, I planned much, silently and unknown to any mind but my own. This silence saved me from pitfalls, and I had wisdom enough to see that my life was to be shaped in the new. When anything was required, it was to be done in the best way, and skilled men were employed. Thus my handicraft in various directions seemed to be unnecessary; therefore after my springing life of industrious girlhood I settled down to modern matronhood, but in the rebuilding of the Margaret structure, or I should rather say Scott structure, it was still plus Arnold and also plus Irwin.*

It was a very great pity that the girls of my day, though good in all the important duties of life, were a little too much rolled up in their own homes and in their parents' surroundings and interests. So it takes time to rub off the impressions of years, but when that is accomplished another stage in one's progress is made, a stage in which the impressions are indelible. So, without that of the girl, the wife's knowledge is nil; but, granted that, her edifice of life is becoming both a greater and sounder piece of masonry.

One thing impressed me very much. We saw a great deal of my father-in-law [William Scott, the founder of the mill] and my brother-in law [Charles's elder brother, also William]. Their conversation was something of a revelation to me. It scarcely ever turned on local events or local people. Events and policies all over the world were discussed, all sorts of inventions and engineering schemes and new books and articles in the reviews. I recollect saying to my sister Mary that in my new home I never heard anything about Omagh or the people round, to which she replied, 'Without knowing it, you have moved into a bigger and better society, and while your body is still in Omagh your mind belongs to the larger world.'

As time progressed I found my husband was far from being a strong young man. I had an idea that, when the days lengthened into spring, he might like to come out to the garden and work there after office hours. I broached this but he promptly said, 'I never worked in a garden and I never will.' I realised very soon he had to rest and sleep on the large sofa in the dining room till the time came to make his nightly round of the mills. This occupied about 45 minutes every evening just before bedtime. I told him to sleep on and that I would be responsible for awakening him at the proper time. Even then I was not aware of how necessary rest and sleep were to him. I had never seen anyone eat so little. I heard afterwards that when he was 18 (through the strain of his responsibilities in the building of a street

*Margaret's mother's maiden name

of shops and houses, for which his father had secured the land) he had gastritis and was taken to Dublin to consult a specialist. He was then ordered to eat nothing but bread and milk for a year – an order which he obeyed rigidly. But he was never properly cured; and an office life was not the best for a slight young man with a meagre appetite. Also this office was far from being a good one. Mrs Scott [Charles's mother] told me he could not eat much food or coarse food, so it was necessary to give him what he liked in every way. I was so obliged to my mother-in-law for these hints. She said, 'I can tell you what your own mother could not tell you, for she has reared healthy, strong lads on plain food. She would never think of Charles being what he is.' All this helped me, and we got on amazingly well.

After some eight or nine months my husband took me to my first theatre. The play was 'Rob Roy'. I was entranced, and to this day I am more at home in a theatre when there is a good play on than anywhere else – except at an opera. My father thought he saw us and watched us into the Court House, where the Grand Jury rooms were used as a theatre by travelling companies. He rushed to my mother saying, 'Maggie and Charles are off to the theatre.' My mother more quietly replied – knowing that motherhood was expected in a couple of months – 'I hope Maggie was walking slowly.' 'Slowly,' my father echoed, 'they were going like hares.' I think this dates my first lecture after marriage, to which, on the following day, I listened dutifully.

Up to the time of my marriage in 1867 I had done much common work with a slight intermingling of uncommon activities. I fear I cared little for poetry and artistic work, tending towards practical things and what was plain and simple in dress and food. In my new home this disposition continued. Mr William Scott, my father-in-law, moved to Lisanelly, leaving Millbank to us. It was a long, old, roomy cottage which had been added to and added to, so that its plan was quaint, suggesting Topsy's remark, 'I 'spects I growed.' It had much old furniture and many old things in drawers that I, in my early ignorance, described as rubbish. It is not easy to make myself out such a barbarian, but 'confession is good for the soul'. When I had got rid of the contents of the drawers, I attacked the walls. There was framed tapestry in silks, but the frame was old, so to my untutored eye how could what was inside the frame be of any worth? Then away with it without a thought; with it went much more which I have often wished for, vainly, since. The last item on the wall of one of the rooms was a boy of eight or nine – the picture perhaps was right enough, but the frame was far past its first youth, retaining only the remains of its former gilding. In the end my festival of soap and suds was completed by sending the whole thing away. I can still remember the picture. It was quite fresh under the glass. It was of a young boy clad in green tartan with stockings to match, with a scarf or plaid brought over his shoulder and fastened with a silver buckle. He had red hair, which I did not like, for no Scott I knew of had red hair. I asked my husband about it and he said it was among the things Mr William Scott had brought from Ballycolman or Carricklee when his father had married again. In after years how much I should have given to have left those old rooms as they were, filled with things of the past. I did confess this to a Scotsman and he said, 'How many thoughtless people have done the same thing. It has been so in my family too, and I often feel sad over the destruction of many old, interesting papers.'

I have said something elsewhere of my father-in-law's schemes for the comfort of his workpeople. Though the firm paid the highest wages in the district and gave constant employment to suitable men, I felt that much could be done for them and their families if the money were expended to better advantage, so I began to try to teach that the wives should try to have a better meal for our workers than the tea and bread they were wont to provide for the mid-day meal. I told them to go to the butcher, where in those days (I speak of the years 1868, 1869) a basket of bones, with plenty of meat adhering to them could be obtained for sixpence [2^1/2p]. These, boiled with vegetables (which were plentiful and easily obtainable or could be grown in the gardens of their houses) would make a good broth, which could be thickened with oatmeal. The meat from the bones, served with broth, would provide a nourishing dinner for two days for the breadwinner, while potatoes could be introduced to give variety. Indeed, almost anything will furnish variety if the woman is resourceful. Alas, I was derided by the women, and my efforts towards progress were called the vagaries of 'Mrs Charlie'.

My mother-in-law consoled me in this sea of disappointment by telling me that, nine years before, a maid she had brought with her from Enniskillen became engaged to one of the workers at the mills. Mrs Scott, being fond of her, taught her so that she should be an example to other somewhat untidy and not always thrifty women. Especially she pegged into her the necessity of a good meal in the middle of the day; and to help her in making a good start, she was to have all the vegetables she wanted from the Millbank garden. 'Well,' Mrs Scott wound up, 'every time I went to see her the diminuendo in her housewifery was on the increase, the perennial kettle was re-instated and the last time I went to see her she was wasting her time gossiping with another woman who was fast making her as shiftless as herself.' As I became a family woman and delicate, I had to cease the unequal struggle, and 40 years went by before I made another great effort to penetrate the rhinoceros hide of slackness and indifference when the fire of her Excellency's (the Marchioness of Aberdeen and Temair) brain lit something in mine from the bygone years.

Between the two dates I have mentioned there was an interlude. In the '80s there were no schools of domestic science, and I found that several girls about Omagh were anxious to learn about cooking and to extend the knowledge they had gained in their own homes about it and the running of a house. So a class was started after we had gone to Lisnamallard, which I enjoyed greatly. I had the idea – if my readers will pardon the phrase – of making cooking scientific. By observation I had found the exact temperature at which each operation in various kinds of cooking should be carried on. The oven doors were bored for thermometers, and my idea was that the cooks should have a scale of thermometer readings, say for the roasting, and the time at which they should be varied. With a chart and a clock all she had to do was to adjust her heat, and she should know that everything was following a normal course. We also did dairying, carving, and laundering. One incident comes back. My two elder sisters were members of this class. I fear they did not take it seriously, for on one occasion, when I had an examination, the answers from one of them consisted altogether of extraordinarily apt quotations from 'The Hunting of the Snark' ...

7

Flood and Fire

MARGARET SCOTT

This second extract from Margaret Scott's writings was originally published in *More Recollections*, privately printed in 1927.

IN MY NEW LIFE AT MILLBANK [from 1867] it might be said that I became acquainted with both flood and fire – the former being a new experience and the latter reviving from time to time the sad memories of the ashes of my childhood's home at Kivlin. As to the first, Millbank lay low; and when the river rose, as it does often in times of storm, we were living on an island with eight or nine feet of raging torrent cutting us off from the town. In Mountjoy Terrace (which is the front of the mill buildings) there were occasions when the residents there had to escape by boats from their drawing room windows.

Fires came too often like a thief in the night, and the way I chanced to be indirectly involved was that, owing to the extent of the mill buildings and a certain danger from fire to some of them, my father-in-law [William Scott] had purchased a powerful fire engine and trained a staff to use it. This with another at the military barracks, were the only provision to fight fire in Omagh, and these remain the only efficient protection down to the present time. [But a town fire engine was brought from Belfast in 1935. Motor-driven, it was on solid tyres and manned by a crew of urban council employees. Developments followed over the years and were hastened by the 1939–45 war.]

Thus, when there was a conflagration of any serious kind the amateur fire brigade of Omagh mills was called upon. As Millbank adjoined the mills my husband [Charles Scott] was usually aroused to superintend the operations. My first experience of this kind was in August 1868. One Sunday night there came a banging, furious and prolonged, at the hall door. The messenger brought news that Mr Matthew's house was on fire and the engine was needed immediately.

Being a Sunday there were only the watchmen at hand; but, while my husband was hurriedly dressing, he devised a plan of campaign. In seconds the alarm was sounding, the engine and horses were being prepared, and first the clerks and then the men began to race to their places. Soon I heard the fire engine tearing along with a terrific clatter and the people, beside themselves with fright, clearing a way for it through the streets. Unfortunately, the season being a very dry one, there was little water in the river, and the efforts made were of small avail. Two houses were burnt out, but the adjoining ones were saved.

My part of that night was the waiting in anxiety. After my husband had left I called the one indoor maid. I told her all I knew, and she was all anxiety for the young mother-to-be – I was expecting my first baby at the end of the month. I got her to come with me to our only window upstairs which commanded a full view of the burning mass, and there we remained until 5.30 am. Then I saw the blaze was becoming less intense, and I asked to be taken down, for I was in an agony of fear for my husband's safety.

Also, I knew I should have tea ready for him. I said to Rebecca, the maid, 'Oh, you must have plenty of hot water ready for the master,' and her answer to this provoked my first smile. 'Well I guess he has had bath enough in the six hours he has been away.' Soon he returned, black as a sweep, cold and overdone; indeed he overworked himself that night, though I never heard any word of thanks from anyone – the willing horse is the hardest ridden.

Another of these sudden fire-calls about 25 years later stands out in my memory. It was one in which my son, Lewis [managing director of W & C Scott Ltd, 1897–1919] and my daughter, Bessie, were involved. This was a fire in the main street of the town. On that occasion the engine was driven right into the river in order to get the greatest volume of water, for the situation was very serious. The wind was raging and it was carrying sparks and burning fragments across the street, so that there was a risk that the houses on both sides would go.

Lewis, with a South African soldier, got up on the roof, while Bessie saw that the line of hose was long and the pumping of the engine was not so effective as it should have been. So she went into the river and stood in the water to direct operations there in order to keep up a full supply of water to Lewis, who was perched on a roof some 60 yards from her. He was saving the side of the street which was endangered by directing the hose on the burning wood and the sparks that blew from the main fire.

One of the houses in danger was that of the Misses Greer, and the two old ladies blessed Lewis every time they heard the rush of a volume of water which he directed on their slates. At the end of several hours he had to be helped down from his high perch; and, after being revived by brandy and having his legs massaged, returned home triumphant...

The mill-workers worked nobly as amateur firemen. The old engine was a manual one, and required about a dozen strong men exerting their strength in working the pump. They could not keep this up for long, and so relays were arranged in which manner, when water was available, a powerful flow was kept up for the time it was required, sometimes for six or seven hours. They were resourceful, too, as was shown on one occasion when a wheel broke and they galloped the engine to the fire on the hubs of what had been the wheels ...

A night attack on the door was not always related to a fire. Some five years after the experience with which I began – that is in 1873 – there was one of a very different origin.

It occurred in the following way. It appears that in the course of their work in loading or unloading wagons at the railway station, some of the mill-workers had discovered some empty hogsheads or puncheons which they found still contained dregs of whatever liquor had been in them. These they drank and it seems these dregs were exceedingly strong, making them not so much drunk as mad.

They had all been dealt with except one, and the first that was seen of this man was a figure reeling up the Millbank avenue. He had the reputation of being violent when intoxicated; and my husband hurried through the back and out to the front of the house in order to intercept him.

The first I knew of this was the sound of a frightful yell. I was undressing at the time, and staying not for skirt or bodice, I seized the poker, flew down the hall and out to the gravel. A glance told me that one or both had the other by the throat. My husband told me to go inside, but I flew in with my poker. The sudden white apparition frightened the man, and he loosened his grip, whereupon my husband shut and locked the door, while the man rambled on outside, 'I could do for you easily, only she came.'

The last I heard of him that night was as he was being conveyed away by policemen; he was crying, and calling for his blue-eyed Annie, the latter being his little daughter. Next morning his wife went to the fountain-head. Mrs Scott [Margaret Scott's mother-in-law, wife of William Scott] interceded for the man with a family, but my husband said, 'I must see my wife before I commit myself.' He came to me, and the man was forgiven, though there was much kindly amusement and admiration in the Scott family for the white apparition armed with the woman's weapon.

William R. Scott, 1868–1940,
in academic robes

8

William Robert Scott
from Proprietor to Chairman

TONY DEESON

IN 1897, AFTER THE DEATH of Charles Scott when he was only 55, his two sons, William Robert (1868–1940) and Lewis Irwin (1872–1946) succeeded him. After the incorporation of the business the following year William Robert Scott became chairman, holding this office until his death in 1940, and Lewis Irwin was managing director until his retirement in 1919.

William, later Adam Smith professor of political economy at Glasgow University, was at that time assistant to the professor of moral theology at

St Andrews. Thus he had already begun to create an academic career for himself, independent of the mill. But throughout his life he found in the family milling business an interest second only to his chosen and distinguished career, and his clear brain and sound judgement were available to his younger brother and his successors whenever required. The 'family-round-the-mill' referred to him as 'the Professor'.

When Charles Scott died intestate, William expounded the desirability of forming a limited liability company and, assisted by the mill's auditors, Hugh Smylie & Co., brought this to fruition in 1898. Thereafter, for over 40 years he managed the mill's real estate and investments well.

Initially the capital of the limited company was small, the five children each taking up a fifth share, in the names of trustees in the case of any not yet of age. For the first seven years, that is from 1898 until 1905, the family were considered 'too young to appreciate the real meaning of the word dividend' and all profits were carried to the reserves of the young company. As Maddin Scott remarked:

> A truly wise policy no doubt, although possibly the persuasive powers of the intended barrister [William Robert Scott] were necessary to put it into practice! In under 20 years reserves, essential to a business like ours, amounted to twice the capital. But for many years, times in our ancient craft, never 'easy', were difficult. Although we had got off to a good start, our fight as a company was on and it was the struggle of an inland mill that these two brothers, both 'bonny fechters', were engaged in.

An obituary of William Robert Scott, published in the *Economic Journal* in 1940, gives the man the high credit he deserved and also helps to explain his strong and lasting interest in the mill of his forefathers:

> By the quite unexpected death of W. R. Scott, in his seventy-second year, the Royal Economic Society loses an ex-president and a vice-president; the Economic History Society, its president; Glasgow, the Adam Smith professor; the British Academy, its treasurer, several other societies, a highly valued officer; and his friends, one whose sheer goodness and integrity of character were as conspicuous as his learning, his industry and his public spirit. He had been unwell for about six weeks, but there was no anxiety. His son and daughter, who had come to see him, went way 'with pretty complete medical assurances', the day before he died.
>
> Scott wrote the most massive book of research in economic history of our time. He served the country on a long series of committees or commissions of inquiry or decision, often drafting the report himself. He was Director of the Glasgow Chamber of Commerce, a member of the Dumbartonshire Education Committee. Nothing economic – speculative, historical or applied – was alien to him. An Irishman by birth, though a Scot by adoption, all through a long, crowded academic life he also kept in touch with

the family milling business at Lisnamallard, near Omagh.

Trinity College, Dublin, gave him that complete training which, one has often thought, made her picked men the best educated people in the old United Kingdom, men of two learnings or more ... He first distinguished himself there in Logic and Ethics. He taught for a time in Dublin, but in 1896, when he was 28, he became assistant to the professor of moral philosophy at St Andrews. Three years later he was appointed lecturer in political economy ... In 1901 he stopped teaching philosophy but not before he had published what those competent to judge – I am not – say is an excellent study of *Francis Hutcheson* (1900) ... As for his special field of work, I fancy it was the mill at Lisnamallard that turned his mind to business history and the origins of the joint-stock company ... His mind once turned, his formidable industry came into play. No scholar who was also a regular teacher and examiner ... can have done so much specialised work in the leisure of ten years as he did between the publication of Francis Hutcheson and that of the three big, packed volumes of *The Constitution and Finance of English, Scottish and Irish Joint Stock Companies to 1720* (1910–12) ... The section on any of the greater companies – East India, Darien, South Sea, Bank of England – is in itself a solid monograph. Hardly one of them has been improved on in 30 years ...

Within two years of the issue he had completed a thorough Report to the Board of Agriculture for Scotland on Home Industries in the Highlands and Islands (1914). This was the sort of contemporary economic work that best suited his special gifts. Next year he succeeded William Smart in the Adam Smith chair at Glasgow. In 1917–18 he published two volumes of lectures, *Economic Problems of Peace after War*, good, but for their day only. He continued to report, and edit, and write prefaces and contribute to journals here and abroad. As fitted the occupant of his chair, he became a passionate student of 'Smithiana', and he made some discoveries; for he had all the qualities of the good bibliophile and bibliographer. His *Adam Smith as Student and Professor* (1937) contained the results, biographical detail of many sorts, with new evidence on the growth of Smith's thought, especially on the early development of his theory of distribution ... But his place among scholars is fixed, and fixed high, by the three volumes of his early 40s.

All the while he taught and administered unsparingly in Glasgow: 'a very good colleague and quite indefatigable', his chief writes. He filled his long count of offices and put work into every one. He examined in most universities. No picker and chooser, anything that he was called on to do he did, and never spared himself in the doing.

I have spoken of his modesty and his goodness. To watch Scott at work with some difficult character was a lesson in patience and applied morality ... He was resolute, pertinacious, yet self-effacing. I think he generally got his way, but he could not be cassant or ride roughshod. He was deeply affectionate; had the strongest family feeling and for many years a home life that was above every other thing to him. The *Memoir* of his wife that he printed for private circulation in 1930 is the record of this. She died in 1929, but happily there were both children and grandchildren. Those who care to meet noble women should try to see the *Memoir*. Of little things, they would learn from it what any who only met the ageing Scott might not have guessed, that for years he and she played together in first-class lawn tennis. To quote the close of the book may seem out of place in the *Economic Journal*. But it tells a great deal about Scott, and there is no reason why economists should not know him as he was. What he wrote ends with these words: 'and so she passed, being all in all to me' ...

Lewis Irwin Scott 1872–1946

9

Lewis Irwin Scott
Managing the Wheen of Wheels

TONY DEESON, MADDIN SCOTT

ACCORDING TO THE *Oxford English Dictionary*, 1987 edition, 'wheen' is from Old English but is now in use only in northern England and Scottish speech. Northern Ireland is not mentioned but the province's country idiom is often derived from the Scots. Its meaning depends on the context. An Ulsterman might say, 'I've a wheen o' pounds about me', which depending on the way it was said could mean 'a few' or 'quite a few'.

The word appears again on page 53 of the present book when W.F. Marshall in his poem 'The Lad' asks:

> An' what's a wheen of medals to me
> When my own wee lad's no more?

'Wheen' in literature is rare but not unknown. The *OED* cites Robert Louis Stevenson's *Kidnapped*, which was published in 1886: 'I wouldnae like the Balfours to be humbled before a wheen Hieland Campbells', which in this case presumably means 'a few'.

There follows an extract from 'Jottings from a Miller's Note Book – 1950' by Maddin Scott. The complete text appears in *A Hundred Years A-Milling* and this part concerns Maddin's memories of his uncle.

One day a boy of 12 [Maddin Scott], fishing the Camowen (pronounced Camóne) left his bicycle at a cottage and was given a drink of 'the guileless champagne of the County Tyrone' (fresh buttermilk). In return, as the good kind woman was obviously curious as to the identity of this wet scarecrow she was entertaining, the boy admitted he belonged to the mill in Omagh. 'Och, dear, that's a quare place,' said she, 'it takes a cart every day to haul the gold they earn to the bank.' This strange saying was pondered by the young fisherman on his winding, riverside road home where he interrupted his father and uncle in deep conclave, with a question if it was true? Never were the two brothers heard to laugh so loud and so long. The boy was packed off to a hot bath, and still hearing laughter indulged in the uncomfortable wonderment of the unconscious humorist ... The conclave (probably whether they could afford a couple of hundred for a 'mill improvement') ended on a happy note, thanks to that unknown benefactress.

This uncle of mine was a remarkable man, greatly revered and respected in the district, particularly by the farmers. He was a soccer international before he left Rossall School. Popular in the best meaning of the word, he was a renowned breeder of dogs, cattle and pigs and a bird fancier as well. The mill office was a tuneful place in his day with many varieties of singing canaries. 'Feather-world' friends used to ring up Omagh 20 to 'listen in' to the trilling of their favourites, the earpiece would be turned to one of the cages and the occupant usually obliged.

He had a mare, Brownberry, famed in the Edwardian jumping ring and a riding groom, 'Mickey', who was a bit fond of the beer. So Lewie would often unexpectedly have to 'take her over the sticks' himself, dressed for the stand and not for the ring, saying it was 'as good as signing the pledge' for the grief-stricken, repentant Mickey.

He had a flair for oil paintings and would often include in his collection paintings of a school which later came into fashion. When tired of them himself he would oblige the eager buyers and reinvest in others that appealed to his taste. He was much in demand in the concerts of his day as a singer of 'Phil the Fluter's Ball' and other Percy French songs.

But we all have a blind spot. Lewie was at times lacking in a sense of direction. One Boxing Day, while he was master of the Seskinores, he gave them a grand run for miles but finally bogged his mare in a field where the rushes were thick and tall. 'What hell-bad farmer owns this rotten land?' cried the master, exasperated, who led a good laugh when told the run had circled back on to his own!

… One of the minor advantages possessed by a family business is that if the chappie running it feels a little like going 'back to Cranny' where we started (later a mental hospital) or even just a bit overworked, he simply sends an SOS round the family to see if there is anyone who could give him a hand. After L.I. Scott took over control on the death of Charles Scott in 1897 it wasn't long before he got his brother-in-law to assist him. This was Percy Gough Dallinger [who married Charles Scott's daughter, Elizabeth]. He had resigned from his appointment as Principal of Government College, Lahore, on grounds of health, and had rented Homelea to recuperate until a suitable appointment arose in these islands. And very useful he must have been.

The mill day then began at seven, the office was opened by L.I. Scott and a clerk at that hour, my uncle Percy coming in with another at eight to let the other two off for breakfast. There was a pillarbox opposite the office with a collection at eight. The routine in those days was for answers to enquiries to be posted, travellers instructed for their journeys by the eight-thirty trains and the first carts from the stations unloaded before L. I. Scott left on his bicycle for breakfast at Lisanelly.

It was noticed that a certain customer always arrived shortly before nine for a load of goods, nothing extraordinary about this but it was rather worrying that the stocks, taken at 6pm daily, frequently showed a deficiency from the book figures. It was suspected that a storeman was handing out a bag extra to the number shown on the docket and receiving a 'back hander' from the purchaser; yet the loads seemed right at the check passing the office. So Percy Dallinger slipped out with the signed docket, unobtrusively, on his bicycle after the cart one morning and trailed it to the point in the country where it was being unloaded.

There the concealment came to light and the deficiencies were explained. The storeman was sacked – one of the very few cases of dishonesty among our staff in the course of our century. Soon after this P. G. Dallinger went to the County Tyrone Committee of Agriculture as its first secretary. He had moved from Omagh before the Kaiser war on promotion to London where he became head of a Department of the Ministry.

Another most useful and hard-working uncle of mine who later helped his brother-in-law, L.I. Scott, in the management of the business was Harold Davis Green [who married Mary, another daughter of Charles Scott and was joint managing director 1920–35], who had been in Lloyd's of London and came to Omagh for a few years before 1914. He and his wife, Mary Irwin Green, lived then at Lisnamallard with my grandmother, Margaret Scott. They were, both of them, most useful citizens of our town. He, a grand office man and a judge of oats, you could set your watch by him, she always ready to help anyone or a good cause. The experience which Harold Green had for a few years under L.I. Scott was to turn out most fortunately ... They went back to England before 1914 but returned after the war.

In December 1907 we took a lease of Newtownstewart Mill from The Maturin–Baird Estate. Mr Moncrieff, the previous tenant, had been milling oats for us for many years but the changeover meant the extra responsibility of running it ourselves. A good country trade, milling for the

farmers on the moutre system (as it was then called), the mulcture of older days, had been done for many years. This is a business rather like that of a laundry, demanding great particularity and care, yet one that was not big enough to justify a regular office clerk. Who would be our resident miller?

We were lucky enough to persuade Alec Mehaffy to move with his family from his corn mill at Castlefin. Honest as the day, fair to us his employers, as well as to the farmers and customers, hard working and clever, with Alec trained to this form of milling (which very few commercial firms would then bother with) we decided to give it a trial. The 'moutre' was done away with and a cash payment substituted. Good organisation and hard work brought success and we have continued milling for farmers to this day, as a department of the business. Alec's brother, Johnston, came to us also.

We put in a turbine to replace the water-wheel ... A present-day map of Newtownstewart would, we think, show remarkably few changes in 104 years. A grinding plant for maize and a producer gas engine for light water periods gave good employment for the business we felt we deserved to do, as employers of labour and citizens of the historic town of Newtownstewart. We lost our good Alec a few years after the Kaiser war, but Johnston stayed on to train Alec's two boys in milling, before emigrating to seek his fortune in America. Alec's sons Sandy and Robert carried on grandly in the family tradition and we think Alec would have been well content also to see his grand-daughter [Anna Jamieson, later Orr] in charge of the office.

That is the end of Maddin Scott's extract concerning Lewis Scott and the other personalities of his era. The Newtownstewart mill continued for many years until its trade was taken over by the mill at Omagh and its site sold to a Mr Maxwell of Urney in 1973. The former mill dam is now occupied by an attractive housing development, and the former mill buildings have become a carpet warehouse.

This four-wheel dray, formerly the property of Johnny Quigley, was used for many years to haul feed ingredients in hessian sacks from the Omagh GNR station to the mill, until the closure of the railway in 1963. Discovered locally by John Chambers in a farm shed in the late 1980s, the dray was meticulously restored by Jack Lynch, Castlederg, and has since had occasional use for promotional purposes. Here it was taking part in a television programme in 1991, at the Ulster-American Folk Park, Omagh. The horse was kindly loaned by Jack Lynch and the other actors were Gerald Little and Ruby Todd.

Like his father before him, Lewis Irwin Scott farmed the land at Lisanelly and directed the Bond Store and markets and improved the shops in John Street, built by his grandfather. In public service he was a grand juror of Tyrone and a JP, again following in his father's footsteps. He was a member of the Tyrone Farming Society and, as we have seen, master of the Seskinore Hunt.

During Lewis Irwin Scott's stewardship of the family business the Scott drier was patented, turbines replaced waterwheels and four-wheel drays the old two-wheelers; in 1903 there was a fire in one kiln but it proved not to be too serious; in 1905–6 a new store designed for bulk intake was built. As already noted, Newtownstewart mill was taken on lease in 1907 and the Mullaghmore mills, bought by Lewis's father in 1889, were destroyed by fire in 1908.

These developments are to be seen against the changing world scene. William Scott shipped oats to France and oatmeal to Scotland. He began flour milling and provender milling of straight feeds for north-west Ulster; his sons, William and Charles, continued these practices, with the exception of shipping oats to France. Charles also became an agent for Chicago milled flour and began the production of flaked oatmeal, which was then sold in hundredweight sacks; he stopped flour milling but continued to sell packeted white flour and wheatmeal. During Lewis's time the packeting of flake began. Flour imports from the USA continued against the background of rising prices; the oatmeal trade to Ireland generally, and to England, was greatly strengthened and the mill contracted for oatmeal supplies to public institutions throughout Ireland.

Family correspondence from the early years of the 20th century shows that, for all his talents and with a country lifestyle that many businessmen of today would envy, Lewis Scott was not content in Omagh. His personal popularity with the local community is attested by a delightful cartoon drawing of him – now framed and hanging in the office boardroom – in hunting gear, and by a large silver cigar box bearing the inscription:

PRESENTED BY HIS FRIENDS
THE MEMBERS OF THE SESKINORE HUNT CLUB

TO L. IRWIN SCOTT, ESQ.
MASTER

MARCH 1912

However, there is a strong family tradition that his Canadian bride, Mary McKean of St John, New Brunswick, did not find Omagh society to her liking. As a somewhat strange individual, and certainly a woman of strong character and of independent means, she did not hesitate to make her opinions forcefully clear, to the detriment of relationships with her husband's family and friends. The result was that, from around 1910 onwards, Mary and Lewis Scott continued to live in the Omagh community on terms of mutual sufferance, and at arm's length from his family.

A sense of duty and loyalty dictated Lewis's active presence as the managing director of the mill until 1919, but he must have felt that this duty was fully discharged when Maddin Scott returned from war service in that year. Maddin's induction training from his uncle was accordingly brief, consisting of three days of familiarisation with the business and the handing over of copious written information, before Lewis and Mary McKean Scott departed from Omagh for south-west England, never to return.

This written material has survived, forming an important and revealing section of the mill's early history as 'Jottings from a Miller's Notebook, 1916'*, in *A Hundred Years A-Milling*. It deals with the now-forgotten arts of oat buying in Tyrone country markets and the conversion of this often unpromising material into a top-quality product that was fit for the finest breakfast-tables of the time, throughout the United Kingdom of Great Britain and Ireland.

There is no mention in Lewis's copious writings of Ireland's 1916 Easter Rising, nor indeed any mention of politics, but as we now write – almost a century later and with the benefit of hindsight – it is interesting to speculate whether his Canadian spouse felt in that fateful year the acute unease of a foreigner living in a country showing evident signs of instability, and fore-

*See Appendix I p.205

saw the likelihood of a greatly changed post-war social and political order.

For whatever reason, Maddin Scott's return to Omagh provided Lewis and Mary with the opportunity to leave their unhappy environment, and they lived together in Summerleaze, a small village near Bristol, in apparent amity until Lewis's death almost 30 years later, in 1946.

Illustration for Scott's
Excelsior Flaked Irish Oatmeal
by Denton de la Cour Ray

In Lewis Scott's writings he mentions the shortages of suitable labour in the First World War, which had a considerable and long-lasting effect on Ulster. As D.S. Johnson writes in 'The Northern Ireland Economy, 1914–1939', in demographic terms it was a disaster second only to the great famine of 1845–1850. Some 49,000 Irishmen lost their lives in the hostilities, of which 24,000 came from the province of Ulster. This represented 12.6 per cent of males between the age of 18 and 40. Yet despite the human misery the war brought considerable prosperity to the whole of Ireland – just as the Second World War would do. This boom was most marked in the northern counties and came about because the war made heavy demands on textiles, foodstuffs and shipping, all of which were traditionally produced in Ulster. Hostilities at sea, and particularly the German U-boat campaign, greatly increased the United Kingdom's dependence on its own suppliers. In beef, for example, by 1917 British and Irish farmers supplied 90 per cent of the country's needs, compared with 60 per cent before the war; butter imports fell from four million pounds (in weight) to 1.6 million in 1918.

But against this background nobody can calculate the effect of the loss of men suffered by Ulster, and indeed the whole of Ireland. It has often been said that England lost the flower of its youth, its future capital, in the conflict. This remark is, of course, no less true of Ireland, or Wales or Scotland. So many did not come back, and lie buried in war cemeteries in France and Belgium. In the poem that follows, 'The Lad', W.F. Marshall remembers one of them:

> They were no great aff-set anywhere,
> The scutchers times ago,
> For drink it follyd the most of them
> That wrought among the tow.
> Plenishment they'd have little or noan
> Except for what they'd stale,
> An' they'd make the childer go out and beg
> Gowpins of oaten male.
>
> I knowed a scutcher that wrought in Shane,
> He was a drunken scrub,
> But he rared a son, an' I mind the son
> A smart wee lump of a cub.

His clo'es were wings, an' his cap was tore,
An' his fire was the fire at the kil',
An' he went to school on his wee bare feet,
An' never got half his fill.

Above the mill was a quare big hill,
He could see to the graveyard wall,
To the market-house, an' the station gates,
An' the new Hibernian Hall.
You'd hear him singin' goan up the hill,
But the dear knows why he sung,
For the people thought they would see the day
When his da would sure be hung.

When the Twelfth was near he'd march the road,
His drumsticks in his han',
Boys, he was prime at the double rowl
On the lid of an oul' tin can.
He played his lone, for the other folk
Were ashamed of him an' his rags,
So he thrinneld his hoop an' waded the burn
An' ginneld for spricklybags.

I mind the year he took up with me,
The ploughin' had just begun,
I'd watch him leadin' the horses roun',
The dhrunken scutcher's son !
Little I thought that afterwards
More than a son he'd be,
For his father died in a water-sheugh
An' he come to live with me.

He was odd in a way; I think he heered
What nobody else could hear,
An' he seen what I could never see,
The more my sight was clear.
The top of a hill bewitched him still,
An' the flame at the mountain's rim,
But a runnin' burn was the best of all
For he sayed it sung till him.

There were some that went that far as to say
He was sure to turn out wil',

But the wee lad grew till he grew man big
An' kept the heart of a chile.
The longer he lived about the place
The less I had to fear.
There was never a word from him to me
But done me good to hear.

I'm feeling oul' since he want away,
An' my sight is gettin' dim;
I nivir axed for to keep him back
When they needed men like him.
He's sleepin' now where the poppies grow,
In the coat that the bullets tore,
An' what's a wheen of medals to me
When my own wee lad's no more ?

The old bridge, Newtownstewart

Four generations of Scotts at Lisnamallard House (1920). Maddin and William Robert, Margaret and Mary with Bobby.

10

Maddin Scott
From Oats to Compound Feeds

TONY DEESON

O N THE RETIREMENT OF LEWIS SCOTT in 1919 (although he did not die until 1946, when he was 74), his nephew Maddin Scott (son of William Robert Scott and great-grandson of the founder) took over the helm and was 'in charge' for many years, spanning the centenary of the foundation of the business in 1950. During the First World War he was a captain in the London Scottish Regiment, serving in France from 1915, followed by attachment to HQ of 56th Division in 1918–19. He came to the mill as a young man of 25, the age at which his uncle Lewis Irwin had taken command when his father, Charles, died. Not surprisingly, perhaps, Maddin Scott's sobriquet at the mill was 'the Captain'.

As has been recorded in the previous chapter, his induction to mill life immediately before he took over was brief. After three days' induction the management of the mill was in Maddin Scott's young and – in business matters – totally inexperienced hands. Over the course of his life at Omagh, Maddin Scott was even more active than his predecessors in public life. Like all the Scotts before him he managed the bond store in Omagh until it was sold, and he was agent for Charles Scott's estates until 1927, which included Carrickaness and Knockbrack townlands and other property. Between 1924 and 1950 he was district or county commissioner of the Boy Scouts; he held various offices in the Omagh Anglers' Association and was its chairman from 1949 until his death in 1962; he was a grand juror; chairman of the British Legion benevolent services committee for over 20 years between 1924 and 1945, and also a member of the Northern Ireland council of the British Legion; chairman of the Tyrone Farming Society in 1949; a member of the council of the Northern Ireland Young Farmers' Clubs in 1950; a member of the egg marketing committee for Northern Ireland 1934–9; high sheriff of Tyrone in 1944 and a deputy lieutenant of Tyrone from 1954. He was also the first president of the Omagh chamber of commerce in 1925.

Like his forebears he also farmed the land at Lisanelly; he was a man of considerable energy and these various 'extracurricular' activities in no way diminished the enthusiasm and hard work he put into the mill. In the Second World War he was joined by the next generation of the family. Rosemary, great-great-granddaughter of the founder and Maddin Scott's daughter, was at the mill for a short time during the war and although her war service in the WRNS (Women's Royal Navy Service) intervened, organised the packing room where at that time oat products were weighed into paper packets before cartoning and dispatch.

Rosemary Scott in her Wren Officer uniform *c.* 1945

To this day Rosemary has a vivid memory of those times, after she had finished her schooling at Liverpool College for Girls, Huyton, and returned home in July 1939. She recalls:

> Within a few days of my return my father began discussing one mealtime his intention of starting up a packing department in the mill. Without

hesitation or due consideration I said, 'I will run it for you.' Just like that and the decision was made.

As yet the packing department was still in its planning stage when the war started. I had the opportunity to hone my organisational skills when I was asked to spearhead the government-initiated drive to collect all the available aluminium in Omagh, whether scrap or not, as part of the war effort. Having done as thorough a job as possible, I was informed that the aluminium would have to be flat. Somewhat non-plussed, but undeterred, I managed to hire a steamroller. Sonny Wallace, a well-known character, helped carry Omagh's contribution, which included a cast aluminium engine, to the municipal gas works on Dublin Road. There it was deposited in front of the steamroller, duly flattened, and transported back by Sonny and his donkey to our base. This experience gave me the confidence to be able to cope with running the packing department.

FIRST USED PRIOR TO 1859

EXCELSIOR

REGISTERED TRADE MARK

Philip Richardson designed the new department and it was built by Jack Anderson and Tommy McCain and every other handy person around the mill. Paddy McBride was my foreman. Interviews were arranged with prospective job candidates and 22 girls and eight boys were employed, nearly all of them in their teens. We were Rosemary Scott (manager); Paddy McBride (foreman); Molly Jack, Matty Martin, Isobel Cuthbertson, Alice Doherty, Vera Adams, Jean McCausland, Bridget Mullan, Mary McGaughey, Philomena Mellon, Mary McKenna, Annie Armstrong, Eva Booth, Maureen Wilkinson, Violet Devlin, Tessie McCausland, Eileen Hall, Bertha Monteith, Alice Colgan, Bridget McGuigan, Jean Rea, Josie Mulholland and a Miss McAlonan, whose Christian name I forget.

The boys were Jack McCausland, Bertie McCausland, Des Coyle, George Campbell, Tommy Hampton, Jim Johnston, Joe Monteith, and Billy McAlonan.

Captain J.G. Ellis, who was manager of the mill at Castlefin, produced the most beautiful design for our 2-pound carton, a great improvement on the 3½-pound paper bag of flaked oatmeal, which we continued to pack for our local markets. Scotts Porage Oats, a Scottish product, was well known all over the country but our distinguished looking SCOTTS ULSTER OATS in this beautiful carton were on sale in Harrods, Selfridges and all high-class grocers in towns and cities across the country. The carton had a seal and a blue mountain in the background, golden stooks of corn in a field on the one side and our Excelsior boy with his flag on the top of a mountain on the other. My father once said on his return from a visit to London that one of the proudest moments in his life was seeing a whole row of SCOTTS ULSTER OATS cartons on display in one of Harrods' windows. The man with the talents to give our products their distinctive and even exclusive edge was my father's agent, Mr Sugarman (known affectionately in the office as Mr Sweetyman).

The packing department was on the first floor (now the boardroom). Up

"EXCELSIOR FLAKED OATMEAL AND WHEATMEAL." SUGGESTION FOR WINDOW DISPLAY.

Shop window display of J.R. Pollock's, High Street, Omagh in 1951. This shows the full range of packaging from one pound to one hundredweight (112 pounds).

above was the electrical hoist. It was my favourite toy! We had our factory line starting with flaked oatmeal being debagged into a hopper, which was positioned near the hoist on the floor above where we worked. The flaked oatmeal poured down a chute into Paddy McBride's care. A girl on the other side of the unit removed any odd flattened black rapeseed or other such non-oatmeal flake. A girl next to Paddy assembled the cartons, which had a clever method of folding to stay closed. After Paddy had filled and weighed the cartons, a girl closed them. We had a board with a large brush and liquid glue of the correct viscosity. We were told this glue was made from beetles' backs! When sticking on the two labels, which took a second or two to apply to the top and bottom of each carton, one's two index fingers got slightly sticky. One of the boys then picked up an assembled row of cartons and popped them into a strong cardboard case, someone else having been assigned the job of forming these cases. They were then glued up along their tops and a third boy used a banding machine to secure them with metal hoop. They were then stacked, ready for shipment to anywhere in the country. We sang as we worked. We were a happy band!

One day while drinking our mid-morning cuppa we noticed a bunch of American soldiers by the window in the street. The USA had just entered the war. Unfortunately, they saw us in our white coats and headscarves, some of us in trousers, some of us in skirts. In a tick the Americans were in our packing department, saying, 'Hey! What! No machinery to pack with. Well, here is how to open a bag. Just hold it. Whoosh it through the air and it opens.' But when we tried what they'd just done we were left with a torn piece of paper in our hands most times. Tea break over, they were

dispatched. This was our first contact with the Yanks.

There was a slack season when the oatmeal ran out and there was only wholemeal to be packed. Some of the girls would be temporarily paid off for a month or so until the next harvest brought more oats into the mill.

Sandy Mehaffey with Eileen Hall (left) and Maureen Walker of the oatmeal packing staff, with Paddy MacBride (seated) at Omagh show c.1953.

Rosemary joined the WRNS and in due course was posted to the Royal Naval College at Greenwich, where she was commissioned. After the war she returned to the mill but although her packing department continued, on a much reduced scale, until the early 1960s her father promoted her to be his assistant. She took a shorthand/typing/bookkeeping course and then her father decided she should learn about the working of the other mills at Newtownstewart and Castlefin. She joined Captain Ellis (whom the family knew as Uncle Binkie) at Castlefin. Every Monday she took the GNR train from Omagh to Strabane, then on to Castlefin by the Donegal railway, returning to Omagh on Friday afternoon.

Her work for the mill ended with her marriage in 1948 to George Duncan, whom she accompanied to West Africa where he was involved in the management of shipping and transport. On retirement they moved back to England and then, in 1988, to Omagh, where Rosemary has renewed her friendship with Paddy McBride, who regularly brings her large boxes of vegetables and flowers from his garden.

Other representatives of the new generations coming into the mill were Walford Scott Green, great-grandson of the founder, whose mother was Nancy Scott – a daughter of Charles, who married the Reverend Ernest Davis Green, a Methodist minister. Walford joined in 1942 and during his war service as a lieutenant-commander became a director and later was chairman of the company. Robert (Bobby) Irwin Maddin Scott, a great-great-grandson, after his war service as a fighter-pilot in the RNVR, joined in 1948 and also became a non-executive director until his untimely death in 1968. They were followed in 1949 by John Richardson McAusland, always known as 'Mr Mac', who married Maddin Scott's daughter Patricia and was a director 1949–81 and managing director from 1960.

Richard Scott has recorded these memories of his father:

My father came to Omagh in 1919, not quite a stranger to Tyrone as he had spent his summer holidays with his grandmother Margaret Scott at Lisnamallard. She doted on him and tolerated – even encouraged – his addiction to angling, which was to last literally until the day he died in 1962. As a boy he would be sent off in the morning with Joe McCullagh, the coachman, in the jaunting car armed with boots, oilskins, rod, tackle, sandwiches and the one-inch ordnance survey map, to be dropped off far from Omagh on some small tributary of the Camowen or Drumragh river. He would then fish his way home, having arranged with the household that he would return in time for afternoon tea at 4pm.

By five o'clock his granny would start to worry about him; by 6.30 she would be convinced he was lost or drowned. She was inclined on such occasions to work off her anxiety by raging at her domestics, nieces, grand-daughters or any other female in range. At 7.30 when her grandson returned, broadly smiling and with his bagful of trout carefully wrapped in rushes, all was forgotten and he wasn't even chided for his tardity or the anguish he had unwittingly caused.

Alongside this harmless spoiling by his grandmother, Maddin had a happy childhood and school career in Scotland ... He was more an enthusiastic player of all team sports than a scholar, but he matriculated into St Andrew's University without difficulty and played rugby for the university XV in 1913, his first year. He then served in the London Scottish regiment throughout the 1914–18 war.

I give these details to demonstrate a point: they hardly constituted the ideal training for a career of any sort, least of all in a technically-related business. Yet Maddin Scott thrived and the mills survived, throughout the tricky 20s and the hungry 30s ...

My father's greatest skill, which he would have ascribed to his experience gained in wartime army service, was in picking his colleagues and sustaining their interest and loyalty thereafter. As a family man he was fortunate in having two very different but complementary characters – Walford Green, his cousin, and John McAusland, his son-in-law – to work with him in his later years and effectively to succeed him and continue building an almost entirely new business after the war.

Advertisement in the
Tyrone Constitution, 1929

From 1948 my father was preparing for the mill's centenary in 1950 and had undertaken the enjoyable task of editing *A Hundred Years A-Milling* for publication in 1951. It is fair to say that Walford and John had mixed feelings about 'the book' – as it was always referred to. At times it seemed to them and the other non-executive director, my older brother Bobby, that time at board meetings was allocated excessively to the problems of authorship and publication rather than to the challenges of reconstructing the mill. However, the great interest that my father took in his own work of literary creation did enable John McAusland to develop his skill and responsibility as mill manager, without frustration or excessive supervision from his father-in-law.

Here is a brief account of some of the notable events that took place at the mill in the period 1920–50; some of them will be enlarged upon in the pages that follow. The first big decision in 1920 was to purchase the first motor lorry and to begin collections and deliveries by road. When the founder went into business the advent of the railway to Omagh was seen as a great blessing and a means of expanding the business, but for some time before his retirement Lewis Scott was disenchanted by the rail services and his nephew promptly implemented his inclinations for change.

Also in 1920 arrangements were set in hand to 'de-register' W & C Scott Ltd as incorporated in Dublin (this was accomplished by a nominal liquidation) and then to re-register with the Ministry of Commerce (Companies) for Northern Ireland, situated in Belfast. The new Memorandum of Association stated that the principal objects for which the company was established were:

- To conduct and carry on the business of mill owners, millers, corn factors, corn merchants, maltsters and flour merchants, and of manufacturers, merchants, brokers, factors and dealers of and in articles of merchandise of all kinds produced from wheat, oats, barley, maize, rice and other grains, seeds or cereals, and also other businesses connected with or allied to the brewing, manufacturing, compounding, or blending of cereal products.

- To acquire and take over as a going concern the business now carried on at Omagh, County Tyrone, Ireland, by and under the style of W & C Scott Limited, and all or any of the assets and liabilities of the proprietors of that business in connection therewith, and with a view thereto to adopt and carry into effect, with or without modification, an agreement dated the 18th day of September 1920 and made between the said W & C Scott Limited and Hugh Smylie, the liquidator thereof, of the one part, and Harold Davis Green, on behalf of this company, of the other part.

The subscribers to the Memorandum were Harold Davis Green of Millbank, Omagh, corn merchant; William Maddin Scott of Lisanelly, Omagh, corn merchant; and Hugh Smylie of Donegall Square North,

Belfast, chartered accountant.

At this time the nominal share capital of the company was £50,000, divided into 10,000 preference shares and 40,000 ordinary shares. In May 1921 the directors were said to be William Robert Scott, Harold Davis Green, William Maddin Scott and Hugh Smylie. The shareholders were the directors and Elizabeth Arnold Dallinger of Southborne in England, sister of W.R. Scott.

In 1921 new drives and plant were installed at the mill and the following year the fee simple of the Newtownstewart mill was bought. In 1924 the business was honoured by appointment as oatmeal millers to the Duke of Abercorn, the first governor of Northern Ireland, and this appointment was confirmed in 1950 by Earl Granville, second governor of Northern Ireland.

In 1925 the first shipment of oatmeal was made to the USA and the following year the company started milling in Co. Donegal; this was followed in 1929 by the purchase of Finn Valley mill in Castlefin. The year before, following a restoration and expansion programme, new plant was installed at Omagh. In 1934 experimental feeding tests with cattle and pigs began and the following year 'balanced rations' were introduced. At the outbreak of the Second World War packing of oatmeal products for the English retail trade began. In 1943 a fire at the Omagh mill hindered production, just when it was most needed. Since Cranny mill was founded in 1847 there had been a policy of day and night shifts for five days a week, and at busy times and in both wars Saturday was added. To add to their burden in trying to provide as much oatmeal as possible, not only for Ulster's needs but to meet English wartime requirements, Maddin Scott and Philip Richardson, a valued colleague, took over the management of a potato-drying factory at Victoria Bridge on behalf of the Ministry of Agriculture.

In 1947 a start was made on a post-war reconstruction of the mill and seed cleaning began at Newtownstewart. The war reversed the mill's attitude to the railways. The founder of the business welcomed their arrival in Omagh but they had fallen out of favour with Lewis Irwin Scott, who greatly preferred road transport. Then wartime petrol rationing forced the mill back to a reliance on the railways, although there were problems here as well and some of the lesser-used branch lines were closed. One of these closures was ironically celebrated by E.O. Byrne and his verses were published in *A Hundred Years A-Milling* under the title of the 'Clogher Valley Railway – Obit. 31 December 1941' ('tarrah', incidentally, is 'terror' or 'terrible').

> They took our oul' railway away, so they did,
> An' sowl' the whole thing for a few thousan' quid.
> They say the ratepayers here are well rid,
> Ahm dambut, boys, it's tarrah.

For fifty long years she puffed to an' fro,
And whiles she wud get there – at ither times no;
She's worth far more dead nor alive, so must go.
Ahm dambut, boys, it's tarrah.

She run down back gardens and up the Main Street,
And scarred all the horses she happened tae meet,
An' now she's been tuk aff tae build up our Fleet,
Ahm dambut, boys, it's tarrah.

I hear they are sellin' the oul' line for scrap;
The rails will make bombs for till plaster the map;
Here's hopin' oul' Hitler's below when they drap,
Ahm dambut, boys, it's tarrah.

They say that the RAF soon will begin
Tae use up our Railway, this war for till win;
They'll drap Clogher Station all over Berlin;
Ahm dambut, boys, it's tarrah.

Them Nazis now boast of a new submarine,
They say it's the finest that iver was seen;
A CVR depth charge will lave it 'has been'.
Ahm dambut, boys, it's tarrah.

We're sendin' out stuff tae Murmansk ivery day,
A while back sure someone heard Joe Stallion say –
'That tankski's frae Clogherski, lads, she's OK.'
Ahm dambut, boys, it's tarrah.

When the Roosians an' us march down Wilhelmstrasse
Ould Hitler will surely say, 'Boys, I'm an ass,
I might have knowed Clogher could still 'houl' the pass.'
Ahm dambut, boys, it's tarrah.

The mill events recounted above took place against the changing wider
scene. Immediately after the First World War, boom conditions prevailed
with maize at £26 per ton. But a slump soon followed; prices dropped

The fourth lorry in the Scott fleet, a 7-ton Leyland JI 4569 with solid tyres, in 1923.

steeply. By 1930 maize was down to £5 a ton and soon dropped to £4. Oats were 5d [2p] a stone and German flaked oatmeal was being imported at £7 per ton. During the 1930s Ulster milling suffered from over-production and the depression in farming hastened the switch from straight feeds to balanced rations. When the second war came, human and animal feed subsidies kept prices down but the immediate post-war period showed rapid increases.

There follows a further extract from Maddin Scott's 'Jottings from a Miller's Notebook – 1950', which appeared in *A Hundred Years A-Milling*.

My uncle Lewis often said that in his time as an inland mill we often found ourselves 'at the mercy of the railway'. A year after he retired, in 1920, we found the combined inwards and outwards rail rates we were paying exceeded by a greater percentage than usual the through rates from the ports to destination stations. Harold Green made out a clear statement showing the excess paid by an Omagh mill over the rate by a mill in Derry or Belfast as much as five shillings [25p] per ton at some stations; an intolerable burden to carry at the selling prices of those days. This was sent to the Traffic Manager and we followed it up by both of us calling on him for a conference.

As this was abortive we made another call in Belfast that day, buying a six-ton Straker-Squire lorry with which we started a collection and delivery service for our own grain and products ... But we did so against our will, feeling that millers should stick to milling and not launch themselves out into transport, an entirely different line of business,

Far from the Mill with its dust and its dunder,
Far from the weir with its wonder of foam,
Far from the sluice with the race running under
We deliver our goods – thinking long for our home.

However much we may regret this unnecessary complication with which the ancient craft of milling has since burdened itself (however profitable and convenient), we must confess it was inevitable and plead that we were unwillingly forced to pioneer this road haulage ... the fourth lorry in our fleet [was] a seven-ton Leyland which we put on the road in 1923. These early, solid-tyred lorries often bogged even on the main roads, which were not yet metalled for heavy loads and were seldom over ten feet wide.

L.I. Scott tells us of the scrapping of the original steam engine, which I can remember working away busily in dry seasons, and refers to the grinding and sale of oat offals in his day. Our first attempt to process these potentially valuable by-products into a useful feeding stuff of consistent quality and appearance, by a grinding plant erected in the old engine house, was a complete failure.

I'm afraid I must plead guilty to turning out seven of our pairs of millstones and replacing with modern machines in 1920, albeit regretfully. [Only one of the millstones survives in one piece in 2002; on his retirement in 1996 Richard Scott was permitted to remove it from the mill yard and it now adorns the entrance to his house. The remaining stones may be hidden in the foundations of the modern mill.]

In 1928 the old engine chimney was demolished and this oat offal processing problem solved. 'A current came no man could see' at first generated by ourselves, later when it came to Omagh from the main electricity supply and drove a 'Miracle Mill' for us, we think one of the first of its type erected in Ireland. It is still humming away happily through most of the day and night hours, as I write this, though it is due to be moved to a new building. It has paid for itself many times over and saved us many a problem in storage of these bulky by-products.

The slump in prices that followed soon after the First World War was survived successfully. The McKenna duties, a revolutionary departure from England's free trade policy, helped to prevent the dumping of foreign food imports. But in 1926 the Irish Free State imposed heavy duties on flake and oatmeal. We decided to mill the oats where they were grown in the Finn valley instead of hauling them by rail to Omagh, and later purchased and equipped as a grain mill the Finn Valley mills at Castlefin in Co. Donegal in 1929.

The Hatry crash in the City of London followed the disastrous slump in the USA about this time. By 1932 not only were there large new milling units started up in Northern Ireland, designed to serve, like the rest of the northern millers, the 32 counties of Ireland, but also all United Kingdom mill products (including those of the Northern Ireland mills) were completely excluded from the Irish Free State. With such competition in 'straight feeds' of all sorts through the millers in Northern Ireland being drastically restricted in their selling area, the crisis created for 'Scotts of Omagh' an opportunity to develop a new kind of 'balanced rations'. We had land and fairly good facilities for farm experiments.

Our chairman [W.R. Scott], who owned the land, was also prepared to finance experiments to demonstrate the advantages he had discovered of feeding stock with balanced rations compared with straight feeds and was in touch with the principals of agricultural colleges in Scotland as regards formulae worth trying out in variations to suit the different seasons of the year under actual farm conditions in Northern Ireland.

First, we had to assure ourselves that the idea was a good one and test the suitability of each formula for Northern Ireland farm conditions such as climate, size of holdings (at that time the average size of a farm in Northern Ireland was 30 acres), etc. and make seasonal grass analyses. Second, we had to convince our very conservative farmers that the balanced rations offered them a saving in their feeding bills and a great convenience, both most important considerations in those days of low ex-farm selling prices and shortage of skilled farm labour. We tackled experiments with pigs and beef cattle ourselves and we got others to do experiments with poultry (chicks, growers and layers) and turkey mashes, and for dairy cattle. But who would lay down for us exactly how our feeding experiments were to be conducted, criticise all the feeding formulae we were working on and generally set us on the right lines in this attempt to teach ourselves as well as the farmers something new and something useful? It would need to be someone trained as an agricultural scientist with, if possible, much practical experience, i.e. years of paying for his own mistakes as millers and farmers have to.

I had just the man in another uncle, F.H. Billington (author of *Compost for the Garden or Thousand Acre Farm*, published by Faber and Faber).

Trained in the old Department of Agriculture and Technical Instruction for Ireland, after war service he became principal of Flock House in New Zealand, a residential training farm institute for the sons of British seamen who had lost their lives in the First World War. When this empire-building and most fruitful appointment ended, Captain Billington came home and farmed in the south of England. Here was the man; if we had searched the world's face we could not have found a better. Well served was the business by its third generation!

From the first we set out to tell the farmers there was no mystery about our Excelsior Feeds; we encouraged them to come and see the feeding experiments and the rations being made at any time they wished. In the case of the beef cattle experiments we had to prove to ourselves that an Ulster blended ration would yield more profitable results than could be obtained by grazing the beasts on grass alone under the conditions actually existing on Tyrone farms.

The animals were weighed every fortnight on the public weighbridge at Omagh and placards put up in the fields with records of the weighings, so that farmers could watch the experiments and see for themselves what progress was made. We advertised in the local press and brought the actual animals under test to pens at our stands at the local shows with details of the experimental test feedings.

As the costs of these experiments and publication of the results were very heavy for a small firm to undertake we had no money to spare for publicity beyond the aforementioned one-and-sixpenny [7^1/2p] advertisements in the local papers. We had tried the films but even with a change of film every fortnight there was a sameness; besides the farmers didn't then often go to the pictures. We wanted some posters which would catch the farmer's eye as he travelled by road. Our mill carpenter put up hoardings at different points where we owned the land beside public roads approaching Omagh and Newtownstewart ... [A] talented member of our staff ... designed our posters ... From ... amusing designs in colour a local poster artist produced the posters, and designs were changed about every fortnight. We think this poster campaign, an original, economical and home-made form of advertising, induced many a farmer to give a trial to something quite new to him. In less than a month each of these pioneering farmers became an enthusiastic unpaid publicity-agent for us among his friends and neighbours; the business grew like a rolling snowball.

When Hitler marched into Poland another ghastly war fell on us, the seventh to affect us since the business started and in many ways the worst. Everything in our little branch of the food industry was 'controlled' almost from the beginning, everything we bought and practically everything we sold. Many of the young people employed or connected with the mill joined up as volunteers and all of them came back safe, except one, young Isaac Hampton, son of our head storeman, Oliver Hampton, himself a disabled ex-serviceman of the First World War. Young Isaac fell gallantly in Burma with the Royal Inniskilling Fusiliers. Among so many we count ourselves fortunate that only one brave youngster didn't come back to his job at the mill – we all miss his cheery ways and happy disposition.

Seven months after the war started we lost my father, W.R. Scott, our chairman for 43 years. Two months later, first Holland and Belgium and finally France fell – who of us doesn't remember the long succession of beautiful days in that Hitlerian summer following our miraculous deliverance at Dunkirk, when we in the United Kingdom woke to find ourselves alone? At the end of June, we in Northern Ireland milling were doing our damnedest to save from starvation as much as possible of our vast pre-war livestock population before the first crops from the wartime 'plough-up' campaign could be harvested. A little granary, a tiny stock farm within the fortress – much depended on the North of Ireland!

In the mill we rubbed our eyes – after nearly a century of just carrying on and attending to our business with hardly anyone in authority seeming to care or know at all whether we carried on or not, we had suddenly become most valuable to the country, and we were told so in no uncertain terms.

Nevertheless, one day they wanted to draw water in vast quantities from our mill lade for a big new military infantry training centre a-building nearby. Another, they wanted to requisition all our mill store buildings. We tactfully showed them how full of food they were for man and beast, and heard no more about it. Next the commander of the district called; the mill must be held and kept going at all costs. As our French friends, then submerged, would have said, we must become a *point d'appui*.

Barbed wire was put up along the mill lade and elsewhere, sniper observation posts appeared in trees, trenches were dug around us. The 'Knoll' [probably the winnowing ground] at the mill-dam in Newtownstewart was honeycombed with trenches and festooned with barbed wire – could it really be possible that country mills could have become *important* overnight, we wondered?

Anthony Eden asked us all to defend ourselves and a platoon of local defence volunteers was formed from millmen and their friends and neighbours, armed with rifles. Its members held the courthouse in Omagh, another strategic point, by turns at night from June to the late autumn of 1940 by which time concrete road blocks were made which we manned at night. [The concrete anti-tank cylinders, weighing about eight hundredweight each, became, like the swords of long ago, very much in the way after the war. The mill collected about 80 of them in Omagh and made good use of them when repairing the 'carry' on the Camowen river five years later.]

The activities of those dark days of the war's second and third years were really a blessing in disguise for all of us in the mill. Even if it was a bit tiring and cold for the elderly to turn out for night's guard in our thin twill black uniforms, soon to be discarded for the familiar khaki Home Guard battledress, it at least left us with no time to reflect on how extremely precarious our situation then was, on the military as well as the food front. It was the same with the Red Cross, St John's Ambulance, ARP, the Fire Service, WVS, War Savings and all the other wartime auxiliaries. The people to be pitied were those with too much time on their hands – 'To sleep; perchance to dream. Ay, there's the rub.'

This platoon held together with few changes until the Home Guard stood down in November 1944, when the service of many of our mill workers in one of the biggest unpaid armies of history terminated. Three of its members, Jimmy Young and Jack Wilson in 1940, and the platoon commander in 1942, were slightly wounded in training. The chaps didn't mean to shoot us, we just must have got in the way somehow. [Maddin Scott's son, Richard, is more explicit about this incident. He writes: 'Some military genius decided that on a particular exercise in 1942 the assembled Home Guards – many of whom were old soldiers of the First World War – needed a spot of 'battle inoculation' by having quantities of live ammunition fired over their heads. In the worst possible sense the fire was inaccurate. The 'platoon commander' was Maddin Scott himself who, having survived the First World War, sustained a body wound in this ill-devised 'engagement' of the Second World War.]

There were no other similar casualties in the 2nd Tyrone battalion, although, alas, our well beloved county commandant [Colonel 'Putney' Hammond-Smith of Edenfel, Omagh] lost his life and some members of other Tyrone battalions were seriously maimed.

The war, with its long hours of working at high pressure, left us with much to do in rebuilding on a new plan, as well as urgently needed plant replacements. We had suffered a serious fire in 1943, also, which made things even more difficult, and we might have decided to cease milling at Omagh during our post-war reconstruction but for the generous way in which other firms came to our assistance, notably our good friends Smyths of Strabane. [The 1943 fire was a kiln fire in the oatmeal flaking plant; this stopped the manufacture of flaked oatmeal, which thereafter was bought in from other mills.]

New storage, new grain intake, renewed mill buildings (necessary to house a modern milling plant): how were these to be provided while the business was kept going? It called for much patience and forethought in organisation of the sequence, infinitely more difficult to carry out than if we had been able to shut down for two years and rebuild from the ground upwards. We believe we shall have when we are finished a well laid out modern mill, efficiently equipped to serve its customers and the farmer for some long time ahead.

Strictly, this is the end of Maddin Scott's recollections of the mill's history until the centennial year in 1950, but he appended some recollections entitled 'Millyard Friends'. This not only is charming but also shows some fascinating insights into the mill of that time – and for this reason surely deserves a place in the present volume.

My grandmother, Margaret Scott, who began writing books at the age of 80, tells us in her *More Recollections* (privately printed in 1927), 'My people were and are peculiar' and I think the same might be said of our family business.

For instance, although we have seen many new and excellent businesses and factories set a-going in this particular part of Ulster, we can be certain that none of them have any dogs, dogs I mean that belong to the place, swear by it and are so to speak carried on its ration strength. Of course any business, old or new, which has an idea of propitiating the gods must have 'doggie' men in it whose dogs will occasionally follow their masters to work, be the rules for or against such a proceeding and with or without the slightest encouragement from the said masters.

But such highly respectable dogs are much more normal in habit than our Skiboo and Hughie, who by their own choice make the mill their home, belong to the mill and are miserable when away from it. Hugh Shearman in his delightful book *Ulster* mentions a Skiboo craze – 'he's here, he's there, he's everywhere' – as having started in Belfast in 1945. We all most seriously take leave to doubt that the credit of starting this craze can be correctly given by a historian to Belfast. Every man Jack and Jill woman of us is convinced it started at our mill, a belief we feel sure Hugh Shearman will generously forgive us!

Anyway our Skiboo is an aristocrat credibly stated to have cost our friend Mr John Keenan, his former owner, the colossal price of £5 as a pup. Now, although people in the mill occasionally sell dogs for sums running up to three figures the thought of any one of us buying one for as much as a fiver was something so fantastic as to put Skiboo into the peerage in our eyes on

Hughie (left) and Skiboo, in charge, off to dinner with some of their millyard friends. From left: Jimmy Fee, Jimmy Mills, Davy Wylie, George Kerr, Oliver Hampton and Joe Quigley.

his first appearance among us – and he was promptly delivered home.

But the first specks of mill dust having adhered to his eyebrows, the dog adopted the mill as his home and his master, having given him away to distant friends several times, once taking him 70 miles away to Belfast, finally forgot all about him and Skiboo, having always found his way back, was content. Now, after five years and having unaccountably lost all his teeth in our service he has acquired seniority on the staff and leads an active and useful life as GOC anti-rat brigade and only wishes he could qualify for a set of 'health teeth' like everyone else, although his efficiency rating is high without them.

Hughie is more robust, more vocal and if less aristocratic is always well groomed and obviously conscious of his appearance. No speck of mill dust was ever on Hughie's eyebrows. Although a permanent resident he loves going places and seeing things. This was noticed at an early stage in his career when he was still only an Apprentice Mill Dog and, lest harm might befall him on No. 1 lorry, his friends the driver and helper made a seat on which Hughie could sit bolt upright between them. He has gone everywhere with them ever since.

Immediately he has brought the lorry safely home he leaps down and does an urgent inspection tour of the yard, disclaiming the office in the true manner of all Big Business dogs, just to see everyone is busy and happy but always keeping a watchful eye on the re-loading of No. 1. If a strong, masterful business dog like Hughie could ever be imagined to waste his time soliloquising, we can fancy him saying, 'Those two-leggers in that office with their telephoning and typing – think they're busy, huh! It's me and my gang up the yard and on the road that hold this place together. A pity they don't stick to a sensible, reasonable trade like brewing or contracting or making field gates! Then we might have made some money and a feller like me could take things easier in his past-middle age. As it is, bedambut I'll have to work till I drop, like the rest of them!'

Finally, having rendered a dutiful report to Skiboo and the lorry having arrived at the weighbridge with all tiresome formalities completed, Hughie resumes his seat with dignity, takes over and gives the 'go' signal. The idea of No. 1 leaving without Hughie simply wouldn't enter anyone's head, the customers would think something wrong and would 'phone us up. Skiboo and Hughie are good timekeepers, they run up the yard barking loudly when the mill bell sounds as if to say, 'come on, come on'.

Skiboo is a good trencherman, he likes his 'meat' regular and can, we think, read a clock. For just before dinner hour and quitting time every day he comes to where he can see the mill clock. At three minutes to 12 and three minutes to six precisely he starts barking and keeps it up till Oliver Hampton rings the mill bell. Then he takes charge of some of his mill-family pals on their way to dinner.

We look on it is a blessing that we have two such energetic veterans to keep a strict eye on us as we enter our second century.

Ed Mc Aleer, driving 'Little Titch', with his sister Eileen, nephew Jim, Michael McGeown and Eileen's dog Lassie *c.* 1949

The editor of *A Hundred Years A-Milling* noted at this point:

As we go to press in this year of grace 1950 autumn has come on after one of the wettest summers in living memory. And a wonderful thing has happened. Skiboo, who all his life disdained dwellinghouse or kennel, has deserted the mill for three weekends running and condescended to our Millbank kitchen, a thing unheard of! We feel we are thus honoured, partly through his old age creeping on, partly by the dampness of the season. But as soon as the mill bell rings on Monday morning he is away like an arrow – 'There's no fun like work, forebye one can't leave all the responsibility to Hughie. Keen enough, but a mere stripling and so inexperienced.'

In the preface to the second edition of *A Hundred Years A-Milling* Maddin Scott adds that Skiboo died in 1953, 'having lived happily with us to a good old age'. Hughie then became the senior dog, 'as dapper as ever' and busily trained Skiboo's son to keep an eye on the doings at the mill.

Oliver Hampton was the much-respected mill foreman in the early 1940s and 1950s. One of his duties was to ring the mill bell, which was regularly accompanied by Skiboo's bark, and he wrote some verses in his memory under the title 'He was Faithful'. Some may consider them to be sentimental doggerel, but they will find an answering chord in the hearts of anyone who has loved and lost a favourite dog:

He is gone, yes he is gone
And his bark we'll hear no more.

The more we think of him
The more our hearts are sore.

We do miss him, yes, we miss him
At the ringing of the bell
He knew the hours and watched the clock
The time, yes, he could tell.
We will never, no we'll never –
For his equals there were few –
We will never get another
Like that little dog 'Skiboo'.

Eleven years he was with us
As I can safely say
And when to us he came
He was just a little stray.
In that peaceful quiet plantation
Just beside the mill
In a cosy little grave
His body now lies still.

He is gone, yes he is gone
And his equals there were few
We will never get another
Like that little dog 'Skiboo'.

In Memory of

Skaboo

In 1950 Scotts celebrated the centenary of its foundation. The local press, too, considered that the centenary year of a local firm deserved a special mention, and this notice appeared in *The Tyrone Constitution* on Friday 18 August 1950:

In 1850, three years after the famine in Ireland, the late Mr William Scott, Lisanelly, acquired what was formerly a brewery. A man of his organising genius might well have revived the brewery and made Omagh beer as famous as any today, in addition to a huge fortune. Having in mind the disaster of the famine, he founded a milling business where grain was milled promptly and cheaply into food. The business prospered, and happily still is under the control of the descendants of the founder. Moreover, many of the workers today are descendants of original workers, indicating happy relationship between employer and employed ... The mills, the Scott family and the workers have their roots deep in the soil of Tyrone, and it is the wish of everyone in Omagh that in the next century they may grow deeper still.

Some of the staff in 1950 – the centenary year

The most tangible and long lasting result of this event was the publication of *A Hundred Years A-Milling*, which appeared in 1951; owing to demand a revised and enlarged edition was published in 1956.

While *A Hundred Years A-Milling, From Country Mill to County Millers* and the present volume celebrate three landmarks in Scotts' history (the centenary, 125 years and 150 years of its foundation), *A Hundred Years A-Milling* had a wider purpose than as a mere journal of record. In addition to the mill's history, which has been drawn on extensively in the present volume, it recorded many aspects of life in the Ulster countryside that have been almost obliterated by the passage of time, setting the mill in the rural life around it.

Richard Scott, later chairman and managing director of W & C Scott, recalls some aspects of the centenary celebrations:

> I was aged 11 in 1950 and during term time was absent at Mourne Grange, a boarding school in County Down, so I suppose that my memories are confined to the school holidays at Easter and during the months of July and August of that year.
>
> My father [Maddin Scott] was then aged 55 and had been recently joined in the management of the business by John McAusland, who was extremely active and competent. Thus Maddin Scott had time to attend to other matters and much of his spare time, particularly in the late evenings, was devoted to assembling the material for *A Hundred Years A-Milling*, which was published during the following year. This entailed voluminous correspondence with the many contributors, holders of copyright and so on, eventually extending to about a dozen large box files which unfortunately have not survived.

One notable event was a large luncheon party that was given for customers, employees and other friends of the firm. It was held in the Star Ballroom, which no longer exists but was sited where McDermotts today have their hardware store, opposite the entry to the Tyrone Farming Society grounds in Sedan Avenue, Omagh. There must have been 300 or so people present and I remember a certain amount of the proceedings:

Centenary celebration lunch at Omagh. From right – Maddin Scott, Mary Scott, W.F. Marshall and Lady (Nelly) Walton

- The slight concern in advance, caused by the fact that we had decided to hold the event on a Friday; it was in the days of 'fish on Friday' for the Catholic participants so there had to be a choice of menu as between meat and fish. To lessen any potential embarrassment, I remember my mother and father both opting for the fishy choice!

- The Reverend W.F. Marshall reading his poem 'The Centenarian', commissioned for the event of the centenary, from the framed vellum manuscript that had been beautifully illuminated by his daughter Margaret. He was quite elderly and I remember his gentle and quavering delivery. Eventually three identical copies of the illuminated manuscript were produced by Margaret Marshall and survive as treasured possessions (two remain in the mill office and I have the third). [This poem is reproduced below, on page 76.]

- Though no alcohol was served before or at lunch one of the millmen had somehow managed to become uproariously drunk elsewhere and interrupted the proceedings at an early stage. I remember him being gently shushed and led away by that good Methodist and lifetime teetotaller Norman Wilson, proprietor of the Carlisle restaurant (and presumably therefore in charge of the catering).

- The 11-year-old was paraded to play music throughout the meal at the Star Ballroom piano. He later thought that the report in the local press, that he had done reasonably well 'for one so young' was just a touch patronising.

- After lunch and the seemingly interminable and laudatory speeches were concluded, everybody proceeded into the showgrounds of the Tyrone Farming Society, where there was great hilarity and 'It's a Knock-Out'-style games of all sorts, ducking for toffee apples, climbing the greasy pole etcetera, possibly in contest for prizes.

Mary Scott presents Nora Madill with a prize at the Centenary celebration and sports.

There were other celebratory events during the year, accommodation for family attending from England being readily available following the completion of repairs and refurbishment to Lisnamallard, which had been in progress since 1948. There are photographs in *A Hundred Years A-Milling* of the 'mill family' and 'family-round-the-mill', which record such gatherings.

I also remember a gathering of family, including the recently returned Mary Irwin Green [the youngest daughter of Charles Scott, who married Harold Green, an executive director of Scotts. Harold Green was a brother of the Reverend Ernest Green who had already married Mary's elder sister, Nancy. Thus were the Scott and Green families well united]. The occasion was a celebratory meal in the restaurant attached to 'The Cake Shop', formerly in Market Street. Other events included a gathering of mill pensioners in the Royal Arms Hotel and another celebration of some sort in the newly-established Silverbirch Hotel.

When *A Hundred Years A-Milling* was eventually produced in 1951, a lunch was arranged in a hotel in Londonderry for family members and all the contributors. I was not present but gained unexpected kudos at my prep school next day when an account of this event appeared in the *Daily Express*.

This press notice had come about quite fortuitously. According to my father the lunch had gone quietly but towards the end was invaded by a staff reporter from the *Daily Express*, who had attended another function locally and evidently wanted the party to continue. The participants in the book launch received him civilly and were rewarded accordingly with a rave review in the next day's national edition of the paper. As a result, according to family legend, all 1,000 copies of the first edition were sold out within six weeks and the second edition was embarked upon. Both editions were subsidised, mainly by the company but also by Maddin Scott personally, so that the book was a critical and public relations success rather

The Centenaria

When I was young I was just a place
  With a wheen of wheels inside,
And a wooden wheel, a wooden wheel,
  A wheel that was my pride.
Black was the wheel on a gray stone wall
  But where was a sweeter sound
Than its rumble up and its tumble down
  As it went splashing round ?

    Hi for the hopper and the clinking v
      And the dunder through the wall
    And the running stones on the b
      stones,
      And the meal dust over all !
    Hi for the kiln and the good turf sm
      And the corn so crisp and dry,
    For the fans that wail and the seeds th
      And the shillen riding high !

They cut corn then with a ringing scythe
  Or a sickle made to saw ;
And a servant man would swing a flail,
  While the farmer bottled straw.
The corn came here in a red farm cart,
  The white corn and the brown ;
'Twas with candles dim or a lamp to trin
  I watched the dark come down.

The red farm cart is a tractor now,
  And the flails are long since fled,
And men must mow ere the binders go,
  But the scythes are rusted red.
On Omagh town the night comes down,
  Yet no man feels his way,
For my lamps are bright with a blinding
  And the darkness turns to day.

'The Centenarian' was commissioned by Scotts to celebrate their centenary in 1950. This illustrated version first appeared in 1951, in *A Hundred Years A-Milling*.

e are steeples three where there used to be
ingle steeple tall,
he old-time kiln with the good turf smell
s vanished past recall :
the drays that crept at a horse's walk,
h burdened from the mill,
orries now no horse could haul,
d they laugh at the court-house hill.

n sallies shade the long mill lade
nowen's streams supply ;
turbines low I face its flow
d keep my old stand-by.
current came no man could see
th a power man learned to tame,
t softly steals to my rolling wheels
d my lamps that have no flame.

ndred years is a hundred years,
d a long way back in time,
who dare say that I'm old and gray
hen I'm in my lusty prime ?
it's here alone, in dark Tyrone,
heart its homestead feels
abide by the river side
nong my shining wheels.

think no shame of my wooden wheel,
the past I've long outgrown,
the wheel went round and the corn was
ground,
d so I served Tyrone :
I made the meal, good oaten meal.
om the day that I was born,
a wooden wheel and the wheen of wheels
d the stones that ground the corn.

W. F. MARSHALL.

Margaret Marshall

W.F. and Margaret Marshall, 1950, at the Centenary celebration viewing her illustration of 'The Centenarian'.

than a commercial venture.

The preparations for two editions and dealing with worldwide correspondence thereafter kept my father fairly busy during the remainder of his business life.

All in all, I feel confident that nothing in Maddin Scott's long and not unsuccessful business career gave him as much pleasure and fulfilment as this late discovery of his own talent for authorship and his seeking-out and encouragement of the other distinguished contributors.

The review from the *Daily Express* is still extant and to this day there survives a large box-file of letters, sent virtually from all over the world, expressing delight at *A Hundred Years A-Milling*. There are also many reviews, of which the following are short extracts from just a few:

> The literary style is excellent and the whole volume lends lustre to the literary history of Tyrone. We look to members of the Tyrone Library Committee to make certain that it will be made available to all readers in Tyrone – as a mark of appreciation and encouragement. (*Tyrone Constitution*)
>
> We can truthfully write that no more interesting chronicle of a firm's fortunes and progress has reached us within the past few years. Here is a book that will stand the severest test of all – it will remain as an interesting and authoritative survey of one of the world's oldest and most fascinating

industries ... Walford S. Green, in an introduction, says of the book that it represents a composite picture, depicting the work of the mill against the background of the local and country environment. This is very true, and unlike most composites the work here has been so skilfully done that the blending of the particular into the general is scarcely noticed and the very necessary duty of recording the founding, development and fortunes of a milling concern has been so interwoven with valuable details of provincial interest that *A Hundred Years A-Milling* represents a treasure-chest of information of many matters. (*The Ulster Herald*)

The book is a fascinating mixture for those who like not only the history, but the lore of their industry. They will find in it much that will satisfy them. It is, indeed, a case in which the reader gets the better part of the bargain. (*Milling*)

This friendly, discursive story of life in Omagh and the neighbouring country during the past 100 years is centred upon the fortunes of a country oatmeal mill, founded after the Irish famine and still managed and owned by the descendants of the same family. A number of contributors have joined in telling some part of the story, whether of people and life in County Tyrone in past and present days or of old and new methods of milling, and the agreeable medley of prose, verse, drawings and maps, has something of the atmosphere of a family scrap book. (*The Times Literary Supplement*)

This volume takes a great deal of material from *A Hundred Years A-Milling* and is greatly enriched by it; indeed, it would not be possible to tell the story of the earlier days of the mill without the research undertaken under the

Gray Ellis, illustrator, William K. Ellis, contributor and Maddin Scott, the editor, with a copy of *A Hundred Years a-Milling* at the book launch in 1951.

direction of the editor. Unhappily both editions are long out of print and booksellers in Northern Ireland and England shake their heads sadly in response to an enquiry for a second-hand copy; apparently it is something of a rarity, only occasionally to be found in libraries or in second-hand book shops. When a copy is to be found, it would surely gladden the heart of Maddin Scott to know that (in year 2002) the asking price tends to be in the region of £20 to £25, whereas the first edition sold at ten shillings and sixpence (52^1/2p in today's currency).

Some additional information on the situation in Ulster and the Scott mills in the immediate post-war years to the centenary in 1950 can be gleaned from Walford Green's *From Country Mill to County Millers*, which is the source of factual material contained in the following paragraphs.

Walford Green making his speech at the Centenary celebration lunch in 1950

> As already indicated, through the war years and to 1950 and beyond, the buying and selling of all agricultural products and the manufacture and sale of animal feeding stuffs were controlled by the Government so that both the farmer and the miller were working in a world of fixed prices. However, by 1950 it was clear that changes were imminent. The period of shortages was coming to an end and a return to the free market, both for farmers and millers, was in sight. To his policy of 'maximum production' the farmer would have to add 'with all attainable efficiency' and it was clear that the emphasis was likely to move away from the production of potatoes and cereals towards the better value livestock high protein products. This would involve a reduction in the acreage under plough in favour of grass for hay and silage and the laying down of permanent leys with a concomitant increase in the demand for animal feeding stuffs.
>
> Already in 1950 the acreage of wheat, barley, oats and potatoes was far smaller than that of 100 years previously when the business started. For the whole of Ulster wheat had fallen from 69,900 acres in 1850 to a mere 1,900 a hundred years later; barley dropped from 16,600 to 5,000; oats from 591,000 to 316,500; and potatoes from 240,000 to 150,000. Against this the density of livestock in Ulster was already higher than ever before: an estimated 960,700 head of cattle; 620,700 sheep; 302,407 pigs and over 19^1/2 million head of poultry.

Walford Green estimated that the probable output of animal feed produced in Ulster in 1950 was in the order of 900,000 tons at a cost of £36 million.

These were the kinds of factors the mill had to consider in laying its plans for the future. At the Excelsior Mill, Scotts was processing home-grown oats into groats, flakemeal, oat feed and offals, handling in all perhaps 1,000 tons a year on average. In addition the mill was mixing animal feed to government formulae to the extent of about 100 tons a week with a supporting trade in straight ground maize and barley meal, and factoring flour and other foods packaged for human consumption. At this time the trade in flaked oatmeal had been boosted by a sales promotion campaign for large flake, sold as a quality product, considerably superior to the small dusty flake then more generally to be found on grocers' shelves.

This larger and largely dust-free flake was presented in 1 1/2 lb packs, attractively designed and distributed by a sales organisation in England, the principle of distribution being to place it in one shop only in the majority of English towns with a population of over 10,000. Although successful, this was a labour-intensive and expensive method of distribution of produce that, during the war, had largely been disposed of to the NAAFI and similar outlets in 112-pound hessian sacks.

Whether the operation was ever really profitable cannot now be established, but it was certainly instrumental in introducing the name of Scotts of Ulster to many people outside the Province. It was also instrumental in enabling them to hold on to their trade in flaked oats against the rising production of ready-to-serve breakfast foods which in the post-war years started to flood the market, whereas before the war there were only 'Force', 'Grapenuts' and 'Post Toasties' to contend with.

At Newtownstewart, Scotts was operating the Trusty Mill under the Mehaffey brothers, where the old grindstones were still in use. This mill processed the farmers' grain in the style of the old mills of Ulster, and provided an outlet for livestock feeds at the Fermanagh–North Tyrone end of the territory it aimed to serve. On the other side of the border, within the Free State, Scotts was still operating the mill at Castlefin in the Finn valley to take advantage of the large oat crop produced in Co. Donegal at that time, although generally this was not a profitable operation.

At this time inward transport was by rail, from either Belfast or Londonderry, whereby substantial storage accommodation was available in the rail wagons at Omagh station, free of charge. Deliveries were made to the stations at Omagh, Newtownstewart and Castlefin and haulage from the stations to the mills was by horse and cart; however, distribution to customers of bagged commodities was by motor lorries. Lewis Scott's opinion of the railways 30 years earlier had been quite turned round, and at this period the GNR was very much in favour. In the balance sheet for 1950 investment in other forms of transport was shown as 'Carts and harness £24' and 'Motor cars and lorries £2,328' – the latter sum including the managing director's and salesmen's cars.

No records of output are available for any of the mills in 1950, but Walford Green estimated that it was around 7,000 tons at Omagh, with the Trusty Mill in Newtownstewart contributing about a further 1,500 tons. The labour force at Omagh, together with the office and sales staff, transport drivers and their assistants, numbered 55.

As for many years previously, the bulk of the trade was between the mills and country merchants rather than direct to the farm, which had been the

case 100 years before. In 1950 water-power was still making a substantial contribution to the total power requirements of all the mills.
In times of good flow in the Omagh mill lade the two turbines located under the oatmeal mill and adjacent to the flaking plant provided
power 'as free as air' to the extent of 44hp. It was, however, not quite
as free as it might at first seem, because the lade banks and the carry at
the head of it had to be maintained, sometimes at heavy cost. As the
need for faster running machinery increased and as a consequence the
demand for more power, water as a powering agent became less useful,
and both turbines were out of use by 1964. One of these was sold
locally and has continued to produce electricity for domestic use for
many years; the other could not be moved and was embedded in the
foundations of one of the new buildings. In 1950 grain drying was carried out on flat-head, coal-fired kilns.

In the accounting year to 31 July 1950 the figures were as follows:

Robbie Gilkinson and Tommy
McKelvey c. 1945 repairing
damage to the 'carry' (weir) on
the Camowen River caused by
severe flooding. This was
necessary to restore the flow of
water to the mill's turbines.
Fellow workers (below) were
from left Tom McCain, John
Johnston, Jack Anderson, Gerry
Rodgers and Ernie Gray.

> Income from sales £198,378
> Production charges £10,441
> Overheads £12,264
> Trading profit £4,361
> Net profit per ton £2.79
> Balance on general P & L account £3,644
> Net worth £46,940

The cash turnover at the Trusty Mill was approximately one-fifth of that at
Omagh, and at Castlefin one-tenth. Twenty-five years later Walford Green
wrote of the mills as they were in 1950:

> The business as a whole consisted of a group of country mills, each serving
> the area over which its outward transport could conveniently operate,
> labour intensive within the mills themselves, though benefiting in the case
> of two of them from the ability to draw imported material both from

Belfast and from Londonderry and to store it at low cost – gradually emerging, while controls lasted, from a period of negative profitability, but likely to run into hard times again when controls were lifted and competition in a free market had to be faced, and perhaps poor in cash resources when compared with larger milling competitors at the ports ...

It was intensely thought-provoking, and an overriding fact had by this time emerged: if we were to continue in business and achieve any worthwhile results we should have to plan ahead against the day when controls were lifted, with a view to achieving a much greater production, and at significantly less cost per ton.

The management team of the time was Maddin Scott as chairman and managing director; Philip Richardson in charge of transport and milling machinery; Cecil Smylie from the company's accountants and Walford Green as non-executive directors. R.I.M. (Bobby) Scott joined the Board in 1948, also as a non-executive director. These were the people charged with making momentous decisions, which would affect the whole future of the business.

The first question to be answered was whether they should continue at all or attempt to dispose of the business as a going concern. As one might expect from what has gone beforehand, that issue was quickly resolved and it was unanimously agreed to continue. It was appreciated that the reconstruction plan would call for substantial borrowing from the company's bankers, and to achieve this with the best possible economy so far as the servicing of capital was concerned, a financial reconstruction was necessary before the physical reconstruction could take place. This was accomplished in 1947.

Jackie McCausland, Jimmy Mills and Tommy Ewing on the mill weighbridge in 1950

As a prelude to the main work of reconstruction it was decided that a weighbridge should be installed to exercise a strict control of what went in and out of the mill gates, and by 1950 a 30ft Avery weighbridge with a weighbridge office adjacent to the mill gateway was in position and working.

Much thought and discussion were given to targets as a necessary preliminary to planned reconstruction. As we have already seen, in 1950 oats were still by far the most important cereal crop for Ulster, so a maintained, but not increased, output was planned. However, it was not thought justifiable to restore the oat-flaking plant, which had been lost when fire swept through the range of buildings served by No. 2 turbine in 1943. The view was taken that the demand for animal feed compounds was likely to increase and the reconstruction planned for an output of 200 tons per week, when working one shift of 45 hours. It was accepted that, if necessary, output could be increased by overtime or shift working.

Also planned was the installation of a Simon 'Master Model' cubing plant with a theoretical capacity of three tons per hour when producing cubes or pellets, and it was agreed to maintain the mill's factoring trade in pre-packed flour and other items for human consumption.

To implement this planning the mill appointed Vincent Murnaghan as construction engineer and Stanley Smith as milling engineering consultant. Under his father-in-law, Maddin Scott, John McAusland joined the team to supervise the reconstruction on the spot. With the intended tonnage figures in mind, the team's brief was to introduce the following improvements (all, naturally, at the least expense compatible with the long life of buildings and efficiency of plant):

- increased bulk storage of raw material
- more efficient drying of grain
- increased grinding capacity
- better handling of bagged ingredients and finished products
- improved storage facilities
- improved out-loading and traffic circulation
- avoidance of flood damage.

At the outset the milling consultant impressed upon the directors two essential requirements for the reconstruction plans. The first was to plan for concentration of the building and processes rather than dispersion. The second was to plan for height in all the buildings to make best use of the force of gravity. Looking back from the year 2002 these appear to be very elementary and obvious requirements, but at the time they gave rise to a lot of heart-searching. During the first 100 years of the mill's existence the buildings had tended to spread outwards to make the best possible use of water-power, rather than upwards. Going upwards meant that many of the old buildings would be obsolete and would have to come down. To condemn an existing building, however humble, was repugnant to the directors but in the end, in the interests of modern efficiency, they all had to live with it.

To meet the storage of grain in bulk it was planned, after demolishing the offal store adjacent to the building housing the Miracle Mill, to erect in its place a silo housing eleven 30-ton bins capable of direct delivery either to the drying plant adjacent to it, or to either of the two new Porteous grinders close by. Provision was made for bulk intake on both sides and the silo was to be capable of feeding out to the new kiln and back in again, in order to condition grain brought in at an unacceptable moisture level. It was anticipated that the silo, together with the railway storage accommodation still available, would be sufficient to meet requirements for the storage of imported wheat, barley, maize and oats, and that the first three of these would account for three-fifths of the contents of most varieties of feeds.

The old flat-head kilns and the old grinding arrangements (at that time there were facilities for grinding at no fewer than four widely separated points in the mill) were to be demolished. Also, the building housing the Miracle Mill was to come down, to be replaced by a new building to house a new Walworth patent kiln for the drying of local grain before further processing. The space occupied by the two flat-head kilns in the back yard of the mill was to be utilised for the formation of a large store on three floors which at the third level would open out into the mixer loft, the bagging of and storage of finished products taking up the other areas. The rubble from the kilns was to be used to raise the floor level of this building above the winter floods and the floor in the large red store in the front yard was to receive similar treatment with rubble available from other sources. The raising of these floors would enable a number of outloading points at lorry height level.

In the mixer loft it was proposed that the existing mixer should be retained and to add in line with it two more vertical mixers, each with a capacity of

Flat head kiln *c.* 1950
The central doorway formed the entrance to the Kil'logie, referred to in the text

one ton and a theoretical mixing cycle of 20 minutes. At the same time a further mixer was to be installed in the adjacent building to serve the Simon cuber. This was to feed out through its sieves and cooling equipment to a bagging-off point on the ground floor of the building containing the oatmeal loft.

In the meantime the existing millstones and other grinders were all to be scrapped and, on the advice of Harris Marrian, Scotts' insurance brokers, the two new Porteous grinders installed, each in its own fire-resistant grinder house. The first was to be erected at the rear of the old oatmeal mill, between it and the Millbank Avenue wall, and the second on the site of the old scrap house adjacent to the miller's house. The flow from both was to be blown by fans, attached to the grinders themselves, to a sacking-off point in the building adjacent to the mixers.

This then was the outline plan, implementation to begin in 1950. It involved quite considerable alterations to existing buildings where extra height was required to accommodate new plant, as well as the rebuilding already indicated, and the estimate of the expenditure involved was £60,000, which at today's prices would mean a commitment nearer £500,000.

In 1950 the first task of the directors was to discuss the plan with their bankers, in order to obtain a long-term reconstruction loan. Such was the mill's reputation of a hundred years' standing that the accommodation was readily granted and generous terms agreed so far as repayment of the debt was concerned. Banks when lending money are often much more concerned with the present state and future prospects of the borrower than anything that has happened in the past, so the bank's directors in Dublin must have been satisfied with the plans that the mill directors laid before them, no doubt with the enthusiastic support of Tom Patterson, the bank's branch manager in Omagh. Perhaps, too, William Scott's petition of 1834 to bring a branch of the bank to Omagh was remembered; after all, it is on the strength of this petition that Allied Irish Banks today (in William Scott's time the Provincial Bank of Ireland) recognises Scotts as probably its oldest corporate customer, though even a banker's memory and records are hard-pressed to extend beyond 150 years.

Nora Madill, Phil Richardson and Lily Taggart, 1950

During 1950 the first item to be undertaken was the construction of the silo and the re-roofing and re-flooring of the burnt-out building which had formerly housed the oat flaking plant, for which the fire insurance money was available and which strictly was not in the reconstruction plan.

Under the able leadership of Maddin Scott, the reconstruction plan went ahead resolutely in the early 1950s. The first year was accomplished successfully and in the 1951 accounts the company was able to capitalise the new expenditure; but costs were increasing, as were grain prices, and at times

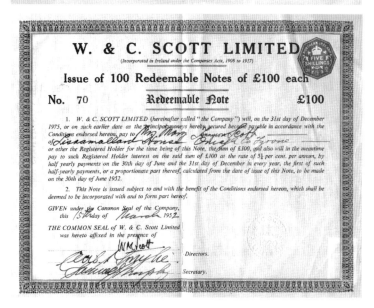

Share certificate, 1950

Redeemable note, 1952

it was dangerously near its overdraft limit. In *From Country Mill to County Millers* Walford Green recalls that for a brief spell in the autumn of 1951, when the harvest had been brought in, they found themselves in the red to the tune of £119,000: 'an unprecedented and horrific figure for those days, which no doubt gave the bank cold feet'.

The directors, together with Tom Patterson, were called to a conference with the bank's general manager in Dublin, where it was suggested that if the bank's seasonal assistance was to continue at the level it had reached, the Omagh mill should introduce some new money into the business. The bank's plan for achieving this objective was to dispose of the Castlefin mill, which had always run at a loss, and to ask the shareholders for more funds. Twenty-five years later Walford Green wrote:

> Looking back to the meeting now, it would seem that we had been summoned to be hauled over the coals for overspending. That could well have been the original intention. However, it certainly turned out otherwise.
>
> There was a very full review of our affairs at the time, of our plans and of our prospects, and it seems that the frank exchange of views which took place, coupled with the undertakings which we gave at the time, and subsequently carried out to the letter, went far to establish that degree of confidence between our bankers and ourselves which was to prove one of our greatest hidden assets of the company during the whole of the following 25 years.
>
> Be that as it may, the bank accommodation was renewed on satisfactory terms and without our pledging our assets as security in any way.

Consequently, the company did undertake to dispose of Castlefin and its plant and equipment, and a series of $5^{1}/4$% redeemable unsecured notes of £100, redeemable in 1963, was sanctioned. Castlefin took some time to sell, producing between £5,000 and £6,000; 80 of the unsecured notes, producing £8,000, were sold to family shareholders.

Another factor helped the company at this time: the passing of the Aid to Industry Act 1952 by the Northern Ireland parliament, which came at just the right moment for the reconstruction plan. By this act, Scotts could recover one-third of its outlay on buildings and plant contracted for subsequent to 31 December 1951.

The mill quoits team, 1952 – from left: Francie Golighy, Christie McCaughey, Jack McCausland, Gerry Hannigan, Davy Wylie, Paddy McBride (captain), George Kerr and Peter McGuigan.

Flooding in Omagh was an almost annual event until completion of flood barriers in the 1950s. Army and mill lorries came into service to ferry passengers on such occasions as may be seen here on the Mountjoy Road.

By the end of 1952 the reconstruction was virtually complete and production rose by 287 tons for the year at only a very small increase in production charges, thus giving a welcome increase in profits. Meanwhile at the Trusty Mill at Newtownstewart the flat-head kiln had been burned out in a fire, which was contained in that part of the building where the kiln was housed. This was replaced by a modern Nu-Way dryer, which used the 'in-sack' method of drying and was eminently suitable for the separate processing of individual farmers' grains. New plant was also installed to clean and dress seed grain for return to the farms.

During 1953 both mills had to learn how to make the best use of the new facilities available. It was a year in which, other breakfast foods having become more plentiful, the demand for oatmeal fell away and oats ceased to have their former attraction for the farmer as a crop, or for the miller as a raw material for his product. However, there was some development in the demand for livestock feeds and this, resulting in an increase of $39^{1}/_{2}$ per cent output, improved profit.

The summer of 1953 saw the end of all government controls over animal feedstuffs and the return to a free market, with all that implied in terms of price variations and enhanced competition among millers. By 1954 the pig and cattle populations had risen at the expense of poultry; oats and potatoes had fallen off; but overall there were few significant changes since 1950. Scotts traded for the next 12 months to its year-end on 31 July 1954 free of all government controls, and held its own against competition. During the first 'free' year, prices of raw materials continued steady with a fairly stable profit margin and the highest volume of production ever. This was not accomplished without heavy wage costs for overtime working, but profit nevertheless shot up. This satisfactory situation was achieved against a continued contraction in the demand for oatmeal for human consumption. Overall, the Omagh mill's output had more than doubled – from 8,055 tons in 1952 to 16,480 tons in 1954. By now it was milling grain from the four quarters of the world: supplies from the United States, Canada, Australia and even Russia came in to the deepwater ports of Londonderry and Belfast.

The year 1955 was the time for the fine-tuning of the new plant and the flow of materials. It was found that, however careful the planning, the slightest change in conditions, or any factor overlooked, tended to produce bottlenecks where least expected and much time and some investment were directed towards smoothing out the flow. It was also noted that when customer demand required the new plant to produce beyond its planned limits overtime charges were incurred which resulted in a diminution of the extra profits that should have been earned by the increased output, so much so that in the words of Walford Green, 'the game sometimes became hardly

Scotts' stand at Omagh Show, 1953. From left – Jack Anderson, Sandy Mehaffey and George Ogle. John McAusland is talking to his daughter Ruth in the foreground.

worth the candle'. One of the problems here was that the milling and mixing process was by no means fully automated. It was also clear that the grinding capacity was insufficient. One grinder milling barley could produce $1^1/2$ tons of meal per hour; the other, milling the softer maize, could go to three tons per hour. Two grinders together capable of $4^1/2$ tons per hour clearly were insufficient to serve a cubing plant with a capacity of three tons per hour and mixers capable of producing five tons per hour.

Thus it was necessary to improve the grinding capacity by a new and more powerful attrition grinder, to give a theoretical capacity of three tons per hour for barley and six tons for maize. It was also clear that the mixer time was being increased and production reduced by delays occurring in the bagging area, where one 'tired' member of a bagging-off team of four could slow down the whole process.

The first remedy was to install an Avery semi-automatic weigher at the bottom of the bin hopper below the mixers; the second was to install an automatic sack stitcher through which the sacks passed before being taken away for stacking. This reduced the manual work to attaching a paper sack to the spout, the actuation of the slide releasing the 56 pounds of feed from the weigher into the sack, the release of the sack on to the conveyor belt leading to the stitcher, and the insertion of the appropriate ticket into the line of stitching as the sack passed through it. From there the storeman took over. This arrangement was rated to deal with the discharge of meal at the rate of 10 tons per hour.

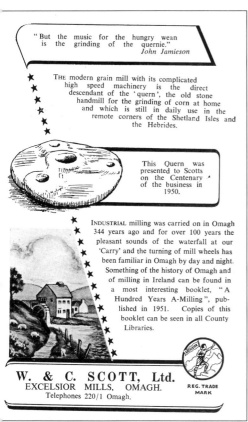

"But the music for the hungry wean is the grinding of the quernie."
John Jamieson

★
★
★
★
★

THE modern grain mill with its complicated high speed machinery is the direct descendant of the 'quern', the old stone handmill for the grinding of corn at home and which is still in daily use in the remote corners of the Shetland Isles and the Hebrides.

This Quern was presented to Scotts on the Centenary of the business in 1950.

★
★
★
★
★
★
★
★
★
★
★
★

INDUSTRIAL milling was carried on in Omagh 344 years ago and for over 100 years the pleasant sounds of the waterfall at our 'Carry' and the turning of mill wheels has been familiar in Omagh by day and night. Something of the history of Omagh and of milling in Ireland can be found in a most interesting booklet, "A Hundred Years A-Milling", published in 1951. Copies of this booklet can be seen in all County Libraries.

W. & C. SCOTT, Ltd.
EXCELSIOR MILLS, OMAGH.
Telephones 220/1 Omagh.

REG. TRADE MARK

1955 advertisement for the company and the publication *A Hundred Years A-Milling.*

In contrast with 1954, 1955 was difficult. While it began well so far as the sales of feed were concerned, it was a year of a poor oat harvest and, as time went on, of widely fluctuating prices for imported grains. In the second half of the year the livestock population of Tyrone and Fermanagh fell back and it was difficult to maintain turnover and margins. Nevertheless, the output from the Omagh mill was up by 1,000 tons compared with the previous year and total output handled in the 12-month period was 17,605 tons, a figure that was not be attained again for 10 years.

During 1955 there were no significant changes at Omagh but improvements were made at Newtownstewart, where new silo accommodation was installed sufficient to hold a 14-day supply of imported cereals and grinding capacity was increased by investment in smaller versions of the Porteous grinders that were in use at Omagh.

This year John McAusland joined the board of directors while retaining

Billy Wylie, driver of the Bedford lorry HZ 316, and his constant companion, Hughie, Skiboo's second-in-command, c. 1955.

his office as mill manager; the second edition of *A Hundred Years A Milling* appeared and was promptly sold out. At the end of the year both the mill-family and the family-round-the-mill were saddened by the death of a popular non-executive director and colleague, Philip Richardson. The reconstruction had so far cost £55,000, of which £17,000 had been recovered by government grant.

Writing of the period from 1956 to 1960, Walford Green comments:

> One is tempted to say that since turnover in cash and in tons, and profit margins and consequently final profit, all remained fairly stable, the years were ones in which we were going through a period of normality. However, to suggest to the executive directors working in the business that at any time a state of normality exists would without doubt arouse their scorn and indignation, and be greeted with a hollow laugh.
>
> It is true; nothing is ever normal in the milling trade; the pattern is ever changing, crises can arise overnight, and can be set off by the simplest occurrence, and one can move from the heights of optimistic anticipation to depths of fear and foreboding within the space of a short weekend.

By way of example, 1957 was the year of the Suez crisis – and swine fever. The first was responsible for a rise of 100 per cent in freight rates for imported grains; a sudden dramatic rise followed by an equally dramatic fall, accounting for a swing of over 30 per cent from high to low in the price of most imported grain within 12 months. The Suez crisis also brought about

Following the success of the first carnival, a trade display was introduced in 1955. Shown here is one of Scott's Excelsior floats assembled in the market yard, Omagh, before the off.

the return of petrol rationing with complications for the running of the transport fleet; nevertheless, a new 12-ton lorry was put on the road to convey grain in bulk from the railway station to the silo. A new grain intake conveyor was also installed at Omagh. There was a silver lining to the fuel rationing because customers of the port mills preferred to travel 10 or 15 miles to Scotts rather than a round trip of 70 miles to Londonderry or 140 to Belfast, and after the crisis some remained as regular customers.

The outbreak of swine fever led to a sharp decline in the pig population and a corresponding drop in the demand for pig rations. Furthermore, as a safety precaution the mill had to suspend the buying-in and re-use of second-hand jute sacks, to guard against the spread of infection. The purchase of new sacks was an added expense – and also a blow to the farmer's wife, who regarded the 'sack money' as one of her perquisites. As the mill feared, the railway line from Omagh to Enniskillen was closed, although the closure of the line to Londonderry, much used by Scotts, was deferred for two years.

In 1957 Scotts acquired the Tyrone and Fermanagh agency for Terramycin and other Pfizer growth promoters and began a series of cattle feeding trials on the mill lands at Mullaghmore. This agreement was followed a year later by one with Glaxo Laboratories for the sale of Amvilac, a special feed to promote the early weaning of piglets. In the same year, Richard Scott on leaving school was indentured as a trainee and provided with a four-year study plan. He was to become an executive director in 1962 and chairman and managing director in 1981.

In many ways 1958 was a year of innovation and new ideas. The directors decided that the time had come to implement a contributory pension and life insurance scheme to provide benefits on the retirement or death of employees. This undoubtedly sprang from Maddin Scott's strong streak of paternalism, in the best sense of wishing to promote and support saving by all members of the workforce to supplement their state retirement benefits, and so to encourage a feeling of mutual loyalty at all levels. Certainly, the pension and life assurance fund has proved to be a valuable benefit to all employees. Though this has been at a considerable financial cost to the company since 1958, it is at least arguable that the pension fund has been an important factor in the encouragement of a stable and loyal workforce over the years.

The directors' thoughts also turned to questions of 'time-and-motion' and method studies, together with the introduction of some reliable method of analysing production costs and maintaining a quantitative control over stocks. Two firms of experts were commissioned to provide reports in these fields, which were the catalyst for prolonged discussions and led to a general updating of management methods. While 1958 was a good trading year,

Passing Carlisle Villas the Bedford lorry HZ 316 is advertising the second edition of *A Hundred Years a-Milling* c. 1957.

the board's eyes were opened to the fact that the net margin of profit earned per ton produced, at less than £1, was far less than might be expected if the mill was working efficiently in all its aspects.

In the same year there were further improvements to the mill. A large tank with a capacity of 4,500 gallons was installed on the ground floor of the building housing the pelleting press. This tank could accept up to 20 tons of molasses delivered by bulk tanker lorry. The miller's house overlooking the lade was converted into a packing room on the first floor with a new canteen below, and the miller went to live in one of the houses in Mountjoy Terrace owned by the company.

At the end of 1959 the estimated acreage of major crops in Tyrone showed a substantial rise in the acreage laid down to barley, partly at the expense of the oats and potato acreage, with a general increase in all categories of livestock. This was the basis for the mill's planning into the 1960s. For two years the amount of home-grown oats coming into the mill had been very low and the swing from oats to barley was continuing; as against this, the livestock figures were on a rising curve, yet whenever an attempt was made to force up the output from the feed production plant the slender working margin was swallowed up by overtime wages. These facts, coupled with the imminent closure of the GNR line from Portadown to Omagh, called for a number of hard decisions.

The first, taken with great reluctance, was to close down the oatmeal milling operations, which had been a feature of Excelsior Mills since their beginnings in 1850; the second was to reduce the labour-intensive nature of the existing plant by reducing the manhandling of ground material in sacks to the minimum. The immediate post-war reconstruction scheme had cut out the manhandling of grain coming into the mill, by the system of bulk delivery to the silo, but had left a bagging-off and handling operation for deliveries from the grinders into the cuber and mixer lofts.

A system of automatic delivery to the mixer loft for all products passing through the grinders seemed to be the answer; the area formerly used for oatmeal milling was available to house some of the additional plant and equipment that would be required. This building, lying between the Walworth kiln building and the cubing and mixing lofts further down the range of buildings, was conveniently situated for the development. By adding to the height of the old buildings and reinforcing the floors and walls it was possible to fit in eight storage bins, each with a capacity of 16 tons. Thus the building was in effect turned into an additional silo, fed from the grinder and capable of holding sufficient ground products to sustain a full day's milling. These bins were planned to feed out at ground floor level through a Richardson weigher, automatically delivering half-hundredweight drops into a 50ft elevator and from there into a 70ft chain flight conveyor with outlets at each of the three vertical mixers in the mixer loft; the fourth mixer was to become redundant.

Up to this point the whole system was to be controlled from a panel located in the loft itself by the mixer loft foreman. By setting up the quantity of the individual ground ingredients required for any formula, he could ensure the delivery from the ground-product bins into any of the mixers of approximately five-eighths of the content of any particular mix; the time taken to carry out the delivery would be four minutes from the pressing of the button. The remaining three-eighths of the content of the mixture would still have to be fed in through the heads of the mixers by hand, tipped in by the mixer gang.

The final planning of this project was completed during the latter part of 1960 and at the same time the opportunity was taken to improve the efficiency of the grinders themselves. These had never given their full rated capacity; the meal was blown by auxiliary fans up and on to the bagging-off point and the fans were operated by the power of the grinders. This method of working set up back-pressure within the grinders, and by absorbing some of the available power slowed down the primary operation. To deal with this defect a system was planned whereby the grist from both of the Porteous grinders was to be drawn up and away by pneumatic suction, created by independent overhead fans which were driven by their own motors. This would have the effect of doubling the grinding capacity of each grinder.

Finally, and in order to ensure that the bagging-off of the mixtures was a

At the presentation dinner in 196 to mark Captain Maddin Scott's retirement are from left: John McAusland, Richard Scott, Jim Graham, Davy Kinnear, and William Martin. Seated are Mary Scott, Jean Darragh, Maddin Sco and Anna Jamieson.

continuous process with an even flow, three finished-product bins were built into the mixer loft building, facing the mixers themselves. These acted as holding buffers by taking the discharged mixtures instead of, as previously, allowing them to proceed direct from the mixer spout to the bagging-off point. This was to obviate the frequent delays that occurred when the rate of discharge overtook the will or ability of the bagging-off team to complete the weighing, sacking-off and stitching operation.

The next step was to get the money to implement these improvements, which were initially expected to cost £20,000 but in practice cost some £5,000 more. It was fortunate that in 1960 repayment to the bank for the first reconstruction was completed and a further reconstruction credit for £15,000 was granted without problems. By the end of 1961 the halfway stage was reached and by 31 July 1962 the mill was fully operational. So, in the words of Walford Green, Omagh entered the era of 'press-button milling'. Taking cubes and meals together, the mill now had an overall theoretical capacity of 250 tons per 40-hour week.

In 1960 Maddin Scott, after 40 years at the head of the company, was compelled to spend a period in hospital and on his recovery he handed on his duties as managing director to John McAusland. At the same time, Richard Scott completed his management training at Magee University College and came into the business. A link with the past was severed at the end of 1960 by the sudden death of Cecil Smylie, which brought to an end the direct association between his family and the business which had endured since his father, as a young man, had set up in practice as an accountant and had been asked by Charles Scott to audit his accounts.

An even more personal tragedy, closer to home, occurred in 1962. To close this chapter it is fitting to quote Walford Green, writing on the death of Maddin Scott:

> At midsummer in 1962, the company suffered grievously by the death of the chairman, and at an emergency meeting of the directors, held on 7 June of that year, the present writer was appointed to succeed him and Richard Scott was asked to fill the vacancy on the board.
>
> I venture to repeat here the opening words of the first report that I wrote for our shareholders when dealing with the year ended 31 July 1962 – words that were written at the time in deep sincerity and with a great sense of personal loss.
>
> When reviewing this year which ended on 31 July last, the factor foremost in all our minds must be the loss to shareholders, those in management, employees, and to customers, suffered with the passing of our chairman – William Maddin Scott.
>
> Many fine tributes have been paid to him and to his achievements in the mill and outside. In writing this report I would only speak of him in relation to the mills themselves, though, when one considers how great a part

of his life and how much of his day-to-day effort he devoted to them, that is scarcely a limitation.

To the mill and to all of us, he gave without stint of all his talents, time, of his magnificent loyalty and of his great affection. My image of him will always be one of Nature's princely givers. Yet in the giving, he himself received the gift of so to weld and bind, that out of elements whose interests of no necessity always marched hand in hand – shareholders and customers at times may seem very far apart – he could create and sustain a corporate whole, a team, or in the words he often used to use himself, 'a family-round-the-mill', on whom he could unfailingly rely.

That, I believe, may well have been his greatest achievement, and I am sure that as success came, that was the base from which it sprang.

That sense of family, of unity of common purpose, of achievement of benefit for all, and not for any one, is surely the most valuable legacy to those who have to follow on.

It is hard for me, remembering as I do the mills since 1919, and Maddin always there as managing director, in times both good and bad, and remembering him too as a greatly loved and respected elder cousin, to feel that words alone can do justice to the man he was. Indeed, mere words must be quite inadequate for all of us. In the mills we can best do honour to his memory by continuing to maintain the traditions which he worked so hard to build for us. Let the mills themselves stand as his enduring memorial, since for over 40 years he was the mills and the mills were Maddin's.

During his 42 years as head of both the mill family and the family-round-the-mill, Maddin Scott saw vast changes in the world and wrought considerable changes in his mills. Taking up the position of managing director in 1920 (and, following the death of his father in 1942, as chairman), he steered the business through the uncertainties of the 1920s, the depression of the 1930s, the difficult war years, and then headed the biggest reconstruction in the mill's history. Most significant, perhaps, was his eye to the future and choice of his successors.

When Maddin joined, Scotts was a country mill; by the time of his death Scotts were county millers, and more. In making this transformation some traditions and customs of the past had to be set aside, which is to be regretted. But if they had not marched forward they would not be in business today and, it has to be said, even if it sounds old-fashioned, that in their development over the years they have sacrificed none of the qualities that informed the business and personal life of their founder.

As we have already noted, Maddin was a keen angler, from those times as a boy when he brought the trout back to his grandmother, right up to his death. Thus perhaps it is appropriate to reprint here the poem, 'Ballintrain' by W.F. Marshall, whose verses reflect the passion for angling that he and Maddin Scott shared.

Long, long ago I lived beside a river,
And, now I'm old, I want to see it still,
To feel the breeze that makes the sallies shiver,
And watch the sunlight flash on stream and rill.
And often in the sweet release of gloaming
I'm thinking long for yon green banks again;
For then my heart, my pilgrim heart goes homing
To that bright burn that flows in Ballintrain.

There's many a river I've found enchanting,
There's many a stream where I have joyed to be;
The tuneful Mourne, with melody so haunting;
The gracious Strule that is so fair to see;
Camowen in its loveliness at Cranny;
The wee Glenelly rushing after rain;
Yet still for me the loveliest of any
Is that bright burn that flows in Ballintrain.

Above Ramackin bridge I used to linger,
When trout-rings widened in the sunset cool;
Below Drumdruff I searched with poking finger
The old tin box before I fished the pool.
But yet no riverside was more endearing,
No road so happy as the sanded lane
That led me from the homestead of my rearing
To that bright burn that flows in Ballintrain.

My folk are gone, but God the kindly Giver,
Has made a place where I shall be with them;
And I shall see one day the shining river,
Whose streams make good the New Jerusalem.
And yet I hope that when the gates are swinging,
The golden gates that shut out tears and pain,
Down past the *Father's House* I'll hear it singing,
– A burn which flows like that in Ballintrain.

Cartoon of Maddin Scott by
Emerson Babington *c.* 1955

11

The Family-round-the-mill

TONY DEESON

BY NOW WE ARE WITHIN LIVING MEMORY of some of those who worked at the mill for Maddin Scott. In the spring of 2000 his son, Richard Scott, taped interviews with a few old employees.

W.T. (Willie) Graham is 88. He started at Scotts in 1934 at Newtownstewart and when that mill closed he came to Omagh, working on until his retirement in 1977. His brother Jim also worked at Newtownstewart:

> I remember Sandy Mehaffey, the head miller at Newtownstewart very well. His father, Alexander, worked at the mill, then Sandy and his brother Bob. My starting pay was 15 bob [75p] a week. My brother worked at the mill for quite a time but he had to give up because of arthritis, but I stayed on to the end and I've been on the pension scheme ever since! When I was at Newtownstewart, Jim McSorley used to give me a lift on the lorry back and forth. He was taking in the grain, and all, at Scotts in Omagh.

John Mehaffey (right) worked his full career at the Omagh mill. Willie Graham worked at Newtownstewart until its closure. He then transferred to work at the Omagh mill until his retirement.

Jim Orr's family has worked for Scotts for three generations. Jim joined in 1971:

> My father was a carting contractor. I looked after the horses when I was a young fellow. I used to deliver to the station and collect grain, which we processed. All of it was in sacks, one or two hundredweights each. These sacks went on the back of a flat cart and the horses had to pull the load up the hill. We used to get a ton at a time from the station. When I moved to Omagh I loaded and drove the lorries, delivering the stuff to customers. Later I worked at the mixer. Then I left in June 1985, taking my pension.

Anna Orr's maiden name was Jamieson, her mother being Sandy Mehaffey's sister. Anna, who later married Jim Orr, started work at Scotts in 1941, after a spell at Omagh Academy, followed by private tuition in commercial subjects:

> I ran the office at Newtownstewart and Captain Ellis came in from time to time to see how I was getting on. I wasn't keen on answering the phone, in fact I was scared of it. Then one day Captain Ellis rang and refused to speak to anyone else. He said he wanted me to come to the phone. It was his way of teaching me to answer it, and from then on I got on with the telephone. I remember John F. Smyth, the auditor from Smylies' office. He was a very nice man and he always said when he was doing the audit, 'I know there won't be any trouble here. Anna always has her books in apple pie order, to the last penny.' My first pay was six shillings [30p] a week. I had an increase to ten shillings [50p] and then later £1. Many years later I got £12.

Jack Anderson and Sandy Mehaffey (right)

After the Newtownstewart mill closed in 1975, Anna transferred her employment to the Omagh mill, working there until her retirement.

Roisín Orr is the wife of Scotts' youngest ever employee, Louis Orr:

> Scotts' youngest ever employee was Louis Orr of Newtownstewart. At the age of 10 years he followed in his father's [George Orr, senior] footsteps and proceeded with his little pony and van to draw meal for Scotts. George Orr [senior] drew all Scotts' meals with his horses and carts from the railway station up to the mill in Mill Street at that time. He was thoroughly shocked and flabbergasted to see his young son, Louis, arrive at the railway station with his pony and van to help him. Louis was loaded with one hundredweight, while his Dad was loaded with one ton. He followed his Dad to the mill where that day he was generously paid the same price for his one hundredweight as his Dad was paid for one ton.
>
> There has been three generations of our family doing haulage for Scotts. Sixty or more years ago George Orr senior, with his horses and carts; then his two sons, Jim and my husband Louis, and now his two grandsons,

George junior and John are carrying on the family tradition, just like the Scott family at Omagh. Jim and Anna Orr's romance began at the mill in Newtownstewart when they were both teenagers. Anna worked in the office there.

Herbert (Herbie) Cockburn left Omagh Academy in 1950 and joined Scotts in 1951:

My starting pay was £2.50 or £3, about that. First I went to learn the seed-cleaning at Newtownstewart with Sandy Mehaffey, and spent between six and eight months there before coming to Omagh. Then I worked on the new silo, which Turners of Ipswich took nearly a year to install. After that I went on to install the machinery. Hard labour!

Later I was taken into the office, on the weighbridge. I can remember in the early days of the expansion there were often 100 wagons at the station. Lorries, but also horses and carts brought it to us. I was also in dispatch, organising orders and reorganising production. Noel Mitchell was head of dispatch and I worked for him for quite a while. When he left, I took over. I had to keep in touch with the mixtures to know what was required. The big change for me was from bags to bins. When I was first in dispatch there were 10 lorries delivering bags. Tonnage was not big in those days but it took time to bag and load and sort things out. The big change was definitely bags to bulk. You take into consideration the amount of men working in the mill handling the bags … The raw material was all coming in bags, up to 14 or 16 stone. They all had to be handled.

My health wasn't too good in the middle '80s and I took early retirement in 1986. I believe I was one of the first beneficiaries of the pension fund that started in 1958. I moved into my house 36 years ago and I love it here.

Paddy McBride is 81 and joined Scotts in 1940, having left school at 15. He is the second generation at the mill because his father, Charlie, ran the flaking plant in the days when it was producing porridge oats. Paddy's father died in the 1940s but Richard Scott remembers Paddy's mother coming to a party that his father, Maddin Scott, arranged in 1950 as part of the centenary celebrations. Before the celebratory meal in the Royal Arms Hotel, they went out to see a film which Richard thinks was probably *Bonny Prince Charlie*, and it turned out that this was the first time that Mrs McBride had been to the cinema (or as it was more commonly known in those days, the pictures). Paddy recalls:

When I left school I went to Tyler's shoe shop for six months and then I went to Campbell's, the butchers. I left there one Saturday night and started with Scotts on the Monday morning. I started at 10/-d [50p] a week and then when you reached 21 you were classed as a man and you got men's pay according to union rates, during the war £2 16s [£2.80] and £4 10s [£4.50] after the war. The mill was very small at that time. We had the flake plant, the kilns and the Greenhill [grinder] at the back. The Greenhill was operated by Tommy Cockburn. He was the head miller, the brother of Sam who used to run the mill water. The mill was driven by water and if it went down the machines would not work well. You knew when it was going down because the lights would go down [there was a generator that was also driven by the water-power] so you had to get the feed off and wait for the water to come up again, there was always work to do when we were waiting. I went to help my father in the flaking mill. The flakes came down the chute, straight off the rollers and onto the table and I had to pack into 2, $3^1/2$ and 7-pound bags. We had a wee small stick, which we moved to get the stuff through.

Then I moved to the packing room when this was opened during the war. Rosemary Scott was in charge in the beginning but then I took over when she joined the forces. The flake came from the back mill in sacks. It was hoisted up in bags and there was a big hopper at the top, which held three hundredweight of flakes, and they came down to me to be examined on the chute. We had about 23 girls and six young fellows working in that department when the mill started to sell direct to shops. I used to fill the boxes that the girls made up. Then some of the others would seal each box and band it up. A lot of this flake was going to England but for security reasons we never knew when it was going so that we had to have about 150 to 180 cases ready. Then we would just get a phone call telling us to get the load to Belfast for the boat. At that time our regular hours were 8 to 5.30.

Sometimes we caught a salmon coming up the mill race from down-river. These were never sold but were divided up for all. They were nice and helped with the shortage of food.

I left in 1947 and went on the railway in Belfast, returning to Scotts, then I left the firm again in the early sixties.

Scotts was known as a family firm and some families worked there for many generations: the Cockburns, the Hamptons, the Hannigans, the Kinnears, the McBrides, the Campbells, the Richardsons, the Mills's, the Mehaffeys, the Wylies, the Quigleys and the Booths.

In my time the night men were Joe Teague and Paddy Rodgers. Johnny Paul, Mickey Doak and Joe Moore were on the kilns. There were no big changes until the start of balanced rations. The Briton grinder came in then to grind the stuff and supply it to the mixer, which mixed in the offals and soya to add to the fibre and protein content. I remember that if we ran out of something we had to go to the office and then Tommy Ewing got something put in. You could not put in what you liked, they were very particular.

Tommy Ewing

I remember that in 1950 I was told the mill was aiming to produce 100 tons a week; now they are producing 2,000 tonnes in a week; machines have taken over. I remember once the Captain [Maddin Scott] told me to gather the men in the big shed. He said, 'Paddy, the big red shed.' And he said to the men, 'I am the captain of this ship and you are all my mates and I am depending on you to keep her off the rocks because the competition is getting very keen. We are the Excelsior men. We have reached the peak, with flake meal to France and the Irish bannocks made with the oatmeal we sell to the Model bakery.' It was a big achievement. I remember Captain Scott coming down the road one day as I was coming up the street and I saw Scotts' oats in all the shop windows. That was during the war. Our oats went right across to America. He was very proud of that.

All our people were good characters. We all worked as a team, they were all families. Everyone helped everyone else. Even if you were going to have a cup of tea we still kept the machines going. It was easier to keep the thing going than turning the whole thing off, you would have to turn the water off.

Apart from the railway I went on to do other things after I left. I became a fireplace maker, for instance. I worked for Masterson after I had done six months' training to learn how to do it.

At this point Richard Scott compliments him on his 'very good golf' and admires the fireplace in his sitting room. 'That is Cornish slate,' says Paddy. 'The water going through the slate gives it the rustic colour, it corrodes it.' Richard says:

> You were always a very handy chap, Paddy. I remember this very well because when my parents were doing up Lisnamallard House [1948 to 1950] there were all sorts of workmen there but when anything turned tricky they always got you in to do the job. They sent for you from the mill. They called you, first because you were handy and secondly you came in light shoes, not big clumpy boots. My mother appreciated that, you had a great name with her.

Paddy replies:

> I Snowcemed the whole of Lisnamallard House outside walls on my own. I used to get Gerry Judge now and again if I was going up high because there was an un-level up-high place and he used to hold the ladder for me. I used to say, 'I do my own decorating at home, I will do it.' I used to tell all the boys and girls that no matter where you go keep the place where you are working clean. Some of the boys used to sweep up and said to me they had done it but I used to go back and do it again.

Thomas (Tommy) Andrew Ewing was with Scotts during the war years and went on to be general manager of Bibby's Northern Ireland, based in Lisburn. He was also a main board director of J. Bibby Agriculture and in 1977 president of the Northern Ireland Grain Trade Association (NIGTA):

> I was at the Model School and then got a scholarship to the Omagh technical college. I did a two-year commercial course and I came out with good results, certificates and so on. The Model School was a nice mixed school,

good for those times.

It was a hard time during the war. We walked up to the station with the bands playing to see the boys off to the army, waving goodbye to their friends and their girl friends. We took time off from the college to see this going on. When I left the tech in 1941 Mr McCoy, the under-sheriff, called at the house one day asking me if I would do a job as a shorthand typist up in the courthouse, which I gladly did for about six months. There was a Mrs Ewing (no relation) who worked for him, a great ex-service lady who was secretary to the British Legion. She said to me there was a job coming up at Scotts. She thought it would suit me and I should apply for it. I applied and I think it was Mr Martin who interviewed me. I got the job. I think it was 30s [£1.50] a week while I was on 15s [75p] with Mr McCoy.

Little did I know that Mr McCoy was very annoyed with Captain Scott for 'pinching' me, his shorthand typist. Mr McCoy spent a lot of time in his office in the courthouse reading about murders. All the books were there from the Omagh Gaol period. I found them interesting to read as well.

I was very happy at Scotts until about 1943. I wanted to join the navy but my mother would not sign the forms, I wanted something in the war effort and I went to Lockheed Aircraft Corporation, which was based at Langford Lodge near Crumlin in County Antrim, on the shores of Lough Neagh.

I spent a couple of very happy years there as a teenager. I was working with the Lockheed technicians. Some of the time I was working in the inspection department with American chaps from California. Very exciting work. We were working on the B18 bombers, which eventually became part of the 1,000-bomber raid. My job was to go out in the jeep – that was thrilling – and collect the log sheets and the pilots' comments. The aircraft were serviced at the base, test-flown and then handed over to the American air force, which flew them to Bomber Command in England. It gave me a good grounding in engineering and, of course, in American methods. Eventually, the American air force stopped employing civilians. We all came under the air ministry and my pay dropped.

I was in Omagh one weekend and some of my friends from Scotts told me there was a vacancy coming up. David Clements, who was the general clerk, was going farming and the captain asked me back and I accepted. That was in June 1944.

We lived in Campsie at the time and in the summer the river was quite dry and I used to get up at 10 to 8 to go to work at eight at the mill. It was opposite just across the river and into the mill. Each morning the Captain phoned down from Millbank to hear the contents of the post and where the lorries were going, that sort of thing, so I had to be ready for the Captain when he phoned. The good thing about going in at eight in the morning was that you could go off at ten for your breakfast and so I was quite happy about it.

The lorries came in and I gave them their loading dockets. The mill was still under wartime control and during my time we had to do a complete inventory of all the equipment in the mill. The captain got Sam Cockburn onto this and I had to go round and measure so many feet of this or that, so many millstones. This was under the food controls of the Ministry of Defence, because we were key manufacturers selling food and they had to assess our ability to produce it.

There was a big demand for flaked oats in England at that time. We used to send hundreds of tons of them to the English agent or his nominee, the Harrods sales company in Northampton. I shall never forget that address: Harrods Sales Company, 3 The Parade, Northampton. I had to type thousands of that address for invoices, packing cases, whatever. Rosemary Scott was in charge of the packing. It was all good fun. The cases went on Johnny Quigley's cart up to the station. It was very exciting.

I was in the Home Guard, but not in Captain Scott's platoon. I can't remember but I think it was Tom Mansell's platoon. My father was staff sergeant in it and we had a black uniform to start with, then khaki. We used to go out on training exercises after parades nearly every night. We did drill parades at the front of the academy on that lovely ground and eventually we went to the range most Sundays. Captain Forsyth was the commander and Colonel Dobbs was the big chief and he insisted on wearing his big Indian hat. At the range we learned how to fire mortars and rifles and how to throw hand grenades. One Sunday Colonel Dobbs threw a hand grenade to show how it was done but it went short of the sandbags. Bertie Anderson had to rush out and throw it again and as it went off we all threw ourselves on the ground.

We had some fun up there. There were some notorious bad shots. I remember Davy McFarland. He was a terrible shot. When we fired we had a signal back whether it was a bullseye, a circle shot or a miss. David's was always a total miss, but we used to stick a pencil through the centre of the circle when he was shooting. This caused confusion back at the rifle bay. We used to play tricks like that.

I gained a lot of experience at that time, just after the war. Rationing was still on. Paddy McGale was looking after coupon points for food, as we were dealing with the Ministry of Agriculture for rationing. Jack Shannon was the man that I dealt with at McCorkell's when a boat-load of grain came in. Maybe we would be allocated 200 tons of maize or whatever. We would send the big sacks to the Derry silo, they would fill them and put on the train to Omagh where they were shunted down to the lower station at the old market yard. Johnny Quigley and Frank McGartland and sometimes Joe Quigley would collect them on their wee carts. I used to get a ride up on the cart with Johnny, which was great. I also remember when the floods came into Bridge Street and around to the bus station, Scotts' lorries and carts were the means of public transport for all and sundry.

Frank McGartland was a carter with Johnny Quigley bringing bagged goods from the railway station to the mill. Frank became a silo operator in later years.

Petrol was rationed and we never had enough allocated because the lorries used so much, delivering oatmeal and feed. Feed was rationed, bran and dust were not rationed, but were in short supply. They were invaluable to the farmer. Captain Ellis used to come from Castlefin to OK the formulae. The ingredients went up to the mixing loft. For most of my time at the mill Tommy Hannigan was the mixing man, assisted by Johnny Harpur. John Mehaffey was the key miller. Billy McCausland was in the flake mill before it burned down [in September 1943]. Billy always amazed me. He could touch electric wires without getting a shock or he could stick a needle in his skin and it would not bleed. He was a great character. The story goes that he got a cradle made for when he got married, but it stood empty forever because he had no family.

David Wylie was the night miller on the night of the terrible fire in September 1943. Jack Anderson was the foreman. His original trade was carpenter; he did all the woodwork around the mill. John Mehaffey prepared the millstones for the winter season. This was a time of great activity, coming and going to the kiln. Grain was often left in by horse and cart but mostly by Ferguson tractors with trailers. The oats were weighed in big sacks – there was no weighbridge at this stage. The oats weighed all different weights and a lot of mental sums were involved. Mostly 1s 9d [9p] a stone. Farmers selling us grain usually wanted the cheque away with them. It was fascinating for me to go up to the kiln to see the oats drying. Once I went up to the top of the kiln and I had to get somebody to help me down, it was quite a height.

The kil'logie was a fascinating place to be. People sat around there at lunchtimes. The oats had to be turned all the time with wooden shovels. It was the first time I learnt about moisture in the atmosphere. We were told to weigh out about 7 pounds light because the oats had been super-dried and they became heavier as they absorbed moisture.

Each year the floods came down from the Camowen waterfalls and the lade at the mill head became flooded. The night before, the generator had to be lifted. It was a physical job in those days and our access was very restricted by the small size of the entry to that part of the mill yard, before the second bridge to the lade was built.

By now the men had returned from the war and I used to be very interested in Mr Martin's stories about when he was travelling in Donegal in a two-seater dickey, with leather seats and a boot which folded out so that there was another open air seat at the back.

Other people who came back were Billy Mills and wee Paddy McBride [known in the mill as 'Soldier Paddy', to distinguish him from his namesake, whose narrative appears above], who had been wounded and taken as a prisoner of war. We all had a great relationship with the British Legion because of Captain Scott and many others. It was a great place for ex-servicemen and there were a lot of good fishermen among them, Captain Scott and Tommy Hannigan among them. Both took their holidays when the water was right for fishing.

It was good fun in the office. Mrs Aukett [a neighbouring farmer and friend of the Scott family, resident at Arleston] was wonderful. She brought

myself and my wife Jean a wedding present when we married in 1951, the year before I left. I remember Mrs Wallace used to come in and pay the rent. She would come in with her son and he would have a few stones of this and that and a bag of wheat. When she paid the rent she always said, 'Put it in the big book.'

At that time Paddy McGale was forever working on the ministry returns. We always had a lot of trouble. We were overdrawn or something, it was getting a balance between animal feed and human feed. I remember the stationmaster used to come round and tell us that we had not emptied the wagons at the lower station. Mr Reavey was fussy about everything. The carriage from McCorkell's silos to Omagh at that time was 7s [35p] a ton.

I used to do a lot of typing. The only thing was that the Captain used to call me in between five and six some evenings and give me a letter. Then I had to transcribe it before I went home. But all in all it was very good. I learnt something about milling, the technical side, and I am a good typist to this day.

Noel Hamilton Mitchell joined Scotts in 1943 when he was 15:

I had primary education, then a two-year commercial course at the technical school and joined the mill at 15 when I was just a lad. I got £1 a week to start with and then when I was paid £2 a week I was paid monthly. I started at nine in the morning until six at night.

One of my first duties when I came in was to light the office fire. Remembering it was wartime and coal was scarce, I had to use the kiln coal used for drying the oats. It was a horrendous job for me trying to light a fire with kiln coal but eventually I developed a technique and I reckon I am still the best fire lighter you will ever get!

My main job was writing out the dockets when customers came in for their orders. The dockets were eventually priced up and typed, you had to do all the accounting in your head. I had done shorthand at the college but

Billy McCausland, Johnny Harpur, Paddy McBride and Paddy McGale hadn't used it. One day I was called up to the office to take four letters, but by then I had forgotten most of it. It really was a tough task for me. I know it was late when I got the letters finished. I did a lot of ad-libbing and guessing. It was the occasion when the regular secretary was off.

David Clements, who was the dispatch clerk, got in early to get the lorries away. Of course, David left when his father died, to run the farm.

Tommy Ewing had been the junior previous to me but had left to work with the American forces. He was persuaded to come back because I didn't have enough experience to take on the job of dispatch clerk at that stage. Later, Tommy got a salesman's position with an English firm [Bibby's] that was expanding.

Willy Martin was the head clerk. His hobby was cage birds, canaries.

In those days it was a traditional office, like you see in old pictures, the old office clock ticking away. The walls were lined with boarding and to say we had a lot of rats and mice is an understatement. It was very dusty and I had to keep it clean. I remember sneezing and my nose running all the time. I used to keep the dust down by throwing water on it. So many people smoked that it was just accepted. The men came into the office with their pipes. They also smoked in the mill although that was forbidden on account of the fire risk. We were not always busy in the office, there was a time when the bosses were away and we played cricket.

I left in the late fifties. It was a very good apprenticeship for me. I learnt a lot of things. I got a good training from Scotts, it was like an extra part of the university for me. I think I also learnt a lot from the top down. It all stood me in good stead when later I was area secretary to the Ulster Farmers' Union.

Andrew (Andy) Cresswell Monteith joined the mill when he was 15 1/2. After he left school he worked for a farmer for a few months.

My mother told me there was a job at the mill and she thought it would be a steadier job than farming. John McAusland interviewed me just six months after he joined the mill. He took me on a month's trial and then I started as an apprentice miller. I was at the mill until I retired. My starting pay was £1 5s 10d in old money [£1.29p].

My first job was clearing up the workshops, putting all the nails where they should be and jobs like that. In those days everything had to go on the outside hoist. You used to put a rope on the neck of a sack, pull it tight and then shout to someone to pull it up.

Then I became a driver. I drove in the yard mostly but sometimes I went to the station or delivered to farmers. It was called 'Little Titch', that lorry. It was HZ 12 … a petrol lorry. I worked mostly on my own but if your load was more than 4 1/2 tons, you had a helper after that.

I got married in October 1956 to Isobel and we went to live at 35 Campsie Road, where Noel Mitchell was born. We started our married life here and we are still in the same house. The thing about this house was the flooding. It is quite low and quite close to the river. The last bad one was in 1987. I had just done up the house. The water was as high as the window-sill – about 4ft. We were under water for at least 24 hours. It destroyed everything, carpets, furniture. In the old days it did not matter so much when the flood came. There was not too much to be destroyed, no carpets or nice furniture and the little there was could be lifted out of the way.

The change to bulk deliveries [from the 1960s] was a big change for all concerned. If you were driving it became a bit of a rat-race. I tried not to let the pressure get to me, but we started very early in the morning to get the loads out and earn our money. The pressure was one of the reasons I retired at 60. Up until that time I enjoyed my work but the long hours and not knowing how much I would earn at the end of the week got me down a bit. Quite a lot of people retire at 60 now and the pension scheme helps them to do it. Aye, the pension scheme was a good thing. Captain Scott had a good insight into that. I was one of the early people to join it in 1959. I retired in 1985.

I remember some of the early characters. There was someone known as 'Tragedy' but I don't remember his real name [Paddy McBride recalls that it was Johnny Harpur who had earned this nickname]. Then there was Eddie Martin. He was always on about the limestone going into the mix. He was always saying, 'Don't forget the limestone.' He was one of six mixer men who worked very hard at night to turn out 12 tons. It took six men to do that – three down and three up. Some nights it was a rush to get the job done!

Oliver Hampton used to ring the bell for starting and finishing and for lunch times. I wonder what happened to the old bell. Probably it's gone for scrap. I remember the millmen standing against the Millbank gate taking in the sunshine and waiting for the bell to ring, in the mornings or after the dinner-hour. The machines were turned down or off for the hour but nothing stops now. I think there's a lot less dust now and no real hard work either. I remember carrying 18 stone sacks up the steps to the wee little door at the top.

Edward (Eddie or Ed) McAleer started at the mill when he was 15^1/2.

Jack Anderson was a foreman at the mill. He was also a part-time farmer and I went to work for him when I left school. One evening he said he had been talking to the captain and the captain said he was looking for a young lad for the mill. I said I was interested so Jack told the captain and I started at the mill as an apprentice. My pay was £1 13s 6d [£1.67^1/2] a week.

Eddie McAleer in his early years as a lorry driver, *c.* 1950

I was with Eddie Martin on the Briton grinder. I think that was from 1948 or 1949, about the same time as John McAusland arrived. Then for a time I drove a very noisy petrol lorry round the yard. I was put on the lorry in the yard to draw some of the mixtures. There were three mixers that handled 50 tons a day. Maize, wheat, barley, all the different mixtures had to be ground and taken from the Briton grinder and the old grinder at the back. You see, there were two hammermills at the back then, you had different grades of mixers around the yard. This was before the elevators and blowers.

So I was 17 and driving in the yard. This lorry was not taxed or insured for the road and then Dick Britton got a new lorry and I took his over. It was called 'Little Titch'. It was taxed for the road and when there was no other lorry I had to go out on the road with it. I was crazy to get on the road.

Later I would collect stuff by road in a bigger lorry. Loose grain came in from Derry and Belfast in the railway wagons. I used to put two chutes onto the wagon, roll the grain into the lorry, draw it down to the mill and drop it off.

The silo was built in 1950. I remember when they were building the silo I used to have to pull the bins off. You see, they were putting the bins down in between the concrete so I was on the lorry in the yard and they got me to pull the bins up and let them down in between the concrete.

At this time I wasn't getting a lot of money so when I went home at nights I was a part-time farmer. I did not get a lot of money. When I had been at the mill for two years I got £2 10s [£2.50], so I gave my mother £2 and saved the 10s [50p] for clothes or going to the pictures. We had three picture houses in Omagh at that time.

My part-time farming was a piggery. A man had 50 pigs and I took it over. I made a bit of money on them. I fed them before I went to work. I would do that about 6–7 in the morning, then got cleaned up and went to the mill at eight o'clock. Sometimes I had to work until seven or eight at night or if I was on the lorry it might be 10 o'clock before I was finished. I had automatic feeders for the pigs. I filled them with meal and water and the rest was automatic.

I married in 1956, my wife's name is Etta. She's a lovely girl. She came from Co. Down. I started broiler chickens in 1961 and built another unit. I built it up until it was 50,000 at that time. I had so much work at home that I left the mill in 1968 and I built the unit up to 80,000 broilers. Paul, a son of mine, runs it now.

I started in the restaurant business in 1990 with the Shoppers' Rest in Omagh. In 1995 we opened another restaurant just before you go on the M1 in Dungannon. My daughter Siobhan runs that. Then we opened another one and Peter runs the village take-away. Paul also started another take-away, 'Flash in the Pan' in Omagh. They are all family businesses. I have the whole family working in them and I've got 14 grandchildren in all.

My training in the mill was a great boost to me because it meant that when I got out in the lorry I could get out into the countryside and see what was going on.

Walford Green

12

Walford Green and John McAusland
Redirection and Reconstruction

TONY DEESON

WALFORD GREEN BECAME CHAIRMAN following the death of Maddin Scott. He was a great-grandson of the founder, William Scott, through his mother, Nancy, who was William Scott's granddaughter and married the Rev. Ernest Davis Green, a Methodist minister. Thus he was first cousin to Maddin Scott.

Walford Green joined the business in 1942, being appointed a non-executive director when he was serving as a lieutenant-commander in a training role with the RNVR, more active service being denied to him because of a serious defect of one eye. Walford's early life was less than stable, in a geographical sense, because he and his family led the peripatetic life of a Methodist minister. His mother died when he was very young and as a result Walford and his sister Noëlle spent their summer holidays with their Irish grandmother. These holidays and the various uncles, aunts and cousins they met must have had a strong formative influence on the young Greens, and possibly explain their later attachment to Ulster and its people.

Educated at the Leys School, Cambridge, where he played hard and well at every sport, Walford nevertheless had sufficient dedication to his studies also to secure a place at Emmanuel College, Cambridge. Although destined to be a lawyer he read history, perhaps believing with Alexander Pope that 'the proper study of mankind is man', before going on to his legal studies. Certainly his early training endowed him with a rigour of approach, a capacity for speed and accuracy and an ability to grasp the vital point in an argument and to take rational and correct decisions which were invaluable not only to him in his chosen profession but also in his leadership of the family business.

A considerable part of his war service was spent on Belfast Lough and this gave him further opportunities of developing the links with Ulster that he had made in childhood. After the war his professional energies were mainly directed to re-establishing his legal practice in the City of London, but in 1962 he was offered and accepted the chairmanship of Scotts, a position that he held for 20 years. All in all he gave service to the company for 40 years, in the latter half of this period as chairman providing wise encouragement and counsel to the managing director, John McAusland, and his colleagues who were charged with the day-to-day running of the expanding business.

Walford Green 1947

John McAusland, who was appointed managing director when Maddin Scott was first ill in 1960, continued in this position under the chairmanship of Walford Green. John McAusland was son-in-law to Maddin Scott, having married his daughter, Patricia. He was born in the West of Scotland, one of six children and the youngest of three boys. His father's textile business failed in the 1930s and the family, once comfortably off, found themselves in reduced circumstances. This early misfortune for the young McAuslands may have been beneficial so far as Scotts were concerned, because John McAusland was always the guardian of the family's business interests and conscious of the need to conserve its assets.

After war service, when he reached the rank of captain and served in the North Africa campaign, John McAusland came to the mill in 1949, charged with the responsibility for carrying into effect the first of the post-war reconstruction plans, at both Omagh and Newtownstewart. He swiftly 'saw off' a milling consultant, engaged earlier by Maddin Scott. Given John McAusland's lack of experience this was a brave decision, but one that was justified and was supported by his father-in-law, as chairman of the board.

It was characteristic of John McAusland that, throughout his years as managing director, a night extension from the mill to Millbank was by his bedside. He always answered the phone, to take orders if a farmer or merchant customer rang, whether late in the evening or before the office opened at 8am, by which time in his early years he would have been in the office for half an hour or so before returning to Millbank to breakfast with his family. This propensity for being early on the job did his reputation no harm whatsoever, with workforce and customers alike.

John McAusland's capacity for accepting responsibility justified an increase in his workload and in 1953 he was appointed a director of Scotts Mills Ltd, with supervisory responsibility for the mill at Newtownstewart. He joined the main board in 1955 and to all intents and purposes under-studied Maddin Scott, who developed full confidence in John's ability to take over the day-to-day management of the business.

On their first meeting Walford Green took to John McAusland and they developed a rapport that was to bear great fruit, particularly in the years fol-lowing Maddin Scott's death. They formed a strong team, even allowing for the fact that Walford was a busy solicitor in his daily job, and resident in Kent. Week by week a bulletin of information was sent from the mill, and almost as regularly an almost illegible handwritten response would come by return of post.

An early piece of advice from Walford, which John much appreciated, was that he should have nothing whatever to do with the mill at Castlefin. Maddin Scott loved Castlefin with a deep loyalty, despite the fact that it had never made any money, and treated it as a wayward child only needing cor-rection for it to change its ways and be good. Maddin's patience partially stemmed from the fact that the manager in charge was Captain J.G. Ellis MC, a comrade-in-arms from the First World War. Gray Ellis was a fine watercolourist and draughtsman and was the illustrator of the first edition of *A Hundred Years A-Milling*, but never seemed quite comfort-able as a mill manager. The bank, possibly prompted by Walford and John, fortunately insisted on the disposal of Castlefin as part of the acceptable price for its financial sup-port for the first post-war reconstruction programme.

In the early 1960s there were three further appointments that have contributed greatly to the prosperity of Scotts to this day.

Desmond Given joined the company on leaving school, on 3 July 1961, and for five years was an assistant in the transport department before becoming a sales representa-tive in February 1966, in which capacity he worked for 15 years, covering Co. Tyrone and part of Monaghan, initially dealing with all types of farmers but eventually specialising in the poultry sector of the market. In August 1981, having gained considerable knowledge and understanding of the farming community, he was promoted to the position of purchasing manager, responsible for the buying of all raw materials essential to compound feed manufacture. Even now, aided by the feed formulation program of the mill's computer, which helps Desmond to decide the most economical mix of products to obtain the required specifi-cation, this is a complex business calling for much practical experience and

The painting created for the cover of *A Hundred Years A-Milling* by Gray Ellis.

FINN VALLEY MILLS CASTLEFIN

Castlefin mill and engine room

Advertisement for the sale of Castlefin mill.

judgement. Desmond remarks: 'Buying at the right price and on the right day is very important, but sometimes good or bad luck can play its part. For example, if I buy a large tonnage of soya bean meal today and the pound sterling strengthens tomorrow, so that there is a drop of £30 a tonne, it creates a lot of problems for us.'

It is not only a matter of purchasing economically. Desmond also has to estimate what is going to be sold ahead, which can be very difficult to quantify. The principle is to estimate to 80 per cent and then top up later. A lot of unrelated factors make estimation difficult: a good summer with plentiful supplies of fodder, a drop in the volatile pig market, the loss of a big customer are just three risks; there are many more. That Desmond has been getting it right more frequently than otherwise is indicated by the substantial growth in tonnage that Scotts has achieved during the past 25 years.

In February 1988 Desmond assumed the added responsibility for the organisation of the transport department and he continues today to carry out the purchasing and transport functions, both essential to the prosperity of the mill. Bearing against the general trend, Scotts firmly retains its own transport on the basis that most of its deliveries are within a 50-mile radius of Omagh, and in this area the company can give a better service more cheaply than if it contracted it out.

In August 1991 Desmond Given joined the board of Scotts Feeds.

A year after Desmond joined Scotts, a young and recently qualified installation engineer came to Omagh representing the Chelmsford, Essex firm of Christy & Norris, manufacturers, suppliers and installers of mill machinery among other types of processing plant. The name of this engineer was Roy Howard. He had served his apprenticeship with Christy & Norris and, after his national service in the Royal Navy, rejoined them as research and development engineer, later becoming further involved as an installation

engineer. The brief from his company was to provide the installation of substantial new plant modifications for Scotts, which took him from February to August 1962.

As Roy was preparing to leave, John McAusland was so impressed by his work and pleasant personality that he invited him to stay in Omagh as mill engineer for Scotts. Having by then fallen in love with the place and its people, Roy accepted and has stayed ever since. He joined the board as production director in 1973. He and his team have provided detailed production planning and were responsible for all the extensive and demanding milling plant developments between 1962 and 1997, when Roy retired.

In 1964 Fred Charters joined Scotts, after training and spending 3 1/2 years as a sales representative with animal feed manufacturers, R. Silcock & Sons of Liverpool. Fred recalls that his starting salary with Scotts was '£800 per annum, plus a Mini car'. In 1969 he was appointed sales manager, and in 1974 sales director. In this capacity, he has had an exceedingly busy life. He has been responsible for the sales team performance of six or seven representatives, serving major accounts personally; he has also had responsibility for Scotts Farms Ltd, with laying units at Inisclan and Aughentaine, Fivemiletown; and the Scott–Smyth pig farm at Fivemiletown. Since about 1980 he has liaised with Charles Crawford, as a Scotts-appointed director of Erne Eggs Ltd. There has also been involvement with the company's customer relations, advertising, shows, calendars and other responsibilities too numerous to mention.

In 1996, following the retirement of Richard Scott, Fred Charters was

Norman Robinson and Desmond Given in front of a new ERF lorry with the new livery adopted in 1986.

Roy Howard demonstrating new technology 1970's style to Giles Shaw MP, NIO minister. Also in the picture left to right are Fred Charters, John McAusland, Willie Vaughan and Eric Reid, a director of customer Moy Park.

appointed managing director. Now in 2002, being himself over retirement age, he is supposed to be part-time, confining himself to mornings, although this is frequently theoretical rather than standard practice and he is often to be seen about the mill in the afternoons.

In his 'spare' time Fred is a keen farmer, largely involved in rearing poultry in partnership with his son, Arnold. He has two farms at Gortaclare and the ever-increasing cost of farming land is illustrated by the fact that in May 1970 he paid £243 an acre for his land; when he acquired his second farm in 1986 the cost was £2,153 per acre.

By the time Walford Green became chairman, Excelsior Mill was very far away from the days when it was a country mill, set in a sleepy country town. Post-war developments had been considerable and the once-rural setting had long since been urbanised, surrounded by housing and by other businesses. In the year Maddin Scott died, the Millbank field belonging to the business was cut in half for a new road to connect the Dublin Road to the Derry Road; and a broiler-breeding unit capable of holding 1,500 laying hens was sited on part of 'Foster's field' lying between Lisnamallard Avenue and the back of the old bag store.

In the early 1960s, two swiftly growing trends were becoming important. The first was the system of delivery in bulk to the farmer's own bins on the farms. These bins had a capacity of five tons and were often bought by the mill, the outlay being recovered by a small additional cost per ton delivered until the bin was paid for. The move from bags to bins was one of the most significant changes to take place in the past half-century. Bags remained available to larger customers who might, for example, want half a ton of feed in bags to feed their calves, and are provided, even if not strictly economic, as part of the mill's service.

The directors judged that bulk delivery should provide a competitive advantage for Scotts. In anticipation of the growth of this system, the mill acquired its first bulk-delivery truck from the proceeds of the sale of Millbank field. There was also a steady increase in the demand for pelleted feeds and the old cuber, or pellet mill in more modern parlance, was by now a well-worn piece of equipment; it was replaced by a new Simon-Barron 'Hi-Flo' 50hp pellet mill with a capacity of five tons per hour when producing 3/8 inch pellets. The plant was completed and became operational in April 1963, but over the next few years refinements were made to perfect the flow of pelleted feed from the machine to the bagging-off and bulk discharge points.

In 1963 trading conditions were not easy. The introduction of the new plant constrained production charges at the level of the previous year, but administrative charges rose and taxation and depreciation bore down hard on the profits earned. Nevertheless, despite intensified competition the mill added 400 tons of sales compared with the previous year, although the trading profit showed a fractional decrease. It was evident that if the work noted above had not taken place the results would have been far more depressed.

About this time the Department of Agriculture estimated that in 1963 the farmers of Ulster spent £44 million on feeds, of which Tyrone and Fermanagh accounted for £12 million. Walford Green commented: 'Of that amount, our slice of the cake was rather under a 24th part – a very small slice indeed.' He continues:

> We now knew we were competitive and it was quite clear that, whether one looked at the statistics in terms of money or of tonnage turnover, there was no reason why we should hold back for fear of treading on the toes of others, or be content with anything less than the slice of the whole cake that matched up with our capabilities. A policy decision was therefore taken to expand into new territory and an additional salesman to explore the areas lying around Dungannon and Ballygawley was taken on.

At the same time an attempt was made to expand the trade in pre-packed human foods, which had fallen back until they had reached an uneconomic level. With this in view a salesman was engaged but his efforts were not successful, and in July 1964 the packing room was closed down.

Roy Howard provides this picture of the mill and its equipment in 1963:

A Redler intake conveyor supplied a 20 tons-per-hour elevator which discharged ingredients into 11 silo bins each of 30 tons capacity. Material was fed from the silo to two Porteous No. 4 grinders which discharged via self-contained fans and piping to cyclones, which in turn discharged the ground material to bagging points on the top floor of the store. Ground raw materials were stored here in two-hundredweight sacks, approximately 100kg in today's measurement. These sacks were wheeled individually by sack truck to three vertical mixers, where they were tipped into the top of the mixer, along with other ingredients to form a one-ton mix.

Mixing time was 20 minutes for each mixer. The mixers and all other associated machinery were driven by lineshaft. At this time, although the potential output from each mixer was 9 tons per hour, the discharge and packing line conveyors only permitted an output of 5–6 tph. Thus mixers had to be stopped, to prevent over-mixing. Finished product was packed, using a semi-automatic Avery scale, and stored in sacks on the middle and ground floors where it could later be loaded onto flat lorries.

A 25hp Simon 'Master Model' press was fed by its own mixer and produced cubes, pellets and 'spangles' – mineral-rich cubes that were so called because of their shape, resembling the popular sweet of that period.

There was also a bulk outloading bin with four divisions and four outlets. One flat lorry had been modified by fitting three removable hoppers, a conveyor and blower for the beginning of the bulk feed market.

Raw materials were brought into the mill by articulated bulk containers to silo and in sacks to store. At that time we also used an old shed to the rear of the mill where grain was augered out of bulkers and stored for later use, when it was augered back into the bulker and thence to the silo. A molasses tank supplied the molasses mixer and the master model press via a pump and pipework.

At this time our products were meals, cubes, pellets, mixed poultry grain and coarse dairy meal.

Plant redesign saw the Porteous grinders converted to a suction pneumatic system along with the associated fans and cyclones which were installed above the blending bins; at this stage ground material was fed into eight newly erected blending bins, from which material was fed out by screw feeders into a Richardson EE50 scale, after which it was elevated to a long conveyor which conveyed it to the three vertical mixers. The building in which the eight bins were housed was named the Bendix building from this date, as the blending system was controlled by a control panel manufactured by Bendix Ericsson. An industrial air-compressor was installed to provide air for the pneumatic slide operation. Bagging and storing ground material direct from the grinders were discontinued and all the associated pipework and cyclones were removed from the site.

In 1963, the long-anticipated closure of the Great Northern rail line to Londonderry and Belfast finally happened and the mill acquired a bulk container lorry with a capacity of 20 tons, capable of carrying out two hauls from Belfast or three from Londonderry in an extended working day.

Closure of the railway line, coupled with the rapid rise in the production of home-grown barley (in 1961 in Co. Tyrone 18,300 acres were sown to barley; by 1964 the figure had grown to 31,300 acres), brought a storage problem and, taking advantage of the great improvement in the storage methods for grain after reduction of the moisture content, a Butler bin with a capacity of 900 tons was erected in the mill yard, 36ft in diameter and 50ft to the apex and made from corrugated galvanised steel. Although, as Walford Green commented, it was 'no ornament in itself', it provided additional storage at a very low cost, one-third of the total outlay of £5,050 being recovered by a grant.

Also, due to an increased demand for cubes in bulk a 50hp Simon-Barron 'Hi Flo' cuber was installed, producing 3/8 inch cubes into a vertical cooler and crumbler.

Delivery to customers in bulk went from strength to strength, increasing 100 per cent in the period 1963–4. In 1965, for the first time, sales of poultry feed exceeded sales of pig meals. One thousand five hundred tons was added to the mill output for this year but a rise in grain costs, with which increased margins did not keep pace, resulted in only a marginal increase in trading profit. This year it became clear that the demand for pelleted feed was again likely to increase and the full rated capacity of the pellet mill would be needed. At that time there was a loss of production as the flow from the pellet mill direct to the bagging-off point sometimes built up and the plant had to be shut down while bottlenecks were cleared. To overcome

Omagh railway station *c.* 1950, at the junction of the lines to Belfast and Enniskillen

Mr McDowell of TBF Thompson handing over a new Leyland articulated lorry to John McAusland and Herbie Cockburn, transport manager, 1963

this situation six buffer-storage bins, each capable of holding 10 tons, were installed into which pellets and cubes could be fed continuously, being bagged off from each as and when convenient, or delivered into the bulk lorry.

By 1966 the clear pre-eminence of barley over oats, particularly in Tyrone, was confirmed. Oats was now the second crop in size, while wheat represented only 230 acres. Livestock changes were unremarkable. Of this time Walford Green says, 'It was a time of governmental change and we had to learn to live with words like freeze, squeeze, standstill and restraint.' This was the time when the Selective Employment Tax was introduced. In the case of the mill, being a manufacturing company carrying on a business in an area classified as one of high unemployment and with more 'productive' than 'non-productive' workers, the tax was collected but repaid (three months later) with a bonus. This *jeu d'esprit* on the part of the government was scarcely understood by Scotts, but its benefit to the company was accepted without argument.

By 1966 the mill could boast an output of 19,300 tons but with a net profit per ton of only £0.84. Nevertheless, steady progress had been made over the decade and automation was paying off. Within the year the sales staff had exceeded a target increase of 10 per cent in tonnage handled, bringing about a total increase of 16 per cent at a time when the volume of feedstuffs in the whole of Northern Ireland had fallen by 5 per cent. Progress had been made when some competitors had fallen back. The increase in ton-nage inevitably brought about an increase in the total of trade debtors, and a policy of rigorous enforcement of credit charges on customers' overdue accounts was adopted as essential when in terms of bank charges the cost of financing credit was both high and rising.

That year a speeding-up of the mixing process, by the installation of new and faster moving conveyors underneath the mixers and above the mixer bins to increase the potential output at this stage to nine tons an hour, was approved. It was implemented the following year. At the same time a 'Cascade' molasses mixer adjacent to the other mixers, through which meals destined for further processing could be passed, was installed.

A new and significant departure was the installation of a Qeleq analogue computer capable of producing the formulae for all the mill's mixes on a least-cost basis. Walford Green commented: 'This was an interesting machine – purpose-built and designed by one of our Northern Ireland miller friends* with a bent for intricate tasks such as this, but manufactured in the Republic. We were able to make it a term of our purchase that further sales in our area were to be restricted for a period.'

The later introduction of a 'Mark 2' and more powerful Qeleq computer in 1973 was most fortunate, just as President Nixon imposed an embargo on the export of soya beans and their by-products. Armed with this new power, Scotts was able to reformulate its diets to better economic effect than the great majority of its competitors, who were without this (then almost unique) tool. Now, of course, digital feed formulation programs are univer-sal and cheap, but from 1966 Scotts felt that for once they were technically ahead of their peers in this important respect.

These items, together with some improvements in the office, called for a capital outlay of £11,000 in 1966, a year when there was a substantial rise in the cost of raw materials. As a matter of policy, sales of straight (unmixed) ground meals, on which the margin was always low, were curtailed, result-ing in a small drop in overall tonnage and a corresponding drop in prof-itability.

In the short term, with the economic situation of the United Kingdom so unsettled, the managing director, John McAusland, proposed, with the agreement of his colleagues, that the further ahead the business could buy the better, and available financial and storage resources were committed to the hilt. When devaluation took place the policy paid off handsomely. For the long term, it was accepted that there was still room to expand turnover, but to do so production would have to be increased and production costs and some overheads would have to be pegged at current levels. To do this called for greater efficiency of method.

This thinking brought about what was in effect a third reconstruction plan, with three aspects: improvements to the operation of the plant; a

*William Marshall, whose grandfather of the same name had been a customer of Lewis Scott's in the early years of the twentieth century.

reorganisation of the handling of the finished product from the bagging-off points to its exit through the mill gates; and an attempt to find further retail outlets.

The plan for the plant was to proceed from 60 to 99.9 per cent automation, involving a complete change of method. The sequence under the new system was 'blend, grind and mix' in one operation, rather than to grind each individual product separately before mixing. By adding augers and dischargers to all storage bins, the silo and neighbouring Bendix building were turned into a blending plant, from which supply could be drawn from 19 different bins automatically and fed into two three-ton batch bins above a new Christy & Norris 150hp 'X26' hammermill. From there, the blended content of each bin was ground, and (by the pneumatic-suction method which had been first adopted in 1961) was taken to the holding hopper at the head of a new horizontal mixer. The operation of the entire system was controlled from an electric panel at a point below the mixer itself. The only hand-additions to each batch of mix were limestone flour and additives such as vitamins, trace-mineral supplements, condiments and flavourings, all of which were required only in very small quantities. The adoption of this system led to two of the old-style vertical mixers in the former mixer loft becoming silent, the third remaining in operation for the production of coarse dairy meal.

So far as the bagging-off and handling problems were concerned, the area occupied by the old red store, described in Lewis Scott's account of the mill in the early 20th century*, was cleared. In its place a single-span building was erected, with a height of 30ft to the pitch of the roof and a floor area of 5,400 square feet. In one corner of this structure was placed the bagging-off point for both meals and pellets. In the remainder of the building, upwards of 300 tons of finished products were stored, stacked on pallets up to five tiers high, with ample space between the tiers for the operation of fork-lift trucks. These changes to the plant had the effect of increasing the rated output per week to 720 tons on one shift or 1,400 tons if an extra shift was worked.

In 1967 the search for retail outlets was satisfied by the rental of a 36,000 caged-poultry laying unit and later in the year by a pig-production unit. These were both sited at Aughentaine, on the farm of Captain John Hamilton-Stubber. The laying unit, known as the Excelsior Poultry Unit (EPU), took an output from the mill of 1,500 tons a year and was managed by Fred Johnston, supported by advice and guidance from Fred Charters. The pig farm was a joint venture with Smyths, the millers in Strabane, whose sales representative, Walter Shortt, gave technical assistance to the manager, Sandy Atwell. Both of these enterprises provided the milling company with a measure of confidence in livestock production that was to bear fruit in later years.

* See Appendix I, p.205

The following year the company undertook a capital reconstruction to simplify its structure and at the same time Scotts Farms Ltd was registered as a wholly owned subsidiary of W & C Scott Ltd, as a vehicle to carry on the farming activities.

At this time, as an enhancement of the pension fund from the members' point of view, action was also taken to adopt the principle of 'controlled funding' for the pension fund so as to provide, after 40 years' service, 50 per cent of the average salary over the last three years before retirement at normal pension age. The benefit to the membership was that, in the inflationary 1970s and 1980s, pensions were guaranteed to reflect salaries in place at the time of retirement, rather than the average of salary throughout the working life. Effectively, therefore, pensions were now inflation-proofed up to the point of retirement, with annual inflationary increases during retirement being applied some years later and back-dated, a feature that has been of great benefit to the membership.

Bobby Scott in naval officer's uniform *c.* 1940

Bobby Scott, OBE, died suddenly in 1968 at the early age of 49. He was the eldest son of Maddin Scott and a great-great-grandson of the founder. A solicitor by profession, he joined his mother's brother Edward Freer in his firm in Leicester, following war service in the Mediterranean as a pilot in the Fleet Air Arm of the Royal Navy and as a lieutenant-commander in the Pacific, later becoming a non-executive director of Scotts under his father's chairmanship.

John W.S. Walton, whose mother Lady (Nelly Margaret) Walton was Maddin Scott's sister, took Bobby's place on the board as a non-executive director. Each of these family members contributed wise counsel and experience during his years as a board member, and each enjoyed the experience and involvement in a business activity that was far removed, both by geography and by occupation, from his main career.

The trading year that ended in July 1969 was in many respects an adverse one for the company. Stocks had to be replaced at post-devaluation cost; demand in some quarters fell off; and corporation tax went up to 45 per cent. Nevertheless, although the trading profit fell back from the high figure of the previous year it exceeded that of 1967, as did the output. Forty thousand pounds of reconstruction expenditure was capitalised and £16,000 was recovered by way of grant. These figures were achieved before the automated plant came on stream in 1970. In that year, output rose steeply to 26,800 tons and the trading profit recovered.

John Walton

At this time a study of production costs and overheads at the Excelsior Mill and the Trusty Mill in Newtownstewart showed how the process of reconstruction had improved the costs of goods produced at Omagh when compared with Newtownstewart. This much smaller mill was something of a one-man band, heavily dependent on the skill, judgement and reliability of Alexander (Sandy) Mehaffey, the head miller, who had been with Scotts for 50 years and was approaching the age at which he would retire. With the increasing production soon to be implemented at Omagh, it was decided – not without heart-searching and regret – to close the Newtownstewart mill.

Another significant change was made, in what proved a successful effort to ensure that future demand would match the new capability in output, in that Fred Charters was appointed sales manager with a brief to ensure that his sales force disposed of all that the mill could produce. This was a challenge, bearing in mind that by 1970 output was 26,800 tons, having risen from 19,100 tons in 1967. There was growing confidence that there was business to be had, on favourable terms, provided that Scotts utilised the strengths that by now were at its disposal.

But the political environment in Northern Ireland was far from happy or stable. In this context, Walford Green should have the last word on the trading year. This is a quotation *From Country Mill to County Millers*:

> It was during this period that the undercurrent of political instability, which one learns to live with in Ulster, came to the surface, giving rise to the disturbances first manifested in the city of Derry, which were to go from bad to worse throughout the province ... This is no place in which to make any but the barest comment. We in the mill bear ill-will to no one, whatever their views, though we are very conscious of the substantial benefits we, as an Ulster business, like many others, receive by reason of our situation within the United Kingdom. Up to the end of 1970 we had weathered the storm without any incident.

As Newtownstewart closed and all production was centred on Omagh, another retail outlet was acquired by the purchase of 45 acres of marginal land at Inisclan, beyond Mountfield, where two laying houses were erected, each with a capacity of 15,000 birds.

By 1971 output had risen again, to 31,500 tons, representing for the first time an income from sales of over £1 million, partly due to an average rise in the cost of raw materials to £30.50 per ton; nevertheless, it gave a trading profit of £53,500. 'This,' says Walford Green, 'was achieved in a year in which the political unrest had gone from bad to worse, and we, like everybody else, stood at risk to the bomber.'

In 1972 the new plant had been at work for a full year; output again increased to 34,300 tons and trading profit soared to £92,500. During this year further improvements were made to the offices. The range of buildings by the old millrace was cleared and the area was graded and surfaced. At the same time a small area of land lying between the lade and Lisnamallard Avenue, bounded on the north by Foster's field and to the south by the rear pathway into the mill itself, was acquired from the executors of William Maddin Scott to provide space for further development.

A new single-span, single-storey building with a floor space of 2,400 square feet was erected here, to provide storage for spares and an engineers' shop for the maintenance of both the mill plant and the transport fleet. Spending on four large electric motors, to provide against any breakdown in mains supply to the plant, and an additional fork-lift truck was authorised. In the mixing area it was decided to install, as an auxiliary to the main horizontal mixer, a 'Schugi' mixer capable of adding molasses and fats to the meals at the mixing stage. The molasses was drawn from the bulk storage tank already in use, but the fats required a new fats tank and boiler so that the stored fat could be maintained continuously in a liquid state at a constant temperature.

During 1973 the curve of rising tonnages flattened as a consequence of the abolition of the Egg Marketing Board. Unsubsidised eggs now had to find their market value according to the law of supply and demand, resulting in the closure of some egg-laying units as prices fell. However, an output of 34,900 tons resulted in sales of £1,639,000 and the trading profit more than doubled to £186,000. In the early part of 1973 it became clear that the old cubing plant installed in 1962 had seen better days and was having difficulty in keeping up with the increased demand for cubed and pelleted feeds. Additional capacity was arranged by installing a new machine alongside the old one; this was a 125hp model with a rated capacity of 10 tons an hour. At the same time plans were laid for the injection of moisture into the meal, as it was drawn away from the grinder, so as to replace the loss caused by the heat of the pelleting process and improve the texture and appearance.

Taken following a poultry conference organised by Scotts in the 1970s. John Mc Ausland, Joe Lawson, Moy Park and Dr David Charles, guest lecturer from MAFF.

During 1973 three separate projects were under study for possible future implementation. The first of these was the replacement of the old weigh-bridge. The increase in the length of road haulage vehicles had proved more than the old bridge, installed in 1948, could manage and as a consequence the control over intake and output had been lost, making accurate stock records impossible. An assessment was carried out of the alterations required to rehouse the weighbridge office and the managing director's office above. The project was implemented some 18 months later with a new weigh-bridge, 60 feet in length, installed on a line parallel to the rear of the Mountjoy Terrace houses. This extended from a point not far from the corner of the old weighbridge, running northward through what had been part of the back gardens of Mountjoy Terrace. It was anticipated that when the lease expired on the lower part of Foster's field in 1976 it would be possible to establish a second entrance to provide for one-way incoming and outgoing traffic to and from the front mill yard.

The second project concerned bins. To quote Walford Green: 'In a period of expansion, the cry had at once gone up of "bins, bins, more and better and bigger bins".' Later it was to be 'computers, computers, more and better computers'. But in the 1970s the cry for bins was heard again with even louder emphasis. So a study was made of the possibility of locating a nest of four cylindrical 'Butler' bins for raw material storage, each with a capacity of 75 tons, in the yard below the silo. On installation this project was reduced to two bins each holding 100 tons, complemented by a line of six 10-ton intermediate storage bins to accommodate the output of the new cuber.

Dr Roger Green

Finally, thought was given to the practicality of adding 'Robo-packer' and 'Robo-former' units at the packing point for meals and cubes. These units had been invented by Roy Howard and developed by his old employers, Christy & Norris, at their factory at Chelmsford, yielding to Scotts for some years a modest licence fee on each sale made by Christy.

In 1973, in a notable departure from previous tradition in this essentially family concern, the board was strengthened by the appointment of two non-family executive directors. Fred Charters had already proved his ability as a sales representative, progressing to be an exceptional sales manager with apparent ease. He was appointed sales director. Roy Howard, who had largely masterminded all the plant developments of the previous ten years, was appointed production director. Fred and Roy thus became the first non-family executive directors in the business's 123 years, and each contributed significantly to its progress during his time.

At the same time, in the interests of family continuity, Dr Roger Green, son of Walford Green, became a non-executive director. Roger, though based with his family in Kent, had followed the Green family tradition of spending holiday time in Omagh during school and university breaks and somehow had become injected with the mill dust that seems to get under the skin of certain family members. His chosen career was that of a surgeon, training in the London Hospital at Whitechapel, with later experience in the Mayo Clinic and a spell at the Royal Victoria Hospital in Belfast, where he developed his skills in traumatic surgery during the most acute years of the troubled times in the province. He was to remain a valued non-executive director and a perennial source of forthright and independent opinion until retirement from the board in 1998, regularly attending half-yearly board meetings at his own expense in travel costs, following a career move to the middle-eastern Sultanate of Oman.

Jimmy Dodds, who retired in 2002, in front of DAF bulk lorry in 1970's livery.

Following a satisfactory year, during which the shell of the old mill at Newtownstewart was sold for £6,000, 1974 proved to be more difficult. First, there was an increase in labour and other overhead costs, coupled with an unprecedented rise in the cost of raw materials; then a politically motivated strike by the self-styled Ulster Workers' Council, involving electricity workers (among others), led to a power crisis and a three-day working week. Output was not seriously affected, however, because the mill was lent two generators, which were installed in a matter of hours. After the crisis had passed, the mill installed its own 390 KVA stand-by generator, with a storage tank sufficient to hold fuel for 14 days running.

Another troublesome event of that year was the detonation of two explosive devices close to the mill's gates. The first of these took place at 10 p.m. on 12 February when a bomb-laden car was driven on to the forecourt of the Crown Buildings, about 100 yards from the mill gate. The explosion lifted all the roofs of the Mountjoy Terrace houses and the mill offices and took the glass out of the windows. First-aid repair was swift and much of it was completed by the following morning, final repairs being completed by mid-summer.

The second incident was far more serious. On the morning of 25 June a loaded car was driven into the car park at the rear of Crown Buildings and parked among other vehicles. A warning was given at 9.30 a.m. and the surrounding buildings were evacuated before the device went off. The explosion set fire to the managing director's hen house containing 5,000 pullets almost at the point of lay. The birds panicked and ran into a mass at the far end of the house, where some 2,000 of them were suffocated. The remainder escaped into the surrounding mill buildings while the fire was being put out.

Damage to the mill was substantial. The office block again suffered damage to roofs and windows, and throughout the mill windows were sucked out by the blast. Corrugated asbestos cladding used to cover voids, whether as roofing or for vertical walls, was destroyed. This left the finished product store, fully stocked at the time, wide open to the weather. Fortunately, plant in the mill was virtually unharmed and was in full production $1^1/2$ hours after the explosion. The damage in this case took longer to repair because of the difficulty experienced in obtaining replacement cladding, but all was put right again by January 1975 at a cost to the national exchequer of £52,000.

Serious as they seemed at the time, in terms of material damage, these events involved no loss of life or injury. They fade into insignificance when compared with the bombing that later took place in Omagh's Market Street on 15 August 1998, resulting in the worst single atrocity and loss of life in the history of the province's troubles.

A further tragedy in 1974 occurred when the office manager, Wesley Wylie, was killed while working on his father-in-law's farm, depriving the business of a valuable and respected member of the office staff. Nevertheless, in business terms, the mill made satisfactory progress in 1974. Sales exceeded the target of a 5 per cent increase over the previous year, to a total of 39,822 tons. In terms of cash the turnover escalated to over £3 million, reflecting in part the huge increase in the average cost of raw materials to an all-time high of £65.35 per ton. Everything rose in proportion, including accounts outstanding, which at 31 July stood at over £0.5 million – an alarming figure at first sight but which in fact represented less than two months' gross takings. Walford Green commented: 'This was an interesting finding, as it went to show that during the whole of the last 25 years sundry debtors had remained remarkably constant in terms of weeks of milling output for which credit was allowed – or taken – the fluctuation was always between eight and six weeks of the current tonnage produced from time to time.'

In 1975, income from sales rose by over a quarter of a million pounds, reflecting a further rise in output of 2,570 tons in the year. At an average cost of £64.14 per ton, feed ingredients showed an increase of only 26p per ton over the previous year's average. However, inflation brought other rises, in both production costs and other overhead expenses. As a result, although the year's operations were far from unprofitable, there was some drop in profit.

In the same year – the 125th since the mill's foundation – a development was put in hand to increase bulk sales, whereby polyethylene containers were acquired, each with a capacity of one ton or a little more, for the use of customers who wished to purchase in quantities of that order. Filled at the mill, they were to be delivered to the farm by a special truck fitted with the appropriate lifting gear and returned to the mill for refilling as required. For this service the customer was asked to bear a small surcharge per ton delivered to cover the cost to the mill of financing the equipment, which nevertheless showed a saving when compared with delivery of the same quantity in bags.

The year ended with the government imposing further controls on prices and wages as part of its anti-inflation policy. Nevertheless, income from sales exceeded £3.25 million, giving a trading profit of £206,104 and a net profit per ton of £4.92. During the five years from 1971 to 1975 output had gone from 31,500 to 42,626 tons.

Unfortunately, the end of 1975 was marred by yet another attack. At 9.30 on the evening of 5 November a bomb exploded in a car left standing at the traffic lights at the junction of Drumragh Avenue with Mountjoy Road. Extensive damage was caused to the County Hall but that building absorbed the brunt of the blast, although the mill again lost its windows and corrugated sheeting.

In 1975 the mill celebrated the 125th anniversary of its foundation, leading to the publication of Walford Green's *From Country Mill to County Millers*, which has been drawn upon extensively in this chapter. To this work of record, Walford Green added a summary that can usefully be quoted here:

> In 25 years [1950–1975] we have come a long way. I hesitate to measure our progress in terms of pounds and pence. In our year which ended on 31 July 1950 our income from sales was £198,378 and we made a trading profit out of it of £4,361. In our last year the corresponding figures were: sales £3,269,423; trading profit £216,104. The figures are impressive by any standard, but they do exaggerate the growth as the pound in 1950 was a very affluent creature compared with its lean and hungry descendant in 1975.
>
> Perhaps so far as figures go we can accept the rise in output over the period, from 7,000 tons in 1950 to 42,000 tons in 1975 as a more accurate account of the progress ...
>
> However, much as one may wish to avoid indulging in our own self-satisfaction and conceit it would be foolish to consider the progress as anything other than remarkable. The result in terms of mill buildings and plant, in mill management and method, and perhaps even more, in the build-up of our great fund of technical know-how, is something in which we can all take great pride. Nevertheless, we must always remember that had it not been for the steady progression also made by the agricultural community, which we exist to serve, this could not have happened.
>
> Nor must we overlook the fact that we have been fortunate in the support which our bankers have always given us, and in the aid we have received year by year in the form of government grants. These two factors, coupled with the flow of cash generated within the business itself, have enabled us to finance our own development, and the increase in our trade, without ever having been compelled to charge our assets in order to secure the necessary funds.
>
> Above all, we can say that throughout the whole period our executives

have served us well. The managing director and his team have been a lively lot, readily receptive of new ideas and not slow to implement them.

At board level it is nice to recall that during the whole of the time during which I have been a director I do not remember the taking of any decision which, after discussion, was not accepted unanimously, and that I am sure is something which the directors of many concerns like ours might greatly envy.

So too, up in the mill yard, the family spirit so well fostered by my predecessor as chairman still endures. As they were in days gone by, so during the last 25 years our mill workers have been second-to-none for their loyalty. We hope that some of the things we have done made life easier for them than it was in the days of continuous shifting of bags by hand, and often hundredweight bags at that.

Whether that be so or not, the fact remains that our labour relations – and the tact and capability of our managing directors throughout the period have had a great deal to do with this – could hardly have been bettered.

I recall that in the autumn of 1950, almost exactly 25 years ago as I write, I was asked to write an introduction to our centenary volume. In concluding it I wrote: 'Northern Ireland in all its parts is a land of opportunity today. If by our efforts now we can, in dealing with the features of the years gone by, point the way to readers to the opportunities of the years ahead, we consider that in this our centenary volume we shall have done a work worth while.' Brave words at the time, written more with the agricultural community of our counties in mind than with ourselves, though to us they also seemed to have their application. I remember being taken to task by certain reviewers for over-optimism at a time of high unemployment, though I think no higher than it is today. I hope that having read so far you will perhaps consider that for once the victim was right and the critics were wrong.

It is nice to find that our faith in the future was justified. You may say: very well; 25 years ago you forecast rightly; what now of the future? What indeed!

In 1950 in many ways we faced the unknown, but we had emerged from the dark years of the war. It was also true to say that due to economic developments in the province as a whole, and possibly the generous spending of the United States' forces while they were stationed with us, there was a great deal more money about than there had been during the pre-war years.

Today we still have to emerge from the troubles which have beset us for the last five years. When that emergence will take place and where it will take us when it does, none can tell. Today, too, there is plenty of money about, at least in certain quarters, but it is a peculiarly-depreciating form of money for all that.

There are still dark waters of uncertainty ahead of us, and, one might think, less reason for optimism than there was 25 years ago. Maybe that is so.

All I would say is that optimism is one thing: a sustained confidence in our own abilities to meet each and every challenge as it arises, is another. It is that which arms us when we have to face the difficulties of future years. Difficulties a-plenty have been met and surmounted in the last 25 years, and as each one has been put behind us, we have gained in strength and stature to meet the next.

Given the will; given the executive man power, and given at least an even distribution of the cards between the players, one can at least say that at the end of the next 25 years our family business could still be leading as constructive, and as profitable an existence as it is today.

So may it be.

And so it has been, as the remainder of this book clearly demonstrates.

The accounts for the year ended July 1976 showed a small decrease on the profit earned when compared with the previous year, although both tonnage and sales were up. However, this drop should be seen in context: 1975 showed the highest profit in the mill's existence. The fall in 1976 was due in part to a subvention payment made by the parent company to Scotts Farms, which had the effect of reducing its overall loss from £28,000 in 1974/5 to £4,000 in the year under review. However, perhaps inflation had a more potent effect in reducing profits. Rising costs of every description were offset to only a small degree by increases in selling prices, which failed to rise far and fast enough to keep place with inflation. Consequently, the margin of profit per tonne sold dropped from 5.6 per cent to 4.1 per cent, notwithstanding a rise of 12.4 per cent in the total tonnage sold.

Part of this increase in tonnage was secured by the development of a new line of broiler food, which found favour with major customers; the remainder was due to the Scott service. Fred Charters, who at that time was sales director, is proud that customer service has always been the factor that kept Scotts ahead of the rest of the field:

The 'dulcet voices' of the mill despatch office *c.* 1990. From left: Sandra McFarland, Helen Lowry and Una McAnenly

We always used the slogan, 'Twenty-four hours bulk delivery service.' That did not mean that we were delivering 24 hours a day but it did mean that if we had an order by 12 midday it would be delivered by 12 midday the following day. At that time the delivery service by the Belfast mills was three to four days. In the early 1970s we had a hey-day when cages were introduced for poultry. The farmer fed his hens and then suddenly discovered he had no meal. If he phoned Belfast for supplies, he would have to wait three or four days. By then his hens would have stopped laying and so we picked up a lot of business on the basis that we could deliver quickly.

Being seen to give good service is almost as important as the act of doing so, and Scotts made a successful innovation, some years back, when it put female voices on the end of the telephone lines to take orders. Instead of a gruff, male voice, well-trained and sweet-talking girls added charm to service and a high degree of organisation, to the delight of their customers. To this day Scotts are one of the few mills in Ireland that employ female staff in the transport department, and have never regretted the change.

Nevertheless, it was only wise and careful buying that saw the mill through the rigours of 1975. In 1975 the average cost of grain and other materials rose from £64.14 to £70.35 per tonne. In the first six months of 1976 the rise was even faster, and Walford Green predicted that by the year end they would be paying on average £100 per tonne for ingredients and the farmer would be paying £125 per tonne for his supply of feeds. 'This must be so,' he said, 'if by the 1st of January 1978 we are to achieve price parity with our Common Market partners as we are bound to do by the terms of our accession to the Treaty of Rome.' He added, 'Price rises ahead will affect our customers just as much as they will affect us. In some quarters the view is taken that the farmer will be unable and unwilling to meet these prices and unless there is a very significant improvement in the prices paid to him for his products we are about to enter upon a period of livestock de-stocking in Northern Ireland.'

In his chairman's statement for the year ending 31 July 1976, the summary was in typical Walford Green style:

> If this is so there is bound to be a consequential fall in the demand for the miller's production. There are Jeremiahs a-plenty who tell us this. For our part while I concede that it is a time for slowing down expansion, for rigorous control – where control can be exercised – over outgoings of every kind, and possibly for exploration of new methods of financing customer credit and capital expenditure, I do not consider that it is a moment for despair or despondency.
>
> It is reasonable, and I am sure it is right, to expect that our steady progression in recent years will now stand us in good stead and that if cold winds are going to blow we will be able to weather them as well as most.
>
> The voices of those in authority are continually heard, reiterating the cry

for industry to achieve more and better production by investigating new and more efficient plant, and that this ought to have been done long ago, so as to be abreast of the times today. I do not accept that it is a criticism which can be made of W & C Scott Limited. With us, re-equipment has proceeded at a steadily increasing rate for the last 25 years and has reached a point at which, if at a time of stringency and uncertainty we have to slow down for a while, it will not harm us to do so.

Cash flow inevitably suffered as a result of the steady rise in output tonnage and the consequent increase in debtors, but at least Scotts could count on reasonable support from its bankers, which was not the case with all concerns at that time. It was also aided by the stock relief provisions of the Finance Act 1974 which absolved it from corporation tax on profits for the years 1977 and 1978, providing its stocks were maintained in value at the level at which they stood at the end of 1976.

Despite the problems, there was still capital investment in 1975/76 – for a new automatic weighing and blending system, a new X26 Christy & Norris hammer mill, a further supply of 25 mini-bins and the purchase of a lorry-mounted hydraulic loader for loading these bins at the mill and unloading them at the farm. The mini-bin system of feed storage had been introduced the previous year to provide assistance to the farmer using perhaps half to one tonne of a particular product per week.

In these circumstances it was not possible for the customer to justify the purchase of 5- or 10-tonne fixed bins, and yet the cost of filling and transporting sacks was increasingly uneconomic. For Scotts this was a case of educating the farmer slowly, but by 1976 it had a total of 50 small bins in use and by 1977 planned to have 100. Apart from handling, the advantages to the farmer were seen as freedom from vermin contamination of feed; elimination of wastage in storage; increased storage capacity at no cost; no capital outlay on bins (which were rented); and a cost saving of £2.20 per tonne over the cost of feed in sacks.

In 1976, 82 per cent of Scotts' output went out in bulk and the remaining 18 per cent in multi-wall paper sacks, the latter absorbing far more than their fair share of production costs and overheads. Over the years these figures improved to 93 per cent bulk and 7 per cent sacks – probably an irreducible minimum. At the press conference to introduce these bins, Fred Charters commented:

> With our mini-bulk system we are using modern industrial bulk-handling methods to bring cost savings to the smaller feed user. Savings of around £150 a year will be made by a farmer using one tonne per week, without his being involved in any capital outlay.
>
> Scotts were a pioneer of bulk feed in the late 1950s. As we are the first in Northern Ireland – perhaps even in the British Isles – in this new field

of mini-bulk, we look forward to the day when the economic benefits of this new venture also gain general acceptance.

The original bins failed but the concept remains, in the form of bulk bags, which are loaded and off-loaded by a fork-lift or tractor. The reason for the failure of the original bins was that the slide at the bottom was not easily opened and closed. As a result the farmer had to take a hammer to it and often missed the opening and hit the side of the polyethylene bin. This caused it to splinter because it had become very brittle in cold weather. In retrospect it is difficult to understand why the design fault could not have been rectified, or another type of bin substituted, but it wasn't.

A local paper, the *Ulster Herald*, gave a succinct account of the mill as it was at that time which is interesting for the record:

> The major proportion of raw materials is brought to the mill in bulk lorry containers. After weighing, each bulk material is directed to a separate silo bin, or, in the case of home-grown barley to the 1,000 tonne Butler bin. (Plans are in hand to increase the grain storage by 2 X 100 tonne bins and to speed up the intake to a rate of 100 tons per hour. Thus a 30 tonne grain lorry will be 'turned round' in under 20 minutes.)
>
> Mixing is carried out by a $2^{1}/_{2}$ tonne batch horizontal mixer, on a three-

Lorry mounted hydraulic loader for mini-bulk bins for the farmer 1975–6

tier system. Mixing requirements are set on the control panel by the mixer foreman, and weighments from the silo of raw materials are blended, ground and pneumatically conveyed to the mixing system. Addition of certain bagged raw materials, including vitamins and trace materials, are performed by hand. The mixing cycle time of four minutes closely matches both the time taken to grind a batch of material for the holding hopper and the time taken to empty the receiving hopper of a batch of mixed material. Thus the only delay between batches is 'clean-down time' and the rated output of the mixer is about 20 tonnes per hour.

Liquids such as molasses and fats are added to the meal after mixing, when it is passed through the Schugi mixer. After this point, the meal can be transferred to a packing-off point or to a holding hopper to await delivery to a farm by bulk lorry. Alternatively, it can be made into cubes, pellets or crumbs by steam treatment and extrusion through a die, again for delivery in sacks or by bulk delivery lorry.

Feed in sacks is stored on wooden pallets holding one tonne each, and these are stacked five-high by means of forklift trucks. The pallets are also of suitable width for loading side by side onto delivery lorries, thus saving further handling costs in the store. A maximum of 300 tonnes is stored in sacks in the 6,000 sq ft warehouse, and stocks are on average held for little over a week, thus ensuring freshness of food to the livestock.

The aim is to provide a delivery to farm within 24 hours of order ... deliveries can also be programmed in certain cases, e.g. to intensive poultry units ...

Aerial view of Omagh mill *c.* 1975

In 1976, work began on a much-needed second access-road to the mill from the Mountjoy Road, thus making possible a one-way traffic system in the mill yard, and before the end of the year the re-roofing of the Butler bin had been completed. A new venture was the laboratory, under Dr Peter Cazalet, which came fully 'on-stream' in 1976 and enabled a continuous analysis of deliveries both into and out of the mill, thus ensuring absolute confidence in the accuracy of formulations. The work of the mill commanded first priority but did not exhaust the full capacity of the laboratory, which, for modest fees, carried out soil and mineral sample tests for the majority of mineral exploration companies operating in Ulster and the Republic.

Plans were also laid for a substantial investment, to be spread over 1977/8, for another set of eight 20-tonne bins for finished products, and to double the cubing capacity so as to be sure of a continuing supply if either of the machines were to break down – a vital consideration in view of the mill's plans to obtain a worthwhile increase in its trade in pelleted dairy feed.

With inflation still a potent force, profits decreased again in 1977 and continued to do so in 1978, matched by a steady increase in overheads. In 1977 tonnage fell minimally but inflation helped to raise sales from just over £4 million to £5.3 million, despite the small decrease in sales tonnage. The farms were reported as having yielded a 'small profit'; Ross Poultry was 'taking an interest in the hens at Inisclan'; and Scotts entered into a partnership agreement, to be known as Erne Eggs, in respect of the marketing of a large proportion of the egg output from Aughentaine. From the start Erne Eggs was a 50/50 partnership with Charles Crawford of Lisnaskea, described to the mill shareholders by Walford Green as 'an egg-packer of good repute'; it was later incorporated as Erne Eggs Ltd.

In 1977 John Walton, a non-executive director for many years, resigned under civil service rules following his appointment as chief statistician to the Inland Revenue. Another notable retirement was that of Patrick (Paddy) McGale, after 40 years with the company. Much of the company's success in the early post-war years had been due to the trust that Paddy had earned in his dealings with customers, as the company's senior sales representative.

Despite disappointing results, the work planned the year before went ahead, or was completed. In addition, a new automatic conveyor system for taking limestone flour and poultry offal meal to the blending bins was installed and eight finished product bins were completed. A new 1,600-tonne capacity bulk ingredient store on the north side of the yard was under construction for completion the following year. Then in June 1977 a substantial drop in protein prices came about; this meant that a substantial provision had to be made from the year's profit to cover this fall in value. As some counterbalance, it was a good year for home-grown wheat and barley. The wet weather made heavy yields of a quality unsuitable for flour milling, but excellent for animal feeds, and Scotts – being in a position to finance substantial quantities of grain when offered at harvest time – profited from the lower prices that were asked for Irish wheat as compared with imported grain of similar feed quality.

Over six years from 1972 to 1977 the figures clearly show the ravages of inflation. In 1972 tonnage produced was 34,300; by 1977 it had risen to 48,021 but turnover had leapt from £1,341,000 to £5,307,888 and the average cost of raw material per tonne from £31.77 to £96.35. Production charges and overheads had also increased by a factor of three.

While Department of Commerce grants were still available at 30 per cent on capital expenditure, Scotts was more than pleased by the announcement of a new source of grant-aid at 25 per cent of expenditure from the European Agricultural Guidance and Guarantee Fund (FEOGA), provided that benefits to agriculture could be demonstrated. Scotts was able to take advantage of these grants when in 1978/9 it planned and began the implementation of a major new £500,000 development, which came to fruition in 1980. Both planning and fulfilment were greatly to the credit of Roy Howard, who was then production director.

In May 1979 William McAusland, son of John McAusland, joined Scotts; he has since proved to be a most valuable member of the management team. Following a course of study at Essex University in electronic engineering, William had a variety of jobs including repairing vacuum cleaners, gutting fish in Iceland and driving lorries from Germany to the UK, importing kitchen furniture.

Rightly or wrongly, Walford Green formed the view that while William McAusland would undoubtedly have a useful contribution to make to the skills-mix in Omagh, and was interested in returning, something was holding him back. Was it merely the joys of an informal, rural Essex lifestyle among his post-graduate contemporaries, or was there more to it?

Likewise, John McAusland wished for his son's return but both he and his wife Patricia worried about the differences of approach to life and work that characterise many father-and-son relationships. John and William greatly enjoyed yacht-racing in each other's company but could they work without friction in the same business, let alone live under the same roof?

William McAusland

After some years of no resolution to these largely unstated dilemmas, Walford Green with John McAusland's concurrence made an employment offer to William McAusland, based on two strict criteria. The first was that the mill would supply him with independent accommodation, on moderate rental terms; the second was that he would report to Roy Howard, rather than to his father. The offer was accepted with little delay, and William never looked back.

He came to Scotts as a technical assistant to Roy Howard, initially involved in the commissioning of the new computerised Chronos-Richardson blending system, completing the installation with a micro-processor-controlled intake system, designed in Lisburn. Since then his primary responsibility has been for the specifying, installation and maintenance of successive electric- and computer-controlled installations. He says, 'As our computer system suppliers progressively went bust, we took on more and more of the support of these systems ourselves.' Appointed to the board in 1988, William McAusland is now production director, having followed in Roy Howard's shoes after the latter's retirement in 1997.

Trading in 1978 was unusually difficult, bedevilled by fuel shortages and power cuts in the winter months. But Scotts had adequate fuel stocks and, with the help of newly agreed productivity incentive schemes, good labour relations and a new capacity, was able to return good profits. The new capacity enabled an increase in the production and sale of cubes and pellets, coupled with a welcome increase in bulk bin sales and a reduction in the sale of bagged products. Another factor was that the new storage capacity made it possible to cut out nearly all payments for rents charged for the retention of imported ration ingredients in the port silos.

Inflation was still raging in 1979 and had an impact on rising trade. Without that factor, Scotts and thousands of other concerns in the UK might have done better. For example, in seven years the average cost of raw materials had risen from £31.77 per ton to £108.10 per tonne (1 ton = 1.016 tonnes); production and packing charges had increased by a factor of four and overheads by a factor of almost five.

Although 1979 was a good year for Scotts despite all the negative factors, customers in the pig and poultry trade found it less so and this affected Scotts' own subsidiary enterprises at Inisclan and Aughentaine. Egg prices remained so low that sales were at a loss throughout the year. Again, Walford Green summed up the year 1978/9 to shareholders in characteristic style:

> At a time when one hears of nothing but woe, woe, woe, so low is the output per man in British industry that ruin stares us in the face, I would like to assure you that, whether that be true or not generally, it is not true at Excelsior Mills. The level of activity which I observe, when I make my visits, is high. In 1950, some of you may remember it took a work force of 53 to produce and sell 7,000 tons. This year with the aid of modern plant and improved technology acquired and applied over the years a work force of 51 have been able to turn out and sell 65,002 tonnes (and the difference between a ton and a tonne is very small). Incentive schemes have worked well and labour relations are good. These things could only be so with efficient management and sales organisations to back up the production team.

In September 1980 Giles Shaw, minister in charge of the Department of Agriculture for Northern Ireland (DANI), officially opened the new plant

extension and was afterwards entertained to lunch at the Royal Arms Hotel, Omagh. The company issued a long and detailed statement which was widely published by the Ulster farming and local press and which said in part:

> The entry of both the UK and Eire into the EEC, with consequent improvement in the prospects for cereal growing in Ireland, has reduced Scotts' dependence on imported grain. Both wheat and barley are purchased for delivery throughout the year from the grain-growing areas of Ireland, north and south. Supplies of maize and soya bean meal and grain from European sources are imported as required, mainly through the port of Londonderry.
>
> The Common Agricultural Policy has also permitted expansion of the firm's economic trading area into the neighbouring Eire counties of Monaghan and Cavan, where there is a concentration of broiler, duck and turkey producers. To meet this new opportunity, and also increased local demand for cattle feed, in 1977 Scotts installed increased extrusion (pelleting) capacity. During the winter of 1978/9, sixteen 30-tonne bulk finished product outloading bins and 1,600 tonnes of bulk raw material storage were completed. In 1979/80, to complete the expansion programme, a major increase of mixing capacity has been added, providing a second mixing system and computer control of both mixing lines.
>
> This year, microprocessor control of the bulk raw material intake and routing system has been installed.

These new developments were supported by the bank, by grants, and by

Giles Shaw MP at an event celebrating completion of mill improvements, September 1980.
From left Richard Scott, Bob McCammond, Alec Ballentine, John McAusland, Eric Reid, Giles Shaw, Hugh Kirkpatrick, George Wright and Vincent Courtney.

profits earned on a steady increase in the tonnages milled: in 1977 48,000; 1978, 54,300; 1979, 58,000; and in 1980, 63,100.

This production was taken up promptly; for example, in March 1979 John McAusland reported to the board that in the previous quarter demand was so buoyant that the mill had been operating at a weekly average of over 80 hours. However, in the final quarter there was some anxiety as sales fell away, the prosperity of their farmer customers suffering from increasing problems as the returns from laying hens, from pig production for bacon and from beef cattle became minimal and their profit margins evanescent. High interest charges and rising overheads due to inflation were at the root of the woes of both Scotts and the farmer-customers.

In 1980 Scotts' profits were notably reduced, although this was, of course, largely due to the costs associated with the new plant. Another cost was substantial redundancy payments that had resulted from automation largely replacing unskilled labouring jobs.

During the year it was decided to cease operations at Inisclan, and in May 1980 the farm was placed in an agent's hands for sale. At the egg production unit at Aughentaine there was better news: although the price of eggs was deemed to be below the safety level, a loss in the previous year was reduced to a break-even position. The Scott–Smyth pig farm joint enterprise did not do so well. The prices for pigs sold at bacon weight when related to the cost of production were described by Walford Green as 'disastrous', and the unit ran at a heavy loss for the first time in its history. Against this, the joint venture in Erne Eggs still managed to show a fair return, despite, or perhaps because of, cuts in egg production.

Walford Green ended his chairman's statement for the year 1979/80 by saying:

> I have never seen the mill in better fettle. During the last 12 months a great deal of hard work, and sometimes frustrating work, has been put in by everyone to make it so. A transitional year is never an easy one through which to live and work. Though the results in terms of profit may be down, having regard to the many adverse factors with which they have had to contend I am thankful to see the profit as it is and to find it there at all. It is greatly to the credit of all concerned that we have come through a difficult year as well as we have and our grateful thanks are due to all, in the office both upstairs and down, up the yard, within the mill itself and to our salesmen and drivers on the road.

On 1 August 1980, in anticipation of John McAusland's approaching retirement as managing director, Richard Scott became joint managing director, sharing this office with John McAusland.

John McAusland retired in July 1981, when Richard Scott became managing director. In his retirement speech at the dinner and presentation held at the Royal Arms Hotel in Omagh, John McAusland said:

> I appreciate the honour and the compliment you have paid to me tonight and no words of mine can express what I really feel. I cannot say that I am glad or sad to have reached this situation in my life, but certainly I have a lump in my throat.
>
> I came here some 33 years ago on a so-called four-year contract to help the post-war reconstruction. I knew a little about general business affairs but nothing about milling. But I have since learned a lot and I am still learning, as I know I can never know it all and neither can you!
>
> Our present chairman, Walford Green, whom I am so pleased to see here with us tonight, first advised me before I came over here ... His advice has always been soundly based and still is. He is a wonderful chap, really, not only in financial matters but in practical things as well. We would discuss some mill plant and its installation and he always puts his finger on the weak spot or even suggests sensible improvements ...
>
> The late Captain Scott showed me a fine example of how things should be done and I have tried to keep to this since he died in 1962. It is hard to believe that was 20 years ago ...
>
> I am convinced that over the past eight years the teamwork, both in the boardroom and the mill, has been a tremendous backing to me and has been successful. It is interesting to note that when I started here the target for feed sales was 200 tons per week. In 1952 we did 152 tons per week; in 1980 we did 1,200 tonnes per week ...
>
> The title of Walford Green's book *From Country Mill to County Millers* is coming true. A very sad development has taken place recently in that one of the oldest mills in Co. Tyrone, Robert Smyth & Sons are closing their Strabane mill at the end of this month, so that the words 'county millers' may now be even more relevant ...
>
> I do not want to forget that all I have been able to do could not have been done without your help and, even more important, without the help, co-operation and understanding of my wife, Patricia. She has had a lot to put up with, including the mill dust, but has always been behind me in everything I tried to do.
>
> It is encouraging to see a few of the older OAPs here tonight. I looked at the photograph of the mill staff taken in 1950 and I think that, of those in the picture, I am the only one still working in the mill today – but not tomorrow! But actually there are two, who were not available for that photograph of 30 years ago, who are still working here: young Jackie McCausland, driver [who joined the mill in 1941] and apprentice Andy Monteith ...

Among the many presentations received by John McAusland on this occasion was a fine painting of square-rigged Thames sailing barges. In his chairman's remarks for the year ended 31 July 1981, Walford Green said:

John came to the mill and Millbank in 1949, charged with the responsibility for carrying into effect the first of our post-war reconstruction plans. He quickly made his mark, stepping smoothly into the Omagh scene, and showing in the mill itself those qualities of leadership and drive, which – together with his sound commonsense and companionability – enabled him very soon after his arrival to shoulder in his appointed sphere the task which his father-in-law, then chairman and managing director, would have found it most difficult to carry on his shoulders, broad as they were, unaided.

His capacity for accepting responsibility justified an increase in his load of work, and in 1953 he was appointed a director of Scotts Mills Ltd, with supervisory duties over our mill at Newtownstewart. In 1955 he joined the main board. There followed a period where, to all intents and purposes, he understudied the managing director, particularly acquiring from him the skill in the appreciation of market conditions, and in the purchasing of raw

materials, which he exercised so much to our advantage over recent years.

When Maddin Scott retired in 1960, John McAusland took over from him and ever since has kept a taut hand on every aspect of affairs.

Nothing that I can say can adequately express the debt of gratitude that we all owe to him. We can be thankful that, when not sailing the high seas, he will still be at Millbank, from where in a non-executive capacity his knowledge and experience will be available to those in the mill office who may come to him from guidance from time to time. And I hope they will!

In the *Tyrone Constitution* of 18 September 1981, announcing John McAusland's retirement, there was a paragraph about the appointment of Sam Bullock to Scotts' sales staff. He trained with R. Silcock & Sons and then joined Smyths, staying with them until they closed their Strabane mill in July 1981. Specialising in the sale of pig feeds, Sam was at one time secretary of Mountjoy Pig Breeding Co. and of the Northern Ireland Livestock Development Co., and a breeder of Charolais cattle. Though past the firm's normal retiring

Sam Bullock   age, he remained with Scotts in 2000 as it celebrated the 150th anniversary of its foundation.

John McAusland went into retirement as managing director but became deputy chairman, no doubt looking forward to having more time for his great love of sailing. But this was not to be. In January 1982 Walford Green felt compelled to resign his chairmanship on medical advice, and John McAusland was prevailed upon to act as non-executive chairman. It was not expected that this appointment would curtail his leisure activities unduly, but they were brutally ended forever only a few weeks later by his sudden and totally unexpected death on 1 April 1982. Richard Scott thus became both chairman and managing director.

In John McAusland's obituaries his keen interest in sailing was remembered. *The Tyrone Constitution* wrote:

> Outside his business he was a lover of sailing, a recreation which he began 25 years ago, and over that period his interest expanded from a small sailing-dinghy to larger vessels in which he went cruising with his family, mainly off the west coast of Scotland. He was a regular competitor in races. He was one of the earliest members of the Lough Swilly Yacht Club and was a past Commodore.

Like other members of the family, he was closely involved in the life of Omagh. He was a founder member and one time president of Omagh Rotary Club; president of the local branch of the RNLI; a trustee and secretary of the local lawn tennis club; a member of the Royal British Legion; and a trustee of the Tyrone Protestant Orphan Society. He was also a former High Sheriff for Tyrone. He was active in the affairs of the Church of Ireland and had been a churchwarden and vestryman of St Columba's parish church, and in a wider sphere was a member of the diocesan and general synods.

Twenty years on, Richard Scott remembers John McAusland in the following terms:

> John's style of leadership, as Fred Charters, Roy Howard and I remember it, was that of a team leader rather than a 'big boss'. He was good at getting the best out of people, was approachable and cheerful at all times, a good delegator and negotiator, and quite fearless – no matter who he was dealing with on the firm's behalf. He somewhat cultivated the image of a hard man but was in reality most considerate of all employees and colleagues.
>
> He and I 'put up with each other's peculiarities', as he memorably said in his retirement speech and I can remember very few cross words during our 20 years of working together. I well remember the gulf of loneliness that I felt for a year or so after his death, at a time when I had hoped that he and I would perhaps have a similar chairman/managing director relationship to that which Walford Green and John McAusland had enjoyed for so many years.

Trading profit in 1980 lifted sharply from 1979, as did selling prices, overheads, and ingredient costs, still affected by inflation. Nevertheless, profit per tonne, aided by increased output, was the best for some years. This year Roy Howard and his production team faced and solved an important problem. Dairy feed customers in particular complained that Scotts' cubes and pellets were too soft, tending to break up in transport and resulting in waste. After extensive experimentation, a harder cube or pellet was found to be achievable only by exertion of increased mechanical pressure in the pellet mill. A Buhler drum fats-coater was also installed, enabling cubes and pellets to be coated with hot fat after production, rather than adding fat to the compound mill before its presentation to the pellet mill.

By early 1981, Scotts was able to produce a cattle cube or a duck pellet of a hardness quality second to none, although the output rate of the pellet mills was reduced. This innovation led to a demand for additional tonnage, which was met by the installation of an additional high-capacity pellet mill. 'Dead on its target date,' said Walford Green, 'an unusual experience for us, and an achievement for which all praise is due to Roy Howard and his assistants.'

During the mill's year to July 1981, there were two setbacks to sales: the Ross Poultry egg marketing organisation at Portadown closed its operations, resulting in a notable loss of tonnage for Scotts. A large broiler-producing concern in the Republic got into difficulties and soon went to the wall. Fortunately, Scotts had sought and obtained a credit guarantee of 90 per cent of the debt from the Export Credit Guarantee Department (ECGD) of the Board of Trade, reserving the other 10 per cent against its profits for this year. However, this – the largest bad debt that Scotts had ever experienced – led to an anomalous situation with Allied Irish Banks, whose advances manager, based in Belfast, somehow overlooked the ECGD guarantee and proposed a reduction in Scotts' overdraft facilities, at a time when they were needed in full. As can be imagined, this brought about a very strong response from Walford Green and his co-directors.

The matter was amicably resolved in October 1980 but, at the bank's insistence, the company went forward to produce a report on its current workings from an outside consultant, John Collinson, a partner in Deloitte, Haskins & Sells. The report provides a very full and detailed picture of the company and its activities as they were in 1980/81. It opens with the situation at 31 July 1980, when the business had a turnover of 63,156 tonnes valued at £8.42 million, of which 43 per cent was in laying poultry feed; 29 per cent broiler and duck; 19 per cent cattle, the balance being divided between pig meals and sundries. As at 1 August 1981, the total number of full-time employees including executive directors was 42.

There is a succinct statement of the purchasing operations of the mill at that time, which are little changed today:

> Buying the main items for the requirements of the mill is a very important part of the operation and factors which influence the buyer are many and varied. He learns mostly from experience and by keeping in constant touch with market values and trends. It is essential that he receives market reports daily and consults other people within the trade regularly. Harvest

conditions and yields not only in Ireland or the UK but world-wide can influence his decisions and he must be fully aware of trends all the time. The Common Agricultural Policy influence of the European Community in recent years has made the job more difficult as the EEC can change things overnight without warning; also international affairs can change the value of goods regardless of supply and demand factors. The grain market is a very speculative one but by using the futures market one can eliminate to a large extent gains or losses and the financial risks.

The buyer is provided with weekly stock details and the average quantity of each commodity used over the previous month. He can then estimate the requirements and ensure that adequate supplies of raw materials are arriving at the port or in the mill to ensure a steady flow so that production can be maintained. Normally contracts are made for monthly requirements but are bought for delivery up to three months ahead. Stock is kept down to 5–6 weeks in order to keep bank borrowing to a minimum, but the buyer may from time to time see an opportunity to buy ahead, or refrain from buying, in order to take advantage of what is, in his opinion, a rising or falling market. Scotts' policy has always been to avoid exposure through speculation.

Supplies of raw materials are purchased mainly through brokers or importers who are acting as agents for shippers and as there is competition for our business from four or five main suppliers there is no question of the business being dependent on any one supplier. The main silos in Belfast and Derry are used not only by the owners, Halls and Barnetts, but by most importers. Of recent years smaller ports such as Warrenpoint and Carrickfergus have been very competitive, also Dundalk in the South. In recent years barley and wheat delivered direct from the Republic of Ireland's grain growing areas has been extremely competitively-priced, particularly at harvest time; it is to take advantage of the availability of this grain, when offered, that we have invested heavily in raw material storage facilities during the past five years.

Certain substitute materials, mainly by-products of human food manufacture, are available to partially replace cereals. In a number of European countries, particularly the Netherlands, this process of substitution has been carried to a much greater extent owing to the greater availability of cereal substitutes at attractive prices, but the cost of transport to Ireland has limited the extent of raw material substitution here, and our distance from the ports limits our use of them yet further.

After describing the all-important liaison between sales and production and stock control, the report has this to say about the mill's customers:

Traditionally, the company used to trade mainly through local merchants but over the past 15 years there has been a gradual tendency for our salesmen to call upon the ultimate customer, namely the farmer, and sell to him, thereby cutting out the merchants.

The past 10 years has seen the emergence of contract farming, whereby individual farmers' production and marketing is organised into large buying groups, e.g. Moy Park in respect of broiler chickens, and Associated Egg Packers, who deal with egg producers. This contract farming, while guaranteeing volume business (and we have all three as customers) puts a lot of pressure on margins. (One of the groups recently stated that we are allowed to have only a contribution to our overheads, not a profit!) However, there is a low sales cost and we have done a lot of business with the groups over the past 15 years, while aiming at not being too heavily dependent on any individual account.

We have a total number of 325 active sales ledger accounts during the summer months, rising to about 425 during the winter months. Our largest customer represents not more than 16 per cent of our turnover. Our proportion of laying poultry tonnage has fallen from 58 per cent to 43 per cent within the last five years, partly due to a reduction of the Northern Ireland laying flock but also because of a conscious effort on our part to develop other types of business.

On pricing and marketing:

At the present time we are in a declining market. The number of cattle, pigs and poultry are all decreasing. The Department of Agriculture 1979–80 statistics show the decline in the numbers of animals. Further study of the figures shows that the western part of the Province is declining faster than the east.

However, while this has been happening over the past four years our sales pattern has been contrary to the market trends. This is basically due to the fact that we have sought to find new markets, e.g. in Co. Monaghan, and also to expand our area a little in Northern Ireland while still trying to preserve our 24-hour delivery service. When expanding our business we have had to be careful to maintain our load size, as this factor becomes increasingly important the further we deliver from the mill.

The proportion of our sales in bulk has risen to between 85 and 90 per cent of our business (according to season), thereby enabling us to save labour and cut costs. The fact that we continue to do a large proportion of our business in bulk shows that we are dealing with a progressive type of farmer and those who are likely to stay in business. Feed supplied in sacks is costing £11.50 extra delivered to the farm, per tonne. This directly affects the customer's gross profit margin, e.g. by £14.50 per cow/year; £4 per pig produced; 60p per hen per laying cycle. These figures are warning signals for the small farmer who buys his feed in sacks.

The report had this to say regarding the farms:

Since the late 1960s, in order to achieve additional tonnage in the mill without corresponding sales overhead expenses, we have carried out farming activities both on our own account and in partnership with third parties. While these activities have succeeded in their primary aim of providing additional profit for our milling enterprise, when considered on their own their fortunes have reflected the difficult times experienced during the past decade in intensive livestock production. However, we have not hesitated to make changes when necessary and at the time of writing our overall farming operations are profitable.

In 1977 we went into partnership with Charles Crawford of Manorwater Farm, Lisnaskea, in his egg packing and marketing enterprise. Our primary aim was to improve the return to our laying unit at Aughentaine by selling the eggs to the partnership, in which we had an equal share of profit on the packing and marketing of eggs, rather than to an outside party ... In 1980 we decided to invest further in the partnership, so gaining a half-share in five acres of land and a 50,000 hen production unit at Lisnaskea, as well as in the fully-modernised egg packing unit. Profit before tax of the partnership in 1980/1 is likely to be in the region of £45,000, representing a return of 25 per cent on capital invested...

The production situation was dealt with in a similarly comprehensive manner:

Because of the decline in the production of eggs in our trading area and our pursuit of broiler and duck feed tonnage in Co. Monaghan, emphasis has changed from production of meals (whether coarsely or finely ground) to the production of pelleted feed. The economic justification for pelleted feed, in broad terms, is that while pelleting adds about $2^1/2$ per cent to the cost of feed it improves the feed efficiency by around $7^1/2$ per cent, mainly by reduction in wastage. It also increases the animal's ability to consume feed rapidly, an essential, for example, in the case of broiler chickens and ducks, where the animals are required to reach slaughter weight in 6–8 weeks from hatching, or of dairy cows where the animal's daily concentrate ration must be consumed in the time taken to milk her ...

After dealing with the demand for cubes of a higher standard of hardness, mentioned earlier in this chapter, the report continues:

Other changes in the past five years have included the increasing use of dietary fat (whether rendered animal fat, or more recently, a blend of animal and vegetable fats) in our compounds. Added fat is now a vital part of most compound feed and there is a necessity for accuracy in its addition and mixing throughout the compound, involving a degree of sophistication in measuring ...

Since the UK and Ireland joined the EEC we have seen a great increase in the cost of cereals. Ireland, despite the encouragement to growers that higher cereal prices has given, is still deficient in cereals and seems likely to remain so. Consequently, compounders have adapted to the use of cereal substitutes, particularly in cattle diets, which now contain hardly any traditional cereal content. Manioc (a starchy root crop, emanating from Thailand, also known as tapioca) has become a familiar ingredient, for example, also corn gluten feed (a by-product of starch manufacture) and rice bran (the shell of the grain, produced when rice is milled and polished for human consumption). None of these were known of, much less in use, 10 years ago and we must assume that their use will continue unless a much greater area of cereals is planted in Ireland in future years. So far as a substitute for our own products is concerned, there is no sign of such development anywhere in the world, even in the most advanced research institutions.

While control of quality has always been an important aspect of compound feed production, our recent development in broiler and duck business has intensified the need for strict quality control procedures. We are fortunate in being able to purchase a full range of equipment for a laboratory from a Belfast compounder who ceased production in 1975, and in securing the services of a PhD, Peter Cazalet, to institute our quality control methods.

Our approach is to treat all incoming feed ingredients with the utmost suspicion and to concentrate the greater part of our effort on monitoring their quality; mill production is closely controlled and our 'critical' finished products are subjected to regular spot checks on a continuing basis. Quality control is treated as 'everybody's business', from the buyer and formulator to the silo operator as he receives raw materials in the mill, through to the driver delivering the finished product to the farm; the quality controller co-ordinates this effort and reports directly to the production director.

Future plans drew this comment:

Within the industry, computers and micro-processors are being used to a greater extent in providing both plant control and management information, computers being the main area in which development is taking place. With regard to development of machines and of new processes, one would say that very little change is taking place relative to traditional products. There are a number of processes allied to the animal feed industry producing such things as extruded whole soya beans, flaked maize, field beans, barley etc., using machines such as the micronizer, Jet-Sploder and extruders, which are relatively new processes. We have investigated the possibilities of entering into these fields from time to time but have not found them to be attractive enough in terms of potential sales to merit the necessary investment.

We are computerised in the following areas: production; stock control; feed formulation; and accounts.

While the penultimate paragraph by implication does less than credit to the continuing expansion, development and investment that was to take place in future years, the report, even in the truncated form in which it appears here, provides a clear picture of Scotts' position and outlook 20 years ago.

13

External Influences
1975–2000
A Changing Trade

RICHARD SCOTT

FOLLOWING THE DISCUSSION in the previous chapter of Scotts' internal review of its business in 1980/81, it is perhaps appropriate to pause and consider events and developments that took place far from Omagh. These had a profound influence on the progress of the business during its sixth quarter-century. They may be conveniently divided into three categories: changes in competing suppliers, both nationally and locally; the effects of European Economic Community (EEC, later to be the EC and currently the European Union, or EU) policies for agriculture; and health concerns and scares.

Dealing with the first of these, it is often said in farming circles that a sheep's worst enemy is another sheep, and the general principle must also apply that a miller's worst enemy is another miller. It is instructive therefore to consider how competing companies – be they national or local – have changed and developed over the years in question. In order to do this effectively it is necessary to step back in commercial history, so as to explain the origins and structure of the UK trade as it stood in 1975.

This was dominated by those companies collectively known as the national compounders, many of which were household names, such as BOCM, Ranks, Silcocks, Spillers, Bibbys, Crosfield and Calthrop. In most cases, they had ventured into feed compounding in order to add value to a by-product of their principal business. For instance, BOCM, short for British Oil and Cake Mills, was a subsidiary of Unilever and its original business was crushing oil seeds for the manufacture of soap and margarine. From the 1920s onwards research work had been carried out in the agricultural institutes to evaluate the benefits of feeding mixtures containing the 'cake', or residue of the oilseed, after the oil had been either expelled by mechanical crushing or extracted by use of a solvent. These cakes were rich in protein and also carried a left-over quantity of high-energy oil. In the case of Ranks and Spillers, the by-product was wheat offals, the residue after rollermills had cracked the grain for flour production. As the nation's two largest flour millers in the first half of the twentieth century, Ranks and Spillers each had a formidable tonnage of wheat offals as a source material for compound animal feeds.

The institutes fed experimental mixtures of cereal, wheat offals and oilseed cakes to different categories of livestock, evaluated the results and the modern compound feed trade was born. It was well established by the outset of the Second World War in 1939, and had its own separate rationing provisions in place within the first 18 months of the war.

The national compounders tended to site their feed mills close to the crushing plants or flour mills, which in turn were sited at the ports of entry for the oilseeds and imported wheat. Oilseeds were grown in such far-off places as the USA (soya beans), West Africa, principally Nigeria (groundnuts and cottonseed), Canada (rapeseed) and China (sunflower seed), which yielded protein cakes known as, respectively, soya bean extractions, groundnut and cottonseed expellers, rapeseed extractions and sunflower extractions. Canada was the principal source of 'hard', or durum, wheat.

The 'nationals' not only had the advantages of having a proportion of their ingredients at first cost, and access to the large-scale finance required to build new feed mills; they were also in a position to exploit commercially the benefits of a scientific approach to animal nutrition and feed compounding. In the immediate post-war years, this was informed by such leading lights as Professor Robert Boutflour, principal of the Royal Agricultural College, Cirencester, who ably demonstrated the productive and economic advantages to farmers of feeding purchased compound rations to their livestock. Since this was a period of agricultural expansion, following the 1947 Agriculture Act, there was a ready response from farmers and this led to the early intensification of British agriculture and a rapid expansion of the tonnage of the national compounders. A price commission report on the animal feed industry, carried out in 1977, showed that there were 235 feed compounders in Great Britain and Northern Ireland but that the seven largest accounted for 60 per cent of the market.

The common agriculture policy (CAP) of the EEC began to exert its influence on British agriculture from 1972, in that its pricing policy greatly encouraged the growing of cereals throughout Great Britain and Ireland. Within five years, this had strengthened the position of those mills that were sited in grain growing areas, and the national compounders were not immune to this trend.

BOCM-Silcock (BOCM-S), which was the result of a 1971 merger between BOCM, Silcocks and Lever Feeds, began to build country mills in the mid-1970s. In 1973, the same company started a 10-year programme of buying up small local compounders, as a move away from selling through independent merchants to direct selling. Of the other nationals, a new force to emerge was Dalgety Agriculture. This unusual company had its roots in New Zealand, as a finance and marketing company serving livestock producers. It entered the UK feed market at a national level for the first time when it won a takeover battle in 1973 for Crosfield and Calthrop against opposition from Bibby, Tiger Oats and National Milling. At the time of the price commission report, Dalgety Crosfields had 4.3 per cent of the GB feed market but this rose rapidly to 13 per cent in 1980, after it took over Spillers in another strongly contested battle, making it the second largest national compounder.

From the mid-1960s, however, nutritional expertise and the scientific approach were no longer the preserve of the nationals. Nutrition service companies such as Colborn and Trouw emerged, to provide technical advice to progressive regional and country compounders on such previously arcane matters as diet specifications and the trace-mineral and vitamin supplementation of feeds. Almost as importantly, these companies provided the smaller compounders for the first time with the confidence that, with their substantially lower overhead costs and closer proximity to their customers, they could compete with the nationals on more than equal terms.

If one had to select a year, in hindsight, in which the band effectively stopped playing for the national compounders and their gradual decline began, it would be the Orwellian year of 1984. This was the year in which the first suspected case of bovine spongiform encephalopathy (BSE) was discovered, a phenomenon that is still casting its malignant shadow over the UK's milk and beef sectors. But of more immediate impact, 1984 was also the year in which milk quotas were introduced, a panicky and ill-thought-out response by the EEC to the consequences of its earlier folly in maintaining artificially high prices for milk. The immediate consequences of milk quotas were little short of catastrophic for the market leaders in dairy feeds, as dairy farmers' early reaction was to reduce milk production drastically by using substantially less compound feed.

As these feeds contributed disproportionately to the nationals' profits, the fall in sales led to 2,000 job losses in compound mills in a single year and a 20 per cent fall in the profits of BOCM-S. Its large mill in Belfast, which had been opened with fanfares of trumpeting in the mid-1950s, was sold to Thompsons in May 1986. This sale was the forerunner of Unilever's somewhat ignominious retreat from feed compounding, which concluded with the sale of BOCM-S to Harrison and Crosfield in 1992. This created BOCM Pauls, which in turn was the subject of a management buyout in 1998.

Dalgety's progress and decline took a different route, both in time and direction. In 1982, the year in which Bibby was taken over by Barlow Rand, Dalgety took over RHM Agriculture, a national with around 8 per cent of the market at the time of the 1977 price commission report, and two substantial regional compounders, Kingsfords of Canterbury and James Wyllie in south-west Scotland. Throughout the 1980s and early 1990s, Dalgety continued to buy up feed and merchanting businesses. But problems in its pet food division and a 25 per cent drop in feed sales at the height of the BSE crisis in 1996/97 led to heavy losses and the resignation of the group chief executive, Richard Clothier. A management team then purchased Dalgety Agriculture from the parent company.

A new entrant, with a distinguished pedigree in flour milling, joined the UK agricultural scene in 1990. This was Associated British Foods (ABF), which bought British Sugar in 1990 and thus became the owner of Trident Feeds. In 1993 it bought Bibby's feed business and in 1998 the nearly-new owners of Dalgety Agriculture departed from the feed marketplace. Dalgety had sold a handful of mills previously, but now sold the remaining feed mills and straight-feed business to ABF, which thus became the equal-largest feed manufacturer with (the new, and reduced) BOCM Pauls, each with a little over 20 per cent share of the market. The remaining 55–60 per cent of the trade, as at the year 2002, is spread among the independent regional and country compounders and the agricultural co-operatives.

The changes in the ownership, fortunes and positions of the national compounders over the past 25 years are mirrored in the reduction in numerical strength of membership of the United Kingdom Agricultural Supply Trade Association (UKASTA). This body was formed in 1977 by the amalgamation of two previous trade associations, which had overlapping memberships. At its inception, UKASTA had about 1,300 member companies. In the year 2002, following the amalgamations and closures of so many businesses – both small and large – UKASTA's membership was around 300, covering approximately 90 per cent of the total turnover of companies supplying British agriculture with feeds, seeds and fertilisers, and marketing their arable crops. Of the 300, fewer than 100 UKASTA companies were now in the business of feed compounding, although they are believed to account for as much as 95 per cent of all UK commercial sales of manufactured feed.

Milk quotas

Milk quotas were introduced under the European Common Agricultural Policy (CAP) on 1 April 1984, as a measure to halt the rising over-production of milk throughout Europe. Milk prices had previously been set, together with tariff duties on imported milk products, at such a level as to encourage farmers in all the EC countries to expand their production without concern for the needs of the marketplace. There was no political will, nor any agreement, among the partners in the EC to deal with the over-production by means of the price mechanism, so it became inevitable that curbs would have to be placed on production by other means.

The politics were grounded in the fact that many EC countries had large numbers of very small dairy farmers, whose businesses and way of life would have been destroyed by severe reductions in the price of milk, which might have taken place by the operation of a free market. It has to be said that Ireland, north and south, seemed to come into this category and thus quotas were broadly accepted – warts and all – as the least bad solution. They ensured at least that milk production would be indefinitely continued at close to its 1983 level, at prices which, at least at the outset, provided a living for smaller producers and a handsome income for specialist dairy farmers with herds of 60 or more cows.

To illustrate why this control by means of quotas had become necessary, it is perhaps sufficient to state that the total expenditure on supporting the CAP dairy regime in 1985 was £4 billion. How did this come about, and how was such an enormous amount of money accounted for? Again, it is necessary to trace the history in order to understand the position in 1984 and the situation that has developed since then.

The EC dairy regime had been introduced in 1964. Its underlying objective was to manage the community market for milk and milk products in such a way that the prices obtained by milk producers met a target, which was set annually by the Council of Ministers. The principal instruments of market management in the dairy sector, apart from the quota system introduced in 1984, were:

- export subsidies
- import tariffs
- intervention buying
- aid for private storage
- subsidies to encourage the disposal of milk and milk products on the Community market.

Each of these mechanisms involved huge sums of money and created distortions that were, at times, almost laughable if they had not been so serious and costly in their effects. To take but one example that affected feed compounders, for many years they were offered the opportunity to buy skim milk-powder, at heavily subsidised prices, for incorporation into compound feeds, including dairy feeds. Meticulous records had to be kept, so as to demonstrate that the milk-powder had been 'correctly' disposed of through incorporation into feed and not sold-on for other purposes. By such Alice-in-Wonderland methods was the fabled milk-powder mountain kept from growing ever larger.

Variable import levies applied until 1995, designed to protect high-priced dairy products within the EC from cheaper imports. The process of dismantling such tariffs meant the variable levies being replaced with fixed but progressively reducing tariffs over the following six years. These provisions, which came about as a result of negotiations under the GATT (General Agreement on Tariffs and Trade), meant that there was a necessity for the EU countries to prepare for something approaching free trade conditions from 2001 onwards. The outcome of CAP reform negotiations in 1999 was that this prospect was further delayed, providing a 'stable outlook' until 2008, subject to review in 2003.

It is arguable that quotas have merely delayed and have not prevented the inevitable concentration of milk production into fewer and larger herds. The statistics bear this out, in that dairy cow numbers in the UK fell from over 3.2 million in 1984 to around 2.5 million in 1999, the average milk yield per cow rising in the same period by over 22 per cent. Dairy production has gradually shifted to those areas, such as the western counties and Northern Ireland, best suited to grass growth.

The Irish agriculture and food development authority (Teagasc) has responded positively to the prospect of the ending of milk quotas, leading to the prospect of 'many of the elements of a free market being in place by 2010'. Teagasc has demonstrated that Ireland and the UK are the most competitive EU countries, in terms both of the cost of production and of the margin between cost and selling prices. It states that a national Irish milk-production target of 1.45 billion gallons would be realistic for 2010, an increase of 30 per cent from current production levels. This level of production is stated by Teagasc to be achievable by means of productivity improvements, rather than an increase in the national dairy herd.

It seems that comparative advantage now lies with Ireland, north and south, in the production and marketing of dairy products, and that the existence of milk quotas has been a brake on the progress that could have been achieved since their introduction in 1984. Irish dairy farmers, it would seem, have more to fear from continuation of the present CAP dairy regime than from the opportunities and challenges that would arise under a free market.

Perhaps the last word on milk quotas should rest with Nick Brown MP, then UK Agriculture Minister, when he was welcoming a study carried out by Manchester University in February 1999:

> The report shows that the total cost to dairy farmers of acquiring milk quota is equivalent to about 12.5 per cent of the revenue from milk production. These costs would be eliminated if milk quotas were removed … The study confirms what we have known for a long time: milk quotas are pernicious, inefficient and add enormously to the cost of milk production.

Bovine spongiform encephalopathy (BSE)

The report of the Committee of Inquiry into BSE was published in

September 2000. The Inquiry heard evidence, between March 1997 and December 1998, amounting to documents exceeding 3,000 lever-arch files from 560 witnesses, and 300 witnesses gave oral evidence. Any comment on its findings is therefore unnecessary, as the report has been fully discussed in the media. However, it would be remiss of the author not to attempt to summarise certain aspects of BSE from the perspective of the compound feed trade, not least as it has been generally accepted that a standard feed ingredient for more than 50 years before 1988, meat and bone meal (MBM), has been the cause of the disease in cattle.

BSE reached epidemic proportions in farms in Great Britain in the mid-1990s, causing enormous cost to the government of the day. This cost was in part caused by the fact that British beef was no longer acceptable to EU or other countries, with which in past years there had been a thriving export trade. Since Northern Ireland is part of the UK, the ban on British beef extended to beef produced in the province. Also, Northern Ireland consumed only 20 per cent of the beef that it produced and 50 per cent of its exports went to countries outside the UK. The economic loss therefore was proportionately greater in Northern Ireland than in any other part of the UK. Since there was no point in farmers producing beef that could not be sold, various compensation schemes were devised for unwanted calves to be slaughtered and so to minimise the economic loss. While some normality has now returned, it will be a long time before consumer confidence in British beef is fully restored and before the export of beef to other countries approaches its former levels.

There is an unfortunate irony, resting on the perception that the Republic's 'Irish' beef was somehow safer than Northern Ireland's 'British' beef, also grown on the island of Ireland. This is bizarre, given that the incidence of BSE throughout Ireland was similar, and much lower than in England, Wales and Scotland.

There was no acceptance, among former customers, politicians or food standards regulators, that Northern Ireland beef was arguably the safest in the world, not least because of its traceability back to the farm where it was grown. Not for the first time in recent farming history, Northern Ireland's farmers continued to suffer a severe and unfair disadvantage because of inaccurate perceptions and mistaken policies elsewhere.

Some comment is also required on the use of MBM in animal feedstuffs (though rarely in beef or calf diets), given that there was a perception in some quarters that this was a modern and undesirable development. In his evidence to the BSE Inquiry, Dr Brian Cooke of Dalgety Agriculture was able to demonstrate that as long ago as 1865, Liebig had recommended the use of meat by-products in pig feeding; in 1926, the Fertiliser and Feeding Stuffs Act included the description of MBM as a feedstuff, and in 1928 Morrison described the use of MBM in cattle feed in America and Europe. In 1934,

Rees described the use of rendered meat meal as a supplement for grass in the feeding of sheep in a number of farms in New South Wales, Australia. In 1939 Hewitt described the feeding of meat meal to dairy cattle in Australia. In 1943, during the war years, Linton and Williamson described good MBM as a valuable complementary stock feed; MBM was included as an ingredient in government specifications for standard diets, both for ruminants and non-ruminant livestock.

With the increase in the export of beef from Ireland after the end of the war, and the later rise in the numbers exported after slaughtering locally, rather than as previously 'on the hoof' for fattening elsewhere, the rendering trade greatly increased its capacity for the production of MBM. This was justifiably seen, given the long history of its use and the state of current scientific knowledge, as an economic and virtuous ingredient for inclusion at maximum levels of around 5 per cent in many farm animal diets, and at somewhat higher levels in pet foods.

Any economic loss, however severe, that resulted from BSE in cattle and from the progressive bans on feeding MBM in, firstly, ruminant diets and subsequently all compound feeds, from July 1988 onwards, faded into insignificance as the evidence developed of the possible but scientifically unproven link between BSE and new variant Creutzfeldt-Jakob Disease (vCJD) in humans. This is a tale which is still unfolding as the incidence of vCJD now appears to be increasing, albeit from a very low base, particularly in younger members of the human population.

The incidence of BSE in cattle in the United Kingdom and Ireland has fallen to the point where it is no longer the scourge that it was in the mid-1990s. The incidence and cost of vCJD are presently unquantifiable and the full extent of that human disaster may not be clear for many years to come.

Foot-and-mouth disease (FMD)

Early in the year 2001 in Great Britain there was an outbreak of FMD, potentially affecting all cloven-hoofed animals, of a severity that had not been seen since the last major outbreak in 1967. Ireland, as a whole, was fortunate in avoiding this, despite some worrying moments.

While the disease is very rarely transmissible to humans, and is rarely fatal to livestock, nevertheless it is so contagious within the affected animal species and of such harmful economic consequences that a draconian slaughter policy on both affected and contiguous farms was seen as the only feasible measure of containment. The distress affecting livestock owners, and images of their animals' slaughter and disposal by burial in mass graves, or burning in huge funeral pyres, was all too apparent to the whole population of the country and indeed to a worldwide television audience.

The economic effects of restricted access to the countryside by tourists and other visitors were even more serious, in total, than those directly suffered by the livestock producers. Morale was not improved by allegations of irresponsible behaviour by very few of the farming community, and by a sense that central government's handling somehow contrived to be both insensitive and indecisive.

There remains also a worrying and widespread sense that the consequences of FMD, given a newly elected government with a fresh mandate, are likely to include legislation that will be unwelcome and harmful to those who live and earn their living in the countryside.

Salmonella

Mrs Edwina Currie MP (who accordingly earned the cognomen 'Eggwina', probably for her lifetime), when a junior health minister raised a political and commercial storm in 1988, by announcing to the world that most poultry flocks in Britain were infected with *Salmonella enteritidis* phage type 4. She had thus disobeyed the first commandment of politics – 'Be careful how you speak' – and paid the price by being forced to resign her post two weeks later.

Had she said, more accurately, that a small proportion of birds in most British egg-producing flocks and broiler flocks were infected with *Salmonella enteritidis*, the comment would probably have passed unnoticed. However, it must be recognised that the widespread existence of the bacterium, which in the early 1980s was a newly discovered strain of salmonella, remains a serious public health issue and should also be a matter of grave concern to anyone whose livelihood depends on poultry production.

It is instructive to take a step back into the history of salmonellosis. The bacterium takes its name from the discovery of the first strain in 1885 by an American vet, Daniel Salmon. Today more than 2,200 varieties have been identified but those most seriously affecting human health are the strains *S. typhimurium* and *S. enteritidis*. In earlier decades, there had been an awareness of salmonella poisoning associated with poultrymeat and eggs, due to infection by the typhimurium strain, but this was known to be transmitted by poor hygiene in the kitchen, or by the use of eggs that were either cracked or whose shells were contaminated by poultry faeces.

In the United States, a programme of washing and disinfecting eggs in shell provided a response to the problem, whereas in Northern Ireland the decision was to ban egg washing and to put the emphasis on the production of naturally clean eggs. It is interesting to recall that this policy was one factor that led to an overwhelming swing to the caging of hens for egg production in the 1960s and 1970s. In cage-laying systems, faeces and the shell of the egg are less likely to come into contact with each other than is the case with eggs produced by free range or deep litter methods. It is only in recent years that the caging of laying hens has been perceived by a majority of the general public as an unacceptable regime; accordingly, the practice is likely to be phased out over the next decade or so, throughout the EU.

The worrying new experience of the mid-1980s was that people were falling sick from salmonellosis in instances where hygiene in the kitchens was of an unquestionably high standard and – where it was related to eggs – only first-quality eggs had been used. Plainly, some new infectious agent was at work. Far from it being a uniquely British or Irish problem – and indeed the incidence in Ireland remained as a small fraction of that experienced in Great Britain – this was a worldwide phenomenon. Outbreaks of food poisoning related to the newly isolated bacterium had been reported in the USA, Yugoslavia, Finland, Sweden, and Norway as well as in the UK. Most notably, 800 holidaymakers went down with salmonella food poisoning while on the Italian cruise ship *Costa Riviera* as they sailed between Corfu and Crete in August 1996.

What gave particular cause for concern was that apparently healthy birds could carry the infection, in contrast to other strains of salmonella, which came from diseased flocks. Research indicated that the contamination occurred in egg yolks, while they were being formed in the ovaries of infected hens. Dr Charles Benson, of the University of Pennsylvania, reported that in his experiments the bacteria were not to be found in the white of the egg, as would be the case when organisms penetrate the shell, but only in the yolk, where the bacteria multiplied explosively when eggs were stored without refrigeration. While *Salmonella enteritidis* is now probably endemic in the majority of the world's poultry flocks, under all methods of husbandry, it still affects only a minute proportion of laying poultry. Even individual hens that are affected produce only a proportion of their eggs with the bacterium in the yolk. It has been reliably estimated that as few as 1 in 10,000 eggs on supermarket shelves may be internally contaminated.

Why then does each summer produce an incidence of outbreaks of salmonella food-poisoning, news of which hits the media with monotonous regularity? The symptoms are, at the least, extremely unpleasant and, in the case of infants, elderly people or others whose immune systems are fragile, can be life-threatening. Clearly, if these are preventable occurrences, greater zeal should be shown in preventing them. Yet how can this be achieved in practice, given the apparent practical impossibility of isolating and removing the very few hens that are carrying the bacterium?

The answer lies partly in amending traditional practices of using raw eggs in recipes and of under-cooking eggs before consumption. Given that the bacterium thrives in the egg yolk, it follows that the yolk, whether fried, boiled or scrambled, should be thoroughly cooked in order to destroy the infection. So far as catering establishments are concerned, danger also lies in the practice of pooling large quantities of raw eggs before cooking and thus infecting a large proportion of the recipe ingredients. The advice of government health departments to catering establishments now states that recipes which call for uncooked eggs, such as hollandaise sauce, baked Alaska, tira-misu or mayonnaise, should substitute pasteurised eggs as a matter of course. Finally, an elementary precaution is that uncooked eggs should be kept under refrigeration, from the time that they are packed, immediately after they are laid, until consumption, thus inhibiting the growth in numbers of the bacteria in the minuscule number of infected eggs that exist.

Regrettably, the eradication of *Salmonella enteritidis* and *Salmonella typhimurium* is impossible; they have become one of nature's hazards, not least as they are present in wildlife populations, and the human race must learn to coexist with them. So far as the feed trade is concerned, the Northern Ireland Department of Agriculture's initiative in calling for the compulsory heat treatment of laying feed in 1992 may have been ill-timed and was ultimately unsuccessful. But the Department sought to give Northern Ireland eggs a competitive edge at that time, by providing certainty that their feed could not possibly be a means of infecting flocks. It was a noble cause that foundered on the rock of practical politics, despite the eloquent and impassioned advocacy of Bill Hodges, who was then the permanent secretary of the Department. Nor is it likely that it would have ensured freedom from salmonella infection in laying flocks, since the more likely source of infection is through the egg of the parent breeder hen.

At the time of writing this chapter in the year 2000, the Food Safety Authority in the Republic has mounted a determined campaign on several fronts, including that of encouraging retailers to buy from 'salmonella-controlled' flocks (note, in passing, the use of the word 'controlled' rather than 'free'). Among other provisions, this requires such flocks to use heat-treated feed. The Authority has also embarked on an imaginative programme of public education. This includes puppet shows for the entertainment and education of children at agricultural shows, featuring two villainous characters Sam and Ella, who, 'when they aren't visiting shows, schools and starring in their own video… spend their time burrowing into food, lurking under fingernails and hanging about on kitchen counters … With their army of bugs, [they] invade homes with the motto, "sick, sicker, sickest".'

According to Dr Patrick Wall, chief executive of the Irish Food Safety Authority, 'Imparting life skills on food safety and hygiene practice to young children must be a priority for the future … if they understand what causes food poisoning now at a young age they will be able to carry these valuable messages through life with them.'

Which leading UK politician was it who stipulated that the three highest priorities of his government's programme would be, 'Education, education, education'?

Richard Scott

14

Richard Scott
Growth and Diversification

TONY DEESON

RICHARD SCOTT ASSUMED FULL CONTROL of the mill as executive chairman and managing director in 1982, following the death of John McAusland. While he could no longer claim the advice of John McAusland or Walford Green (who by that time was in failing health), he had many years of experience at the mill to support his new responsibilities and the loyal co-operation of a strong senior management team, comprising Fred Charters, Roy Howard, William McAusland, Desmond Given – who assumed responsibility for material purchasing and transport – and Noel Donald, the accountant and office manager, who had joined the firm following the untimely and tragic death of Wesley Wylie in 1974.

His connection with the mill went back to his childhood and he once recalled:

> My earliest memory of the mill is that I was not allowed in it. This was because with its carts, lorries, high piles of grain in sacks, watercourses, sluice gates and turbines, it was a very dangerous place for a hyperactive, inquisitive, and unbiddable youngster.
>
> In 1943, when I was five, there was a serious fire, which destroyed the mill's flaking plant. The previous week the fire brigade had paraded

through the streets of Omagh and given a display, complete with a military band. While the mill was on fire – from 6 a.m. or so – I was not woken up, but when all was over at breakfast time I was allowed to witness at close quarters the damping down process and vividly remember my father [Maddin Scott] in the mill yard supervising the proceedings in his dressing gown and slippers. I am recorded as having said, 'Oh, we've got a fire brigade, too! But where's the band?'

Richard Scott is in the direct line from William Scott, the founder of the business, and is his great-great-grandson. He was educated at Omagh Academy as a small boy, and from there went to Mourne Grange School, in Kilkeel, and Loretto, in Edinburgh. He continued his education at the Royal Agricultural College, Cirencester and Magee University College, Londonderry, in courses of study considered to be relevant for a future feed miller. In 1960, when he was 22, he joined the family firm in management and in 1962 was appointed a director, a position he continued to hold until his retirement in 1998.

He is currently a Deputy Lieutenant and sometime High Sheriff of County Tyrone. Richard, like all the Scotts, has throughout his life been much involved in public appointments, trade associations and voluntary service to the local community. He was president of the Northern Ireland Grain Trade Association (NIGTA) in 1984/5 and until 1997 was the convenor of the NIGTA compounders' committee. Successively, between 1991 and 1996, he was vice-president, president and treasurer of the United Kingdom Agricultural Supply Trade Association (UKASTA). His period of office as vice-president and president involved him in a great deal of work, based in UKASTA's office in London, necessitating his partial absence from the mill during 1991/2 and 1992/3.

Richard's first year of full responsibility at the helm, 1982, was a fairly unremarkable year for the mill. Plant investment continued steadily. A CPM 7000 pellet mill and associated plant were installed to meet the need for greater output of pelleted products. The Qeleq Mark 2 computer was retired and replaced with a Digital Equipment Company (DEC) minicomputer, used to update office methods, including formulation.

Overheads, ingredient costs and selling prices all continued to rise, although more slowly than in previous years, but profit per tonne and trading profit declined, although tonnage increased to 74,200. Smyths had closed down its Strabane feed mill in 1980 and the closure of the Scott–Smyth pig farm partnership at Aughentaine followed.

Erne Eggs became a limited company in 1982. Richard Scott and Fred Charters were appointed to the board to represent Scotts' 50 per cent interest in the venture.

Fred Charters

But the year 1983 was a very different story. Tonnage was up by 10 per cent; margin up 2.21 per cent, with production costs and overheads falling by 0.7 per cent. The net result was a 'best-ever year' with a trading profit for the mill of £493,000 on a turnover of just over £13 million. The spending on plant amounted to £153,000. Another press line was installed to improve the quality of crumb production, particularly responding to the needs of Moy Park, which had been a substantial customer of the mill since the late 1960s. The quantity of steam that was required for the new rates of production proved too much for the existing water main, and a new one with enhanced capacity was installed. It was also necessary to install a new Thompson-Cochrane horizontal boiler to meet the increased requirement for steam. The spending on plant was reduced by Department of Commerce grants of 30 per cent, plus a £12,000 grant from FEOGA*, with more expected.

Scotts Farms had an unprofitable year at the Inisclan farm, reducing the group's consolidated profit, and its future was held under review by the directors, who at that time were Richard Scott, Fred Charters, Roger Green and Roy Howard.

Plant expenditure in 1983/4 included an additional Christy 150hp X-Mill-Extra hammermill, plus ancillary equipment such as Rotafeeds and Airmaster reverse-jet filters with conveyor and elevator discharge, chosen in preference to a suction-pneumatic system. To house this equipment, a new grinder-house was built. The hammermills were also fitted with an auto-screen change system of 8mm, 5mm and 3mm screens to provide a series of screen combinations, which could be changed automatically without the need to stop the grinders or employ any manual intervention, thereby allowing screen changes to be programmed into the plant computer.

Grain was in short supply in Northern Ireland in 1983 and after lobbying by NIGTA, through the Department of Agriculture for Northern Ireland, the EEC decided to move 50,000 tonnes of German wheat of bread-making quality from intervention stores to Belfast silos.

Plans were made to spend £256,000 in the forthcoming year, half in the pursuit of greater efficiency and the other half in increasing capacity to produce higher volumes. In fact the 1984 figure for expenditure on plant, machinery and buildings was £304,000, less 30 per cent from the Department of Commerce and £85,000 from FEOGA. Most of this was spent on the provision of a new conveyor route from the mixer to the pelleting presses. At the same time the opportunity was taken to change from worm conveyor to chain-and-flight, to avoid molasses build-up on the worm flights, reduce cross-contamination of products and decrease transfer times.

Profits for 1984 could not match the record of the year before; they were nevertheless extremely satisfactory, being a 'second record' not to be surpassed until 1991. Sales tonnage fell by 4.5 per cent but increased in cash

*The European Agricultural Guidance and Guarantee Fund.

terms by 6.5 per cent as a result of the continuing inflation in ingredient costs. During the year, ingredient costs increased on average from £137.49 to £155.83 per tonne. Inflation was still a disturbing feature of the external economy, putting constant pressure on borrowing limits for Scotts and, presumably, most other businesses.

The year 1984 was saddened for many at the mill by Walford Green's death. Giving the funeral address in Kent, Richard Scott said:

> There are several people here today who are better qualified than I to speak of his distinguished legal career but I think few whose combined family and business links with Walford were of such closeness and long standing. He was my father's first cousin and, from the early 1930s his close friend, as a result of which he became my godfather ...
>
> In 1942 he had accepted a non-executive directorship in a small family business of grain millers in Omagh, Northern Ireland. He became chairman in 1962 and retired in 1982. This bald recital of positions and dates cannot give any indication of Walford's outstanding contribution over 40 years, by counsel and encouragement, to those charged with the day-to-day running of the expanding business, nor of his generous gifts of time and talents to three generations of my family. It does not surprise me to learn that he was also regarded by many in this county as a wise and kind adviser.
>
> Walford was not much given to talking about himself or his achievements; in his virtue of reticence he was truly English. But in his evident joy and pride in his marriage, his family, his home and his garden Walford Green showed us where his treasure lay. It is indeed a privilege to have known, and today to remember with affection and gratitude, such a gentleman and true friend.

Milk quotas came in, at three weeks' notice, on 1 April 1984. Their likely effect was debated at length in the report to shareholders, as must have been the case in all feed mills throughout Europe. There was, necessarily, constant concern about the steady drop in Northern Ireland compound feed sales ever since 1970. As we have already seen, Scotts did what it could to enlarge its share of a diminishing local market, in part by increasing sales over the border. In this it was generally successful. In 1970 it had 2 per cent of the Northern Ireland market and by 1985 this had increased to about 6.5 per cent. That year, the board welcomed a reduction in corporation tax from 50 to 35 per cent although this was offset by less generous tax allowances on capital expenditure.

A year following Walford Green's death, Scotts suffered a blow of a different kind on 8 February 1985, when a serious and damaging fire broke out in Plant 1 mixer room, in which the mixer plant and the building were totally destroyed. The damage could have been much worse but for the fact that an army patrol had spotted smoke and alerted William McAusland and Jimmy Dodds, who were two of the residents of the mill houses on

Mountjoy Road. William McAusland was aware of the proximity of the fat storage tanks and duly informed the fire brigade of this particularly combustible material. In a truly professional response to the information, a foam tender was dispatched from Derry, covering the 34 miles in 45 minutes, and this was successful in suppressing the fat fire and limiting the total damage. Only a few hours were lost on the following day, as mixer Plant 2 was available for extended use. Nevertheless the cost of the damage was estimated at £400,000.

In 1984/85, in cash terms turnover fell by 30 per cent, sales tonnages having been reduced by $22^1/_2$ per cent, and profit before tax fell by 45 per cent. The total production of compounds in Northern Ireland was just over one million tonnes, the lowest annual tonnage since 1975.

Scotts was not alone in experiencing a miserable trading year. Many of the changes that have since occurred in the compound feed trade nationally had their origin in the experience of the year following the introduction of milk quotas, as has been discussed in a previous chapter.

However, the following trading year proved to be very different, and it was a case of the old saying, 'It's an ill wind that does nobody good.' All over Ireland, west Scotland, Wales and the west of England, the summer of 1985 was unseasonably cold and very wet, resulting in an acute shortage of saved fodder. Owners of ruminant animals were advised to buy in concentrates rather than expensive, low-quality fodder. Up to July 1986, the end of Scotts' trading year, its cattle food sales increased by 158 per cent against increases in the province of 32 per cent. In monetary terms this increased Scotts' sales to very nearly £14 million, a high point that was not reached again until 1996.

As Richard Scott remarked at the time, this superb relative performance 'did not merely happen' but was the consequence of a sustained effort by the sales force, backed by the ability of the production and transport staff and drivers to produce and organise the prompt delivery of good quality feeds at the right price. This achievement was good for everyone's morale and self-confidence during a year made difficult by the fire. The profit for the year ending July 1986 increased by 50 per cent over the previous year.

It is interesting to compare production figures for 1950 and 1986. The output in 1950 was a tenth of that achieved in 1986. In 1950 the workforce, including management, was 55 working a 45-hour week; in 1986, 37 were employed on a 40-hour week. In 1950 18.33 man-hours were required to produce one ton of product; in 1986 the figure had dropped to 1.07 man-hours per tonne.

These figures show quite clearly the increase in productivity, achieved by a programme of continuous development and efficiency savings. Less apparent, perhaps, but no less real, was the development of skills at all levels in the workforce, which had become essential to the smooth running and profitability of a much more fine-tuned and sophisticated system of operation, with greatly enhanced productivity.

In 1986 Erne Eggs – now a limited company – was steadily increasing profits from a low base in 1982 and Charles Crawford had developed a plan to 'add value to the egg', which was supported by an initial optimistic market survey by Coopers & Lybrand. In the same year (1985) Bell Communications, a joint venture between Scotts Feeds, Eddie Scott of Scotts Fuels (no relation) and Billy Pollock, started up. The name 'Bell' came from the mountain known as Bessy Bell beside Baronscourt, ten miles from Omagh, and the objective was to sell radio-telephone services to small businesses in the west of Northern Ireland.

In October 1985 David Scott, who was later to play a major role in the business, joined the board, and so a second member of the sixth generation of the family (William McAusland being the first) entered the business.

Following the fire, Scotts was confronted with what the chairman described as 'an intriguing choice'. Should they rebuild the plant according to the 1969 design, where possible taking advantage of recent improvements in individual machine design? Or should they take the opportunity of re-designing and upgrading the whole of the mixing plant to an entirely new layout? The major advantage of the first approach was that it could have been achieved within the sum obtained from their insurers. However, perhaps not surprisingly, they decided on the second option at a net additional cost of approximately £110,000.

The new mixer system, including Le Coq sifters, the Schugi mixer and the day tanks, was re-sited and for the first time the main mineral additives – salt, limestone flour and dicalcium phosphate – which previously had to be manually assembled, weighed and tipped-in to each batch of the mixer, were automatically weighed out of four bins, via a dial-hopper scale. The new control-room was built on the same level as the redesigned tip-in point, where vitamins and trace minerals were added to the mixer. The undamaged Plant 2 was incorporated into the overall design, thus giving a plant that had three nests of bins each fitted with a hopper scale. The existing silo contained the ingredients that required grinding. The former Bendix building was renamed the bulk material building and contained bins of ingredients that did not need grinding, such as soya bean meal and herring meal, which were always received in ground form at the mill. As Roy Howard, who masterminded this complex reorganisation, remarked, 'If a material does not need grinding, why grind it? To do so wastes expensive electricity.'

The Plant 2 bins were reorganised to contain easily ground materials such as corngluten meal. These were passed through an X26 hammermill fitted with a large screen, again saving electricity. A fats sprayer was installed at the die of press 2, so as to enable fat to be sprayed on the outside of pellets while they were hot. A Siscan sieve was installed to improve the quality of pig food, by ensuring that the maximum grist size was always consistent.

Modifications were also carried out to the Sizer cooler, whereby existing air-ducting was removed and a new air-duct constructed on top of the cooler. Air-flow was then reversed so that air was pulled upwards through the product, greatly improving the cooling operation and overcoming the earlier problem of 'blinding' the base of the cooler's conveyor bed, which was constructed of wedge wire. A new 30-tonne fats storage tank was installed to keep up with the increased demand for fats and oils in the higher energy diets.

Included in the additional cost was a new Instem computer to control the process of ingredients intake, weighing and blending, grinding and mixing, replacing two smaller and obsolete computers installed in 1975 and 1979. Unfortunately, the company supplying the software went out of business during the course of the contract and the anticipated advantages of the new system were delayed by over a year.

In 1986 it was announced that two of the largest mills in Belfast, John Thompson and BOCM-Silcock, would merge and that one of the mills would be closed in 1987. Richard Scott remarked to his shareholders that 'while showing a certain lack of confidence in the compound feed market on their part, [the merger] does at least promise to remove one major competitor from our territory'.

Richard Scott took this factor into consideration when preparing a strategy report for his co-directors on 'The Northern Ireland Compound Food Market and Us':

> As you are aware, we are one of many suppliers into a feed market which has been broadly static in volume terms at one million tonnes to 1.3 million tonnes during the past 10 years. There seems to be little prospect of growth from this base; Ireland continues to be deficient in feed grain, particularly wheat, and our main export market, Great Britain, has developed its livestock production and feed-milling industry to utilise their plentiful and cheaper grain and so to supply their own local market for food products, thus limiting Northern Ireland's prospects.
>
> Throughout the past 10 years there has been over-capacity in mills; however, those mills – mainly distant from the ports – which managed to modernise their capacity and to avoid over-manning of their mills, have prospered reasonably well, in some cases aided by FEOGA grants on capital investment. As one of the early mills to modernise, we have had our own measure of prosperity.

He then went on to analyse the competition, ranging over Dalgety, Wilson, Thompson, BOCM-S and Clow, reaching the conclusion that the development of Wilson Feeds should be the only serious concern for Scotts.

This mill, an independent, had had the good fortune, some years previously, to be compulsorily moved from an outdated mill on a bad site to a brand-new mill beside the docks. Since then it had raised its weekly tonnage of 800 to, reputedly, about 3,000. Wilsons had developed its business by aggressive selling and price-cutting and by buying-out the trade tonnage of retiring or ailing millers and merchants. Richard Scott then asked:

> What are the implications of all of this for us? It seems to me that our major concern must be the Wilson development, unless we can manage to be fully competitive – in terms of costs and product quality – with them.'
> He concluded: There are risks in all choices which face us, so it seems worthwhile to consider two clear alternatives:

a   Be defensive – this implies an assault on our own overheads, staffing etc., conserving cash resources and looking to our future prosperity in diversification of effort and investment (Erne Eggs, advertising, *ad hoc* developments, e.g. property possibilities, using the mill's cash flow as banker).

> The attractions of this are that we would be diversifying into more buoyant markets than agricultural production and feed milling. However, a critical detraction, so far as I am concerned, would be that such a decision must suggest the running down of our milling operations over the next ten years or so, as we would have made an implicit choice not to re-invest. It would also present problems of multiple choice in areas where we have little expertise.

b   Be aggressive – I think that last year's experience has shown that we are capable of aggressive selling and thus winning new business. I think that by autumn 1986 we shall have as good a mill as any of our competitors and better than most.

And Richard Scott concluded:

> Let us use the early summer months to plan our counter-attack against all-comers. I think that this process must include the following:

a   An analysis of our marketing strengths and weaknesses.

b   Decisions on sales representation and advertising policy, area by area.

c   A critical look at volumes and margins of all product groups.

d   A look at our overhead costs. Are they appropriate to a mill of our present output? Can we increase output without further overhead increases?

e   Set aggressive but realistic sales targets by product group and sales representative and let these be known throughout the company.

> I hope that we can complete this searching and no doubt painful process by the end of April and then set about implementing the decisions reached,

so as to ensure that all our wheels are humming from September onwards. I believe that terms of trade still favour us and that we have a sufficiently good team, if we can lead them properly, to beat the hell out Wilson's or anyone else. Let's give it a go!

These comments were backed by Scotts' steady progress over the previous 10 years. In 1976 48,000 tonnes were produced; in 1986 (not a particularly good year), an output of 70,000 tonnes was achieved. Turnover rose from £5.3 million to £9.9 million and profits had more than trebled, though this comparison takes no account of the cost inflation that had taken place in the interim.

Although Maddin Scott once quoted a famous piece of doggerel to his shareholders:

> He who mumbles down a well
> About the goods he has to sell,
> Never makes as many dollars
> As he who goes to town and hollers!

it could not be said that Scotts had ever been 'big' on publicity. But by the autumn of 1986, no doubt following the board's agreement with Richard Scott's analysis of the situation, a public relations and advertising budget of £20,000 was allocated. The old logo of the 'Excelsior boy' climbing the mountain gave way to a new windmill emblem, which appeared on letterheads, badges, ties, pens, lorries, posters and advertising, the company increasing its representation at a variety of agricultural shows and gymkhanas, and there were a number of sponsored events.

Arising out of the 1982 Finance Act, an important letter was sent to all shareholders on 6 October 1986, giving them the opportunity to sell their shares to the company. All shareholders were minority holders and a low value had been placed on their shares because until the 1982 Finance Act allowed a company to purchase its own shares there was no market for them. The ordinary share value had been agreed at 21p for inheritance tax purposes but the company now offered 80p per share.

Sam Bullock and David Dunn, sales representatives, in conversation with Fiona Cathcart, quality controller, *c.* 1987, outside the mill's show caravan at Omagh Show.

In order to understand why the shares had been valued at so low a figure in former years, one has to appreciate that a minority shareholder in a private limited company, particularly if unconnected with the management, has very little power. He or she cannot single-handedly appoint or dismiss the directors and so has minimal influence on the direction or management

of the company, much less the dividend policy. Also, shares cannot be transferred without the concurrence of the directors of the company. The Inland Revenue, when agreeing a value of shares for inheritance tax or any other purpose in a private company, realistically accepted that the valuation of a minority shareholding in a private company is based on the flow of income derived from dividends.

Clogher Valley Show with the new windmill logo fully implemented

So far as the latter influence was concerned, in Scotts' case, in past years the shareholders had become accustomed to the fact that the company had a need to re-invest the bulk of profits after tax in the development of the business, whether to add to the plant and buildings or to finance the growing trade against a background of inflation in ingredient costs. Shareholders had had to accept, and did so ungrudgingly, that this set of circumstances had continuously meant that dividends were modest in the extreme. It was of some minor consolation that when a shareholder died, the tax to be paid on the inheritance of mill shares was based on a modest valuation and was not a painfully large sum.

The new generation of directors, led by David Scott, saw that this state of affairs could not continue to be justified. The group's cash flow, from the early 1980s onwards, was such that the company was likely to start to accumulate cash, yet the directors had plans for the development of market share and other enterprises in related trades that were both worthy of consideration and likely to demand capital. David contended that those owners of shares who had no connection with the management should be given an opportunity to choose whether to retain their shares in a growing but cash-hungry group, while being afforded the opportunity to sell their shares. If the second option was to be seen to be fair by all, it must be on a basis that was more favourable to the potentially departing shareholders than a calculation based solely on dividend yield.

While there was debate in the board of the company as to whether this largesse could be afforded, there was little dispute as to the correctness of the policy. Not least on the basis of anecdotal evidence, there were many family businesses where a rift had arisen between the shareholder-directors and the outside shareholders. Such a situation had at best provided a severe distraction from the core business, and at worst had led to a forced sale of the family business concerned, so that the outside shareholders could be satisfied that they had obtained the true value of their inheritances. Not least on the basis of 'fair play for all', the Scotts board wanted to pre-empt such a situation arising among the group's numerous and geographically scattered shareholders, and it was this that led to successive offers to those shareholders who were not members of the management team.

The same opportunity was eventually afforded to directors who, on their retirement from the business, were enabled to realise a price for their shares which reflected the growth in value that had been achieved during their time with the company. But in order to avoid any potential suspicion that directors were being given more favourable treatment than other shareholders, which would have been out of step with company law as well as natural justice, the same offer had to made to all shareholders at the same time. The process was therefore not without risk from the company's viewpoint, in that an excessively enthusiastic acceptance of a cash offer might have depleted company funds to an unaffordable extent. The setting of the share price, from time to time as offers were made, was something of a balancing act and it was pitched at a level at which some individuals became buyers at the same time as others were sellers.

In the event, the uptake of the offers was gradual, and indeed some of the non-director shareholders of both the fifth and sixth generations have chosen to remain with the company. This appears to denote confidence that the treatment of shareholders by the directors has been and will continue to be fair and reasonable.

Such transactions in the company's shares had become possible only because of changes in company and taxation law under successive Conservative administrations. These changes permitted the sale of shares at the time of a director's retirement from a private company on a favourable taxation basis. They also enabled, for the first time, the company to buy in its own shares, having made a case to the Revenue for doing so. Thus, for the first time in the company's history, there was something approaching an open market in the shares, and a closer relationship between the balance-sheet value of the group and the value that would be placed on minority shareholdings, though with the directors retaining control over the identity of any potential external purchaser of shares.

1987 was reported as 'a very busy year'. Sales increased by 3.2 per cent and resulted in a consolidated profit of £243,000. The delays to the installation of the Instem software led to continuing plant inefficiencies and these were not finally solved until the end of the year. Despite considerable capital expenditure as a result of the fire, 1987/8 showed continuing investment activity. A new bag-store was built and a Medway automatic packer installed with a roller-conveyor for transferring loaded pallets to a fork-lift pick-up point, from where the loaded pallets were later transferred to the new bag-store. This greatly improved packing efficiency and speeded the outloading of feed in paper sacks. A third pressline was installed during the year and two new intake conveyors, rated at 120 tonnes per hour, were installed to improve the intake system so that two lorries could be discharged at the same time, whether containing the same or different materials.

Another significant development took place in 1987, in that McCorkell Ltd started trading during the year. Scotts had been instrumental in forming this new trading company, in co-operation with three other mills in the north-west of Ulster, to purchase their grain requirements through the port of Londonderry. The four mills had the common aims of maintaining a supply-line that was independent of the Belfast importers, and of developing a trade in grain throughout the north-west of Ireland. The new company rented a 60,000 sq. ft store in the Londonderry enter-

An unusual form of sponsorship was to support Billy and Carmel Patterson's trans-Sahara expedition in the late 1980s.

prise zone and obtained the co-operation of the harbour commissioners in making suitable arrangements for the discharge of ships. As the largest of the partners, Scotts made an investment of just over £141,000 in convertible preference and ordinary shares, representing 35 per cent of the equity. Richard Scott was elected chairman and John McCorkell managing director.

As it happened, this collaboration continued a tradition that dated back to earlier generations of both families: in the nineteenth century Charles Scott and Barry McCorkell had been involved in an earlier importing company, known as William McCorkell, which had sold its business some years previously to Andrews, in Belfast, and Maple Leaf of Canada.

Concern continued to be expressed about milk quotas, which it was thought would cause a drop of around 20 per cent in ruminant tonnage in 1988. Indeed, 1988 was not a good year for Scotts. The mill showed a profit before tax on a slightly increased tonnage of 67,200 tonnes but there was a consolidated loss of £6,000, the first loss for over 35 years. Erne Eggs, still intent on developing into egg products, made no contribution to profits; the McCorkell operation made a small profit on the first year's trading. It was said to be too early to forecast success or otherwise for Bell Communications, but here Scotts had no capital involvement. In this otherwise somewhat inauspicious year, William McAusland was appointed technical director.

Capital expenditure was £799,000, for which a FEOGA grant of £400,000 was in prospect. Among the improvements that took place in the years 1988–90 were a substantial extension to the raw material flat store, to allow the plant to run for longer hours by the increased storage of a greater number of raw materials, which also saved on port storage charges; a Bobcat bucket-truck for the raw material store; bridge-breakers for the meat-and-bone meal bins to facilitate discharge; bin division plates to provide bay divisions in the raw material store; and a substantial amount of transport.

About a third of the shareholders who had been approached in 1986 had responded positively to the company's offer and now another letter was sent, renewing the offer and extending it to preference shareholders, the terms being 80p per 25p ordinary share and £1 per £1 preference share. Later in the year the purchase date was specified as August 1989, when the company bade farewell to erstwhile owners who between them made over 233,670 ordinary and 5,552 preference shares to the company, at a total cost to the company of £192,500.

In 1990 a further letter was sent to the remaining non-director shareholders, exploring the possibility of offering high yield (14 per cent) preference shares in place of ordinary shares. The aim was to give a higher income to those wishing to remain shareholders; the proposed arrangement had the added advantage that the transaction was not a 'disposal' for capital gains tax purposes.

Profits for 1989 returned to a substantial and satisfactory level with continued considerable capital investment. Erne Eggs was thought to have put in 'a creditable performance' with a loss for the year of 'only' £33,000, partly caused by the cost of attempting to develop the market in 'value-added' egg products. But relief was in sight; it was agreed that egg products would be produced in a new company, in which Scotts would not have a shareholding. No figures are extant for McCorkell, while Bell Communications made a 'very modest' profit.

Mrs Edwina Currie's injudicious intervention in the salmonella controversy, previously referred to, was less than favourably received by the company at a time when eggs sales were already unsatisfactory; a further downturn could damage the prospect of Erne Eggs' return to prosperity or indeed, at worst, threaten its survival.

In 1989 Robert Scott, the elder brother of David and thus another Scott of the sixth generation, joined the board as a non-executive director and, like his brother and their cousin William McAusland, played an important part in the development of the company towards the middle and end of the 1990s.

In 1990 Scotts considerably increased its profitability over the previous year on a slightly reduced tonnage of 66,800. Profit per tonne was also dramatically increased from £2.57 the previous year to £3.97, the highest for 15 years. Capital spending of £231,000 was capitalised and dividends were raised by 10 per cent. The chairman commented:

> Truly, the livestock farmer's lot is not a happy one at present, for the most part. Having last year shared the tribulations of Curried egg and chicken farmers, we now look forward to the consequences of mad-cow disease and continental lamb wars upon the business of our customers. The cost of the EC's common agricultural policy borne by the taxpayer is largely blamed on 'greedy and inefficient' farmers, even in semi-respectable newspapers. Any farmer with a memory or even a sense of history might conclude that, like the soldier, he is considered a hero only in time of war ... But, to balance these gloomy thoughts, it must be remembered that people still continue to eat and are unlikely to become vegetarians. Life will never be easy for us or for our customers, but I feel reasonably confident that we shall survive. Perhaps the Scott motto should be amended from *Pacem Amo* to Profitable Survival. It would, I am sure, be overly ambitious to match that of the Rothschilds: Buy Cheap, Sell Dear.

Erne Eggs had been 'outstandingly successful' in its core business of producing, packing and marketing eggs in shell.

As referred to earlier, since 1984 Charles Crawford, the managing director and driving force of Erne Eggs Limited, had developed his conviction that it was necessary to capitalise on the productive efficiency of the company by somehow enhancing the value of what was essentially a commodity product. The hen's egg could justifiably be regarded as a remarkable combination by Dame Nature of nutritive value and economic packaging, but the fact remained that comparative advantage in a commodity market lay with those producers who were situated close to cheaper grain supplies than were available in the north-west corner of Ireland.

Such thoughts – in relation to the whole of the province and affecting many other livestock products as well as eggs in shell – were exercising the minds of senior people in Northern Ireland's Department of Agriculture, such as Bill Hodges, the energetic and voluble permanent secretary, at much the same time. The department had earlier found the wherewithal to provide added-value food production equipment and training facilities at Loughry College, near Cookstown in County Tyrone. A certain Harry Steele, former Irish rugby international who had become one of the department's senior food technologists, was the acknowledged expert in turning fresh eggs into food products. Surely Harry Steele's expertise and Charles Crawford's vision, eventually to be matched by substantial investment in a specialised food factory – to be called Ferne Foods Limited and sited within half a mile of the production unit at Erne Eggs itself – could be profitably harnessed to provide 'added value to the egg', a phrase that was to become familiar over future years.

It undoubtedly had a more positive ring to it than 'the old egg equation', a well-worn phrase beloved of George Wright, managing director of Associated Egg Packers, friendly rivals of Erne Eggs and for some years layer feed customers of Scotts. The egg equation, George seemed to suggest, was a conundrum wrapped in an enigma and contained within a mystery; its gloomy answer was a zero sum, an apparent impossibility of making money locally in egg production and marketing, given that producers here were mainly suppliers to the market in Great Britain. They accordingly suffered from the dual handicap of higher grain costs and lower egg prices than their competitors on the mainland. Yet local egg producers and egg packers somehow seemed to continue to survive.

Ferne Foods was also seen by Charles Crawford as an important potential contributor of profit to Erne Eggs itself. The trouble with being the producer of a commodity, let alone a commodity whose market was evidently in gradual but steady decline, was that the substantial trading profits which were earned in the good years tended to be matched if not overshadowed by losses in succeeding years, as the terms of trade turned in favour of the buyers. If eggs could be taken off the market in the lean times, at cost of production rather than being sold at a loss, Charles's argument ran, and be turned into profitable food products, there would be a dual benefit. Even in prosperous times for the sale of eggs in shell, there would always be certain sizes of first-quality eggs that were less profitable than others, and again these could be applied to the production process so as to maximise profit in the egg-producing company.

There were also, from the early 1980s, concerns about salmonella infection in laying poultry that were eventually to erupt in 1988, with the outbreaks of acute food poisoning caused by *Salmonella enteritidis* phage type 4 that were associated with both eggs and chicken meat. So far, these concerns had not affected consumer confidence, but it was already apparent that there was the potential for housewives increasingly to regard eggs in shell as an unsafe commodity to put into their fridges. What then could be better, from the angle of food safety, than that food products with eggs as their main ingredient should be cooked in a specialised factory, for the busy housewife to rapidly re-heat from the frozen state for her family? Such products, given the quality of the ingredients and the expertise that was available, would certainly be flavoursome and competitively priced.

After some months during which work was carried out at Loughry on developing the sort of egg products that might become marketable, Harry Steele was duly seconded to Erne Eggs and in course of time was employed by the company on a full-time basis. The first product that was brought to the market-place was called 'Scramblers', a combination of scrambled egg and shredded ham that tasted better than its appearance, being shaped like a burger.

Work also continued on the development of filled omelettes, using a variety of complementary ingredients, and by 1990 there was sufficient optimism to embark on the enormous step of building a 40,000 sq. ft factory at Lisnaskea. It was recognised at an early stage that the market for egg food products was likely to be slow to develop, and so the factory was designed with equipment that could if need be make food products based on pig meat and chicken meat as well as from fresh eggs. This later proved to be its salvation.

Scotts' directors considered that all of this represented one step too far from their experience as feed millers; there was also an evident need for a marketing partner and the outcome was that Ferne Foods Ltd was now established as a separate company, producing food products for the supermarkets. Its equity was capitalised at £1 million but its total capital, with grants and loans, amounted to £3.5 million. The ordinary shares initially were held by Charles Crawford and Harry Steele (50 per cent); Erne Eggs (25 per cent); and Unipork (25 per cent). Unipork was seen as supplying the previously missing link, being a company with marketing capability in value-added food products and established contacts with supermarket customers. Ferne Foods undertook the manufacture of some Unipork food products, based mainly on pig meat.

In the mill itself, a third pelleting press was installed and a Milltech rotary sifter was installed to remove fines, transferring them to the blending bins, the coarse fraction of the sieved material being used in the manufacture of a new range of blended ruminant feeds. Four new finished-product bins were installed, additional to those of 1983/4, and were later divided into eight 15-tonne capacity bins to help with the increase in the number of smaller load sizes and variations in finished products. A new entrance to the mill and to Millbank was constructed via the former front avenue to Lisnamallard House, which facilitated an increase in numbers in the queue for discharge of bulk vehicles, especially useful when a ship was being unloaded.

A valuable addition to the management team took place in July 1990, when Siobhan Kelly joined as group accountant and company secretary. In the previous year, Noel Donald had departed from the company, on the most amicable of terms, in order to capitalise on his self-taught expertise by establishing KVS Distribution, selling office computer systems to small and medium-sized businesses throughout the west of the province.

Siobhan Kelly's initial brief was to provide effective financial reporting and planning to the group, in accordance with best accounting practice, and soon after her appointment she presented the first ever financial budget to the board and introduced monthly cash flow reports to the management team, which were followed by monthly sales forecasts. Only too often non-financial directors become a trifle glazed when figures are discussed at meetings, and it was Siobhan Kelly's aim (in which she succeeded) to make them both interesting and intelligible, relating them to the life of the company. Not only did she educate her executive directors in financial forecasting, she also trained her staff to respond to the new challenges that she presented to them. In 1995 she was appointed finance director to Scotts Feeds and in 1997 she became the administrative trustee of the pension fund.

The group now consisted of W & C Scott Ltd, trading as Scotts Feeds, with the associated companies Erne Eggs, Scotts Farms, McCorkell and Bell Communications. In 1991 an extensive financial reconstruction of the group took place and the company's share structure was rationalised. Four new ordinary 25p shares were exchanged for each old 25p share and five new 14 per cent cumulative preference shares were given in exchange for 20 of the old ordinary 25p shares relinquished. W & C Scott Ltd became the holding company for the group. The milling activity passed to Scotts Feeds Ltd, a new wholly-owned subsidiary, and the holding company also held the Scotts shares in Erne Eggs and McCorkell.

Closer to Scotts' main concern with feed milling, Glenpark Poultry Ltd was formed in the same year, as a joint venture between Scotts and Gordon Jones, an existing customer of the mill. It was planned that Scotts' involvement and capital contribution would enable an expansion of chicken production by investment in broiler houses. The expectation was that there would be 5,000 tonnes of feed purchases from the mill each year and a reasonable profit from the business of rearing broiler chickens on contract for a poultrymeat marketing company.

In August 1991 Desmond Given was welcomed as a director of Scotts Feeds and Robert Scott became company secretary of the holding company, Siobhan Kelly remaining in that office for Scotts Feeds.

With the dawn of the 1990s, Scotts was entering into a period of unprecedented prosperity, the result of continuous development and investment over a number of years. The consolidated profit before tax in 1991/2 was £470,000, of which Erne Eggs and McCorkell contributed £139,000. In his chairman's report Richard Scott said that Bell Communications 'continues to wash its face' under the eye of Fred Charters. Expenditure of £270,000 in the mill was capitalised in the accounts. The sales volume of the mill was 67,695 tonnes, an increase of 4 per cent on the previous year.

For years the peculiarities of the Common Agricultural Policy (CAP) had been a source of despair and even desperation not only to farmers but to compounders and many others in Northern Ireland seeking a modest competence in matters agricultural. Richard Scott took up the cudgels for the free-marketeer, encouraged by the General Agreement on Tariffs and Trade (GATT) round of talks then in progress, in an article that appeared in the trade journal *Feed Compounder*, extracts from which are reproduced here:

> Perhaps I had better explain why I am a free-marketeer, after 20 years of trading under the CAP. First of all, it is a matter of instinct, almost of heredity, as I represent the fifth generation of my family in this business and am the grandson of an academic who was both an economist and an economic historian. Secondly, it is a matter of experience and observation. One does not have to be foolishly nostalgic, a believer in a lost golden age, to come to the conclusion that the CAP has been both unjust and unhelpful to the intensive livestock producers in Northern Ireland and other remote, grain deficient, areas of the EC. In the 20 years following the post-war de-regulation of feedstuffs, millers here were able to purchase grain supplies at world-market prices through the deep water ports of Belfast and Londonderry, converting them into competitively-priced compounds for our farmers to produce profitable livestock products for the markets in Great Britain.
>
> Since 1972, however, while the CAP's managed market for cereals and resultant levies on US and Canadian cereals have led to Ireland being self-sufficient in barley, our farm structure and high rainfall have combined to ensure that we are deficient of around a quarter of a million tonnes of wheat each year which we must purchase from the EC countries. Effectively, therefore, for poultry diets and increasingly for modern higher-energy pig diets, our customers operate under the dual handicap of the cost of haulage of English wheat to the mills here and then of the livestock products back to England. The second of these factors is manageable and is the price we cheerfully accept for living in God's own country. The first is an almost unmanageable burden and is down to the CAP cereals regime.

It is no wonder that we have had to be innovative in the use of unusual and exotic (though wholesome) feed ingredients from time to time; nor that we have lent support to our customers in their frequent and necessary lobbying for assistance out of this or that crisis.

However, I wonder if help may be at hand in the shape of the likely consequences of the GATT round. The casual reader of newspapers and particularly of the agricultural press in recent months could be forgiven for a feeling of confusion. On the one hand, the urban chattering classes are informed that the breakdown of the GATT round, if unresolved, will lead to greater protectionism, trade wars and general mayhem. On the other hand, commissioner Ray MacSharry's monumental efforts to achieve EC consensus on a modest reduction of 30 per cent in agricultural support costs over ten years were pilloried by the agricultural press and greeted with cries of *Parturiunt montes, nascitur ridiculus mus!* (which may be roughly translated as, 'The mountains have laboured to produce this ridiculous mouse').

At this point I recall accompanying a party of farmers on a European study tour in about 1971 to look at the consequences of the UK's and Ireland's then impending entry to the EEC. The question in every Ulster farmer's mind was 'What is the price of land in the Common Market?' and he was greatly cheered to discover that it was three or four times the current price of equivalent land in Ireland. Instant capital gain!

Now, as many a houseowner in south-east England is aware, a meteoric rise in the value of one's property produces a feeling of euphoria. It is, however, merely illusory if the gain cannot be realised, or otherwise translated into greater prosperity. Worst of all if it leads to an ill-timed decision to 'gear up' on the presumption that the roller-coaster will run uphill forever. What is the point in sitting on a million pounds of assets if your farming business cannot produce the cash to buy a new tractor? I exaggerate, but only to emphasise the point which I am trying to make.

Let us assume that the GATT round will produce a free-market result or something close to that; in other words, perhaps the worst picture that the agricultural press can envisage. Further, let us assume that the changes will be phased-in over a five-year term, and examine the likely consequences.

One's natural presumption might be that land prices would fall. However, there is an alternative view from a body of informed and responsible opinion – as represented by Peter Day, FRICS, writing in *Bidwell's Review* 1990–91 who predicts: 'During the 1990s the asset value of all but the poorest land within the UK, with little or no amenity, will undoubtedly increase.'

Mr Day's thesis is that it all has to do with farm size, recommending reform of the Agricultural Holdings Act so that farms of uneconomic size may be permitted to merge into larger units and, by spreading overheads, create better and more viable farming businesses.

To quote him further, '... farmland values are related only in small part to the fortunes of farming, and much more to the fortunes of national and international economies'.

If the GATT solutions included a dismantling of milk quotas, which are the antithesis of a free market, this would sort out a few inequities and distortions, such as the current price difference between land of identical quality 'with quota' and 'without quota'. The cost of freehold farm land without amenity or development potential might even fall to the level where it could justify its purchase price in relation to the economic return to be derived; though not, I think, in Northern Ireland where about one in every two town dwellers wants to possess his own 'wee bit of land' and no farmer ever wants to sell …

So, with all due regard to present uncertainties, I finish on a cheerful note. People will continue to eat and continue – in our relatively free market – to be able to afford to eat. If the result of price reduction is a lower acreage of cereal production in the UK and Ireland and consequent changes in land prices, so be it. The good news is that there seems to be a prospect of a larger quantity and a wider variety of oilseed and cereal by-products world-wide, as far-Eastern countries in particular raise their standards of human nutrition. Compounders should welcome the prospect of obtaining cereals at world market prices, wherever they are grown.

Let us continue to use our native wit and develop our scientific knowledge and our milling skills to convert all of the suitable and available ingredients into wholesome, nutritious and value-for-money compounds. Perhaps Adam Smith would be proud of us.

On the whole, the year 1992/3 was a good one. The consolidated profit before tax was £437,000; capital spending in the mill amounted to £259,000 including an expander which was installed over the existing CPM press, to improve quality of pellets and to enable an increased inclusion rate for molasses; and £225,000 was invested in Glenpark. Sales volume during the year was 76,586 tonnes, a 13 per cent volume increase over the previous year despite the loss of sales to Moy Park, a substantial customer with which Scotts had been trading for 30 years. This was something of a blow, but it proved to the directors that they were fortunate that the sales tonnage was now well spread between ruminant and non-ruminant feeds; it also served to reinforce their long-held view that it was important never to be too dependent on a single customer, whose buying policy might alter at short notice as in this case.

Of the subsidiaries, Erne Eggs showed a modest profit but anticipated an upturn, largely due to the currency devaluation of 'Black Wednesday'; the Ferne Foods factory had been equipped and was in production and Richard Scott was appointed a non-executive director on behalf of the Erne Eggs interest; Glenpark returned a disappointing year but McCorkell had 'a very profitable year'. Largely on the personal initiative of John McCorkell, it had formed a new trading company, McCorkell Scotland Ltd in Clydeport, Glasgow, requiring a £500,000 rights issue, of which Scotts' share was

£190,000. The Lisahally port, some miles downstream of the old harbour facility on the quay of Londonderry city, had reopened and it was felt that there were 'exciting times in prospect'.

This was the year that heat-treated food for poultry became an issue. The Department of Agriculture for Northern Ireland (DANI) had previously required that feed for laying hens should be heat-treated with the aim of eliminating *Salmonella enteritidis* in eggs from Northern Ireland laying flocks. Scotts had complied with the requirements of heat treatment but there were practical difficulties, not least the cost of the treatment, and a substantial number of egg producers refused to obey the law, taking DANI to judicial review. DANI won the judicial review but lost the battle, and Scotts and other law-abiding compounders lost a great deal of layers' feed tonnage as a result.

Richard Scott had been deputy president of the United Kingdom Agricultural Supply Trade Association (UKASTA) in 1991/2 and was president in 1992/3. In his annual report for the latter year he expressed gratitude to his senior colleagues who had deputised for him during his many necessary absences on UKASTA work.

The year 1993/4 showed a fall-back of both profit and tonnage on previous excellent years. There had been considerable difficulties because of currency swings between the pound sterling and the Irish punt, in which about 25 per cent of sales were made. Seeking to neutralise such uncertainties, Scotts Feeds decided to buy future supplies of Irish grain in punts, aiming to match the total value of purchases with its sales of finished feeds to customers in the Irish Republic. While Scotts Feeds sales, at 69,000 tonnes, had fallen in comparison with the previous year, it was generally felt that they were 'creditable' in view of Moy Park's earlier decision to place all feed purchases with a Belfast compounder, and also in view of the loss of sales associated with heat treatment of layers' feed. Nevertheless, during the year Scotts Feeds spent £263,000 on buildings, plant and machinery and £115,000 on vehicles.

In the wider world, outside the agricultural supply trade, the shenanigans associated with currency fluctuations in the summer of 1992 probably had little immediate impact on the general British public, apart from the daily news bulletins on the radio and television. Successive senior government spokesmen seemed to be appearing, almost constantly, to express their solid and ever-increasing conviction that sterling's place within the European Monetary Union (EMU) was secure for all time. Norman Lamont, as the Chancellor of the Exchequer, and John Major, the Prime Minister, have subsequently made it plain in their memoirs that the break with EMU, forced upon them in September 1992, was a most significant moment of the Major government's tenure of office. It seems probable that the 15 per cent devaluation of sterling, which occurred as an immediate result, was the start of the electorate's increasing loss of confidence in the Conservative administration that ultimately led to Tony Blair's overwhelming victory at the polls in 1997. It is also arguable that this devaluation was the start of the economic recovery that had for so long been forecast but had proved so slow in arriving.

Possibly of even greater historical significance than either of these has been the British public's disenchantment with the euro, the latest and most powerful attempt at harmonising the economic and taxation policies of the European Union, a loss of confidence which can be argued to stem from the events of September 1992, which at the time were perceived as a humiliation for the UK and its government.

'Black Wednesday', as sterling's eviction day swiftly became known, had a most immediate effect on the business of the group companies and their profitability for that year, but in ways that varied widely from company to company. The effect on Scotts Feeds was probably favourable, on balance, to the extent that supplies of grain and other ingredients for a fair proportion of the winter's requirements had been contracted during the summer months, when sterling was at its pre-depreciation value, whereas a substantial proportion of the company's products were sold throughout the ensuing winter to customers in the Republic whose currency was relatively strong when the time came for them to pay for their supplies. So far as our northern customers were concerned, the selling value of their livestock products had the benefit of the fact that their competitors in the UK food market were to some extent based in France and Holland, as well as the Republic of Ireland, all of whose currencies were now stronger than they had been in relation to sterling and whose goods were accordingly more expensive.

In line with this scenario, Erne Eggs was helped to a record profit of £187,000. But McCorkell suffered severely, its managing director claiming that the considerable loss arose because the company believed that the UK government would not devalue and decided to make a 'prudent' covering of foreign exchange. This misjudgment, or misfortune, transformed an operating profit of in excess of £½ million to a profit before tax of only £79,000. David Scott and Peter Simmonds – previously the managing director of Pauls Agriculture – joined McCorkell's board at about this time, John McCorkell having expressed a need for 'more professional' non-executive directors than he felt his existing team to be.

Unrelated to currency fluctuations, Glenpark yielded a modest loss after what was described as 'an unhappy year', and Ferne Foods made a budgeted small loss in its first year of operation. A point of interest and a considerable achievement at Ferne was that its filled omelette was now being sold to British Midland and British Airways for serving on breakfast-time flights out of Belfast.

This year the pension fund's 'contributions holiday' came to an end and the scheme's actuary signalled that the company should resume funding at 12.2 per cent of members' total salaries, plus employees' contributions of 5 to 7 per cent. The company's contribution now involved an overhead of around £100,000 a year, or, as Fred Charters was inclined to express it, almost £2 per tonne of feed sold.

The new group structure was under review; it was eventually agreed that the holding company and its subsidiaries were to be separately accounted and separately banked, with the aim that subsidiaries and associates would become self-financing and cash would be accumulated in the holding company. It was noted that the group was financially strong but lacking in liquidity, and the board sought to redress the balance of cash.

In this endeavour, they were almost immediately successful, perhaps fortuitously. Group borrowing in the year ending 31 July 1993 was £700,000 but in the following year to 31 July 1994 dropped to £200,000, while the consolidated cash flow statement showed a remarkable net cash inflow of £474,000. In 1994, the consolidated profit before tax rose steeply to in excess of £1/2 million. Scotts Feeds' tonnage was 78,769, showing a 30 per cent increase in compounded and blended ruminant feed.

Blended feeds were a fairly new concept for Scotts, having been introduced some three years earlier, and at least at the outset were not seen as an entirely welcome development. Many feed ingredients for ruminant diets in particular are by-products of items used in human nutrition. For example, when soya beans are crushed to yield the oil used in cooking and margarine, the by-product used in animal feeds is soya bean extraction meal. Such examples are extensive because almost every human food ingredient has a by-product that is economically useful in creating animal feeds. Instead of

Staff photograph 1994

re-grinding, mixing as ground meals and re-pelleting the resulting mixture, materials could be roughly and unscientifically mixed in the form in which they are received and sold as 'blends', having a price-competitive effect on the businesses of 'traditional' compounders like Scotts. From the beginning of the 1990s, Scotts began to produce its own blends to compete in this marketplace, which fortuitously they found to be an addition rather than a substitution of tonnage for ruminant feeds.

Capital investment continued with the installation of a new high-voltage supply to reduce electricity unit charges. Soon afterwards a third transformer was added to meet the increased demand for electricity and a new method was evolved for making blended feeds in the ingredients store, using the intake conveyors for this purpose. At a higher technical level, for the first time enzyme spray was used on broiler feeds, as an aid to the digestibility of the starch component of the diet.

The subsidiary companies also enjoyed a successful year. Erne Eggs began a large investment in new laying accommodation, surrounding land and a dwelling house; Ferne Foods returned a profit, although it was still looking looking anxiously for the 'big order' that could secure its future; and McCorkell enjoyed an 'extremely successful year'. The company purchased three 1,500-tonne ships, within the framework of a new subsidiary company, aiming to be a fresh profit centre, as well as carrying goods for the trading companies in the group.

But as the calendar year 1996 dawned, McCorkell was struck with a disaster that affected the whole group. The centre of the débâcle was the shipping activities. In the financial statements the directors' report reads:

> The performance of the associated company McCorkell Holdings Limited has been extremely disappointing and substantial losses have been incurred,

Mill yard in the 1990s, showing a lorry discharging grain.

mainly as a result of a poor trading year and the provision by the company for losses on the realisation of ships since the year end. Since the year end, the company [W & C Scott Ltd] has taken up its proportion of a rights issue by McCorkell Holdings to raise £500,000.

The rights issue was a requirement of McCorkell's bankers (Ulster Bank) as a condition of their continuing to fund McCorkell with loan facilities.

John McCorkell resigned as managing director in February 1996 and the

remaining directors decided that the company should return to its original aims. Anser Laboratories Ltd was sold to John McCorkell at net book value; McCorkell Scotland Ltd was sold to Nidera Handelscompagnie BV, an international trading company based in Rotterdam, at a small premium to net asset value; and the trading activities of McCorkell Shipping Ltd were run down in an orderly fashion and the three ships sold.

Kevin MacAllister, seconded by Coopers & Lybrand, was appointed as administrator and manager of McCorkell Holdings to assist the directors in re-focusing the business. Richard Scott and Winston Patterson were appointed as part-time executive directors, having previously been non-executive directors. John Keon, chief executive of Donegal Creameries PLC, provided invaluable support and advice, as the sole remaining non-executive director of McCorkell.

McCorkell's losses in 1995 were £592,000 but by 1996 determined if painful decisions reduced the loss to £108,000, and the directors estimated that an annual profit of £500,000 should be achievable within two years.

Despite McCorkell's trading woes, 1996 was a good year for the group, to which Scotts Feeds made a substantial contribution. In the chairman's statement 'a steady growth in tonnage' was noted, from 72,769 tonnes in 1993 to 81,143 in 1996. Pelleted feeds increased by 10,000 tonnes over the same period and Fred Charters, the sales director, stated that blended ruminant feeds were 'now profitable'. Erne Eggs returned a record profit owing to the very favourable market conditions for the sale of eggs, which encouraged it to consider further plans for expansion.

In 1996 Ferne Foods increased sales dramatically, following the purchase in 1995 by Moy Park of the Unipork 25 per cent holding. Moy Park brought in vital new business, subcontracting Ferne Foods to manufacture its food products, which were almost entirely based on poultry meat. Erne

Eggs continued to have a minority shareholding in Ferne Foods, all share-holdings having been diluted by the new ordinary capital introduced by Moy Park, when it took up its option to increase its shareholding to 50 per cent.

Alone, Glenpark Poultry was said to present 'an unhappy picture', with a hint of possible closure. This company had had a short and unsuccessful history. In the autumn of 1996, there were two fundamental problems. First, the market for broilers was ruthlessly competitive and margins were, at best, very modest. Despite much debate around the boardroom table, there appeared to be little that could be done about this. Secondly, it became quite apparent that no-one at board level was taking responsibility for Glenpark and that not enough attention to detail was being given on the farm. Unless this management issue was resolved, there would be no prospect of making Glenpark profitable, and the inevitable exposure to losses was clearly an unattractive and unsustainable proposition. The directors needed to find someone to buy the company or its assets, preferably an established customer of the mill so that they would have a reasonable expectation of retaining feed tonnage.

A solution to the management responsibility issue came from an unexpected quarter. This was in the form of Roy Howard, although he was in his last year before retirement. However, his volunteering of assistance was gratefully accepted. While Roy did not have any experience of managing livestock, what Glenpark needed was someone to give close support and supervision to the farm manager.

Given Roy's characteristic enthusiasm for the task in hand, and his by now legendary attention to detail, his approach worked wonders; the farm was tidied-up, and a number of management control systems were installed and carefully monitored. The all-important food conversion ratios improved, likewise, as night follows day, the financial performance. With Roy's imminent retirement, this could only be a short-term solution, but it gave the directors the time needed to secure a buyer for the assets of Glenpark Poultry. The subsequent sale to Silverhill achieved the objectives of eliminating risk while retaining the prospect of holding onto the tonnage.

On 31 July 1996 Richard Scott stepped down as executive chairman and managing director of Scotts Feeds Ltd, but remained non-executive chairman of W & C Scott Ltd. He took the opportunity to express his strong confidence in the management team at both W & C Scott and Scotts Feeds, which had been built up so successfully over the past decade and more. While his own daughter and sons had careers outside the company, he remarked that he was fortunate in 'having more nephews in the business than the Borgia Popes', an allusion to William McAusland, soon to be production director, Robert Scott, who became non-executive chairman of Scotts Feeds from 1 August 1996, and David Scott, later to become chairman of the holding company in August 1998. On Richard Scott's retirement as managing director of Scotts Feeds, Fred Charters was appointed in his place.

The chairman's report for 1997 showed a consolidated loss for the group of £423,000, the worst ever to have been recorded. The reason for this unhappy result was the group's share of the continuing losses from McCorkell. In part, this was due to a poor trading performance in difficult markets, the remainder being the cost of closing down the grain trading operations during the year. The board recorded 'considerable disappointment' but felt strongly that the decision to depart from grain trading removed an important element of risk from the group overall.

For some years past there had been no guarantee by the group to McCorkell's bankers and thus the risk was limited to the capital invested in McCorkell's shares and loan stocks, although that in itself was a substantial sum. McCorkell had retained the port services company in Derry, 'which (had) good prospects of profitability', trading under the style of Burke Shipping Services. W & C Scott had purchased its due proportion of the shares held by the departing managing director at £1.29 per £1 ordinary share, a price fixed by an independent valuer. The directors of McCorkell were currently seeking offers for the Belfast office and the Campsie (Londonderry) grain store.

BSE, mentioned above, had been a concern both to the farming community and to the feed compounding trade for several years. Scotts' sales tonnage across the border was about 30 per cent of total output. When the EU countries decided to ban British beef and cattle products from their markets in 1997, at short notice, the Republic of Ireland with equal speed was obliged to put out a ban on feed products containing MBM taken from UK cattle. Scotts had the task of convincing the authorities in the Republic that its feed did not contain any meat-and-bone meal(MBM), in which endeavour it succeeded after an exceptionally stressful 48 hours for William McAusland in particular, during which the prospect of losing the vital Eire sales tonnage seemed all too real. All animal by-products had by now been eliminated from all feeds and this restriction was later the subject of a European directive, the effect of which was somewhat to increase the cost of feed as other more acceptable, but also more expensive, sources of protein were introduced. Ironically, compounders in the Republic thereby gained a significant, if temporary, competitive advantage as for several months they were allowed to continue to include home-produced MBM in non-ruminant diets.

Despite such short-term emergencies and in contrast to the gloomy results of the group overall, Scotts Feeds returned a 'very creditable' profit of £216,000 for 1997, particularly in view of what Richard Scott described as 'a tumultuous year for our trade, principally on account of the consequences

of BSE ... very creditable and a tribute to the team led by Fred Charters and Robert Scott as managing director and chairman respectively.' There had been a 5.5 per cent fall in sales output to 76,414 tonnes, but better gross margins and lower overhead costs had been achieved.

Des Given viewing the transfer of supplies from ship to grain lorry at Londonderry Harbour, Campsie

It is interesting to glance at a series of figures that show the progression of the mill over the years 1951–1997. In 1951 sales amounted to £238,000; in 1997, virtually £13.5 million. Tonnage in 1951 was only 7,000 tons; by 1997, 46 years later, it had grown to 76,400 tonnes. Overheads, a mere £14,000 in 1951, had risen by 1997 to a formidable £1.8 million. The cost of raw materials rose from £28 per ton produced in 1951 to £148 per tonne in 1997; consequently the average cost rose from £34.60 per ton of processed feed in 1952 (no figures available for 1951) to £175 per tonne in 1997.

Over the years, trading profits had risen from £2,047 in 1951 to £273,000 in 1997, and profit per ton from £1.53 in 1951 to £3.56 in 1997. These, of course, are only snapshot figures and the results of each year rose and fell. The directors would be the first to draw attention to the inflation that had taken place over these years, but even so the numbers depict the consistent rise of a small mill to one of considerable importance and influence in a considerably enlarged trading area.

Erne Eggs also showed satisfactory profits in 1997, but the continued high value of sterling was a cause for concern. Nevertheless, a substantial investment in layer housing had been capitalised. Ferne Foods' performance was summed up as 'consolidation, further investment, modest profit'. Moy Park was now owned by OSI, a multinational food supply company and a worldwide supplier to (among others) McDonald's.

Glenpark passed to Silverhill Foods, which had purchased the land, buildings and equipment for the rearing of ducks on the site. This was a welcome development since Silverhill, a family business based in Emyvale, County Monaghan, had been a substantial and valued customer for many years. Its highly specialised business of rearing Pekin and Barbarie ducks for markets in Ireland and far afield was both progressive – the company was the winner of many awards for marketing innovation – and successful, as this substantial further investment demonstrated. Silverhill justifiably demanded, and obtained, from Scotts at all times a high level of product quality and service and has never allowed its custom to be taken for granted.

In his chairman's report, Richard Scott expressed his own opinion that the present site of the mill, where the company had been since 1850, was becoming less suitable as a site; this suggestion was subjected to close scrutiny and discussion over the next two years.

On Friday 14 March 1997 a dinner party was held for the combined mill family and family-round-the-mill, at the Royal Arms Hotel, Omagh, to mark the occasion of the retirement of Richard Scott as managing director and Roy Howard as production director.

In November 1998 the chairman's letter was prefaced by three short paragraphs on the Omagh bombing:

> On 15 August 1998, as the world knows, Omagh suffered an atrocity that is probably without parallel even in the bloodstained recent history of Ireland. I cannot add anything of meaning to the millions of words that have been spoken and written between then and now. Every one of our family and staff knew people among the dead and injured. A cousin of one of our employees was killed, as was one of a local family firm of steel erectors who have worked on many projects for us. We were indeed fortunate that none of our employees was among the casualties.
>
> The world has wondered at the resilience and strength of the community in Omagh and how it was drawn closer by the tragedy. The 'kindness of strangers', from all over the world, in response to the event, has been almost breathtaking.
>
> The sadness remains with every one of us and we await the healing that only time can bring to the bereaved and injured.

The group had returned to modest profitability in 1998; with a strong control on overheads, Scotts Feeds did well, although sales tonnage again fell; the sales turnover in money terms also fell because of a substantial drop in the price of feed ingredients. The sales performance was particularly cred-itable at a time when so many areas of grain and livestock production were so depressed. In local terms, producers of pigmeat, sheepmeat, beef, chick-en and eggs had been forced to accept prices for their produce lower than any experienced during the previous 20 years.

The prime cause for this sorry state of affairs was the strong pound ster-ling, the effect of which was twofold: exports of grain and livestock products were hampered and imports sucked in, both being harmful to prices at the farm gate. There was also a strong suspicion that the overweening power of the supermarkets, controlling the major proportion of all food purchases, had been detrimental to the normal market-clearing effect of low prices. The farmer's perception was that his prices had been driven down, in many cases to below production cost, while the benefit was not passed on to the ulti-mate consumer, the housewife.

McCorkell, now trading as Burke, was slowly making progress: the Belfast office had been sold and loan stock capital had been repaid to shareholders, following the close of the trading year. Unfortunately, all was not well with Erne Eggs. Poor market conditions and heavy borrowing costs had resulted in a loss before tax of £331,000, the worst in that company's history.

By now Ferne Foods was almost entirely a manufacturing supply compa-ny of poultrymeat products to Moy Park, but there was still 'no substantial success' in developing the market for egg products from eggs supplied by its sister company, Erne Eggs. Thus, Charles Crawford's vision of adding value to his commodity product had remained something of a mirage, despite the years of effort and innovation on the part of himself and Harry Steele. But this resilient team was far from downhearted, as the factory was capable of making good profit from the manufacture of bespoke products for Moy Park, or any other large outfit that happened to be in need of efficient food production facilities.

The group chairman's thoughts on moving the mill's production site had blossomed, in the sense that the directors were seeking outline planning per-mission for a change of use for the mill site and the Millbank house and gar-den. It was thought that the proceeds of a sale, with planning permission attached, might be sufficient to fund a newly built mill to modern standards of design and production on an out-of-town site.

Richard Scott and Roger Green retired as directors of W & C Scott with effect from 31 August and 31 October respectively. David Scott was nomi-nated to succeed Richard Scott as chairman of the holding company. Robert Scott took over Richard Scott's roles as chairman of McCorkell and as a director of Erne Eggs. Thus, for the first time, the sixth generation of the family was in the driving seat, having proved itself fully capable of the responsibility.

In his first chairman's report, following Richard Scott's retirement, David

Scott said of his uncle:

> I would like to pay tribute to his lengthy period with a business which he joined in 1958 and which he led as managing director from 1981 and executive chairman from 1982. Over that time, the group has grown and developed very substantially, for which Richard must take great credit.

A cartoonist's view of future events for the retiring Roy Howard, Shirley and Richard Scott, March 1997.

David Scott

15

David and Robert Scott
Dilemmas and Decisions

RICHARD SCOTT

DAVID SCOTT, THE YOUNGEST OF THE THREE BROTHERS, joined the accountancy firm of Peat Marwick Mitchell (since evolved into KPMG) when he left school at Wellington College, Berkshire. He must have been one of the last chartered accountants to qualify in one of the big firms without first taking a university degree. One of his early jobs, as a junior manager in the firm, was to manage supplies by ship to the island of St Helena, usually remembered as the remote island where Napoleon lived and died in his last exile. When preparatory work was started for the new Channel Four television channel, David was seconded to it. The channel started in business with Jeremy Isaacs as chief executive, Justin Dukes as managing director and David Scott, who decided to leave Peat Marwick Mitchell upon being offered a permanent position with Channel Four as financial controller. He has survived various changes of chairman (Edmund Dell, Richard Attenborough, Michael Bishop, the current chairman being Vanni Treves) and of chief executive (Jeremy Isaacs, Michael Grade and Michael Jackson). Justin Dukes left at the same time as Jeremy Isaacs in 1988, at which time David Scott was appointed finance director. When Michael Grade left in

1997, David Scott was appointed to the position of managing director.

David's elder brother, Robert, came to feed compounding by a very different route. On leaving Wellington, he spent six months as a pupil with a firm of chartered land agents, Fisher & Co., followed by six months' practical work on an arable/beef/sheep farm in Rutland, before undertaking a three-year course in Rural Estate Management at the Royal Agricultural College. On leaving Cirencester in 1973, he was appointed assistant agent for the Duke of Abercorn at Baronscourt Estate, Co. Tyrone. He went on to spend a year as a partner's assistant with Drivers Jonas, chartered surveyors in London, and then spent a year farming in Australia and New Zealand before seven years' farming at Carrickmore, Co. Tyrone. Meanwhile, in 1977 he returned to Baronscourt as agent and factor to Abercorn Estates. This is a demanding, varied and responsible position and it is a tribute both to himself and to the understanding of his employer that he has been able to give valuable time and energy to the business affairs of the Scott group of companies over the ensuing years.

Robert Scott

One of Richard Scott's reasons for retiring early was to give the next generation of Scotts the opportunity to build the new management team. In September 1996, Robert Scott and Fred Charters invited David Garrett to join Scotts Feeds as sales manager. David Garrett had formerly been with Dalgety Agriculture in Belfast, where he was field sales manager in the east of the province, managing a sales team selling a wide range of farm requirements, but principally feed and fertiliser. As he says, it was a move he has never regretted and perhaps was even wiser than he knew at the time. The latter half of the 1990s saw a considerable consolidation of the Northern Ireland feed trade: among others, Dalgety in Belfast closed down, the mill site was sold and the tonnage transferred to Thompsons. Jordan sold its mill site in Lisburn and transferred their tonnage to Bibby, and Wilsons sold its business to Andrews Milling.

Almost inevitably, as Fred Charters and Roy Howard had done 30 years previously, David Garrett brought a fresh approach, which from 1996 onwards led to increased sales to dairy and pig customers in particular. He and his team successfully targeted dairy buying groups in Tyrone and Fermanagh but also developed the tonnage sold through merchant outlets, both locally and south of the border in Monaghan and Cavan. Because of the Omagh mill's flexibility, David Garrett also developed sales of contract-milling tonnage to two substantial merchants situated north of Omagh. Likewise, the Progressive Lean Pig Group, who co-operate both to buy their contract-milled feed and to market their bacon pigs, started to buy from Scotts and have proved to be loyal customers over many years.

In 1996/97, with his retirement imminent, Roy Howard and his team carried out an extensive analysis of the mill, its machinery and organisation, particularly directed to satisfying a series of criteria: improving quality and traceability; satisfying customer requirements; and increasing throughput. Product quality and integrity were judged to be vital: for example, the control of salmonella by heat treatment; minimising cross-contamination in conveyors; reducing particle discharge to the atmosphere by changing from cyclones to dust separation units and reverse-jet filters; and improving the quality of steam by adding separators and traps to steamlines.

It was characteristic of Roy Howard's approach to life, and to his sense of responsibility as Scotts' production director in the final six months of his business career, that he should still be driving himself and William McAusland in the processes of studying, assessing and revising, investigating and planning future plant developments in minutest detail. He then concluded that if a new mill could be built somewhere on the edge of Omagh, his non-technical co-directors needed to understand and embrace all that was the latest and the best available in feed technology, for the business's future survival far into the twenty-first century. His colleagues, in 1996 as in the previous 30 years, appreciated his analysis and wondered how all the proposed changes were to be paid for.

Roy Howard's mantle, as the company's technical seer and gadfly, floated gently onto the able and by now experienced shoulders of William McAusland, on Roy's retirement in January 1997. There can be no doubt

The Scott family group at the 1997 retirement party for Roy Howard and Richard Scott at the Royal Arms Hotel, Omagh

STANDING: William McAusland, David Scott, Charles Scott, George Duncan, Robert Scott, Richard Scott, Sullivan Scott, Roger Green

SEATED: Moy Scott, Suzanne Scott, Patricia McAusland, Marie-Christine Scott, Shirley Scott

that the work which Roy had done during his last six months with the company was of enormous value as a point of reference to William. Looking yet further back, the terms of William's recruitment in May 1979 as Roy Howard's technical adviser had been instrumental in the younger man's development as a future production director.

In 1997, sales remained steady but margins were coming under pressure and the prospects for farming were not improving; in particular the beef sector was being hit hard by the loss of export markets as a consequence of BSE. Accordingly, the directors of Scotts Feeds took a number of decisions aimed at reducing costs. A company-owned retail outlet in Enniskillen had never made a profit, and the decision was taken to close it. Similarly, the office near the bag store was relocated to the mill office, leading to one redundancy, and overtime for production staff was phased out. The union representatives were quick to accept the need for these adjustments and the directors appreciated both their understanding and that of their own staff. A new generator was installed, enabling the company to make considerable savings on electricity costs.

Strategically, the time had come to address the major issue as to whether the mill should remain on the site, chosen almost 150 years previously, or relocate. The arguments in favour of relocation were, first and foremost, the likely costs of upgrading plant to comply with requirements for single-species production lines, environmental regulations, etc. While considerable investment over the years had resulted in significant reductions in noise, smell and dust emissions, the fact remained that the statutory requirements were becoming stricter. This trend was perceived to be irreversible; indeed, for the first time in its long history, under new legislation the company was obliged to apply to Omagh District Council for a licence to manufacture its products.

The second argument in favour of relocation was that it would create an opportunity to realise the redevelopment potential of the site upon which the mill was located. What was a rural location in 1850 had by the 1990s become enveloped by the expansion of the town. The board concluded that if they could build a new mill somewhere on the edge of Omagh this would be in the best long-term interests of both the town and the company.

The first approach was to examine the Omagh area plan, published by the planning service. This identified all sites that were currently zoned for industrial development, the most suitable one being on the industrial estate at Doogary, about two miles from the town centre and owned by the Industrial Development Board (IDB) for Northern Ireland. Robert Scott contacted the IDB, which told him that IDB sites were reserved for client companies of IDB or its sister body, the Local Enterprise Development Unit (LEDU). Scotts Feeds was a client of neither, and with fewer than 50 employees was too small to be of interest to the IDB.

The only other site zoned for industrial development that might have been of interest to the company was at the junction of the Drumquin and Derry roads, but there were technical reasons why they rejected this. Meetings with representatives of the planning service yielded the advice that no more land would be approved for industrial development until all areas already zoned had been developed. It transpired that the planners were not aware that IDB sites were available only to IDB/LEDU client companies, and that the IDB did not realise that the planners were reluctant to zone additional land until existing sites had been developed.

Robert Scott concludes:

> A solution to this 'Catch 22 situation' was found, with assistance from LEDU, for which we were most grateful, and we were eventually offered a site at Doogary. We felt that this experience identified a weakness in current government policy regarding industrial development in Northern Ireland, which appeared not to be as helpful to established manufacturing industries as it was to higher-risk inward investment projects. Perhaps the authorities felt that we feed millers, and others like us, were lacking in glamour. Maybe we were naïve in thinking that our proposed relocation of the mill away from the town centre would be warmly welcomed by both local and central government.

The IDB attached a number of restrictive conditions to its offer of a site at Doogary. However, Scotts was told that some grant aid might be forthcoming if the relocation was combined with some rationalisation within the feed-milling industry. In any case, the cost of the project, estimated to be of the order of £7m, was too much for Scotts to contemplate alone, particularly at a time of economic crisis within the agricultural sector and the growing pressure on margins. A partner was needed, and in due course a suitable one was identified and approached.

The purpose of Robert Scott's and Fred Charters' first meeting with David Graham, chief executive of Fane Valley Co-operative Society Limited, was to explore the possibility of sharing the cost of building a new mill. David Graham had a similar problem, namely that the Fane Valley mill, located at Newry, would require considerable capital expenditure, and was also on a site with redevelopment potential. While discussions made good progress, it became apparent that there were some fundamental differences, which proved impossible to resolve, and these discussions concluded amicably but without agreement.

In the meantime (February 1998), the board were being advised by James Burgess, a Holywood-based chartered surveyor who specialised in retail development. A planning application for a supermarket and petrol filling station was about to be submitted, when Mr Burgess was contacted by J. Sainsbury, which in early 1998 was expanding its business in Northern

Ireland and was actively considering building a superstore in Omagh. Sainsbury submitted an offer for the mill site, without planning permission. However, the deal collapsed when Sainsbury decided against investing in Omagh, and Scotts' planning application, which had previously been withheld at Sainsbury's request, was finally submitted at the end of July.

The financial results for the year to 31 July 1998 showed a profit of £234,483 on sales of 78,223 tonnes.

As previously mentioned, on 15 August 1998, Omagh was devastated by the bomb that took 31 lives and injured over 300 people. While none of the mill employees was caught up in this barbaric incident, everyone knew several people directly affected. The mill did not sustain any structural damage, although two windows at Millbank were shattered by the blast, and part of the car in which the bomb had been placed landed on mill property.

In October 1998, David Garrett was appointed sales director of Scotts Feeds Ltd in recognition of his success since joining the company two years previously. The following month, Charles Scott, the eldest of the three brothers, was appointed a director of W & C Scott, bringing a wealth of property-related experience to the board.

At the end of November 1998, Pattons' mill in Monaghan was badly damaged by fire. This created two opportunities for Scotts. Firstly, it was able to provide Pattons with a contract-milling service, which during the next eight months to 31 July 1999 increased the mill's output by over 8,600 tonnes. Secondly, it opened the door to negotiating a possible merger: like Scotts, Pattons was a well-established company, still owned by the descendants of the founder of the business. Scotts' proposal was that the two companies should jointly finance the cost of a new mill at Doogary, but Robert Patton appeared determined to rebuild in Monaghan. He eventually sold his business to Paul & Vincent, whose mill at Edgeworthstown in Co. Longford had recently been expanded and was hungry for additional tonnage.

Scotts' future strategy was now becoming clearer. Building a new mill without a partner was not an economically viable proposition, and there were no more likely partners, though from time to time there had been discussions with a number of possible partners that turned out to be fruitless. The directors therefore narrowed down their options to two courses of action: either to re-equip on the present site or to merge the tonnage into another established milling business. These strategies were worked-up concurrently, the former driven by the directors of Scotts Feeds and the latter by the directors of W & C Scott.

David and Robert – and indeed every director, manager and employee in the group – were delighted when the results to the year ending 31 July 1999 were announced. The operating pre-tax profit was a record £577,069 compared with £234,483 for the previous year. In his first chairman's statement, David Scott described it as 'a tremendous outcome [that is] due to a combination of favourable circumstances in a difficult market'. Sales were a record 93,581 tonnes, partly because of the fire at Pattons' mill, but also because of the success of the sales team under the leadership of David Garrett in gaining new business from other quarters. Another favourable factor for the mill was the shortage of good quality fodder in the 1998/9 winter.

Erne Eggs, in which Scotts continued to have a 50 per cent shareholding, returned a reasonably satisfactory year, with a level of profit providing some compensation for the previous year's large loss. Ferne Foods, in which Erne Eggs had a minority holding, traded profitably throughout the year. After a number of worrying years McCorkell/Burke, of which W & C Scott held 41.6 per cent, finally freed itself from debt and started to trade profitably, making a cash return to the group, the first for several years.

In his chairman's statement, David Scott wrote:

> We are fortunate that Fred Charters succeeded Richard Scott as managing director of Scotts Feeds in 1996, but now, sadly, he has also reached retirement age after 35 years of loyal and dedicated service to the company. His leadership in recent years has been quite outstanding and we shall all miss his wisdom and experience. I am however thankful that he has agreed to remain at the helm, albeit on a part-time basis, until July 2000. [The arrangement continues as this book goes to print, in 2002.]
>
> Whilst I succeeded Richard Scott as group chairman, Robert Scott succeeded Richard as chairman of Scotts Feeds. In addition Robert has taken Richard's roles as chairman of McCorkell and as a director of Erne Eggs. He has put substantial time and effort into these non-executive roles and I am most grateful for his dedication and clear thinking, and close attention on the spot to our activities in and around Omagh.
>
> Roger Green, who has been a non-executive director since 1973, resigned from the board on 31 October 1998. His contributions to our board debates and experience gained over many years were invaluable to our discussions.
>
> Charles Scott became a non-executive director on 1 November 1998. On Richard Scott's retirement he decided to sell his shareholding and the company purchased most of his shares on 5 April 1999. Roger Green also chose to sell his shares, which were purchased by existing shareholders ...
>
> The group is fortunate at present to hold a significant cash balance, which provides us with the resource to reinvest and sustain the business for the future ...

Earlier in his statement David Scott made the following cautious observation, despite the record year just completed:

> Looking further ahead there are some formidable challenges to overcome. Our competitors in Belfast are consolidating and getting stronger, and continuing severe limitations on farm profitability will result in greater

pressures on businesses supplying the agricultural industry. Margins are likely to be squeezed ...

Relocation from our present site in Mountjoy Road is becoming an increasingly unlikely option. Over the next few months the board will evaluate a substantial programme of capital expenditure on plant renewal, which will have to be incurred to enable us to continue manufacturing animal feeds for the foreseeable future.

Since Roy Howard's retirement, William McAusland had been producing a series of capital expenditure options, which assumed a number of different time scales. In conjunction with Jim Wilson of Turner Grain Ltd, he now started working-up an ambitious proposal on the assumption of another 15 years in Mountjoy Road. This included the construction of a new tower, over 90 feet in height, into which a pair of hammermills would be installed. Planning permission was required and an application was submitted in January 2000. Scotts had been fortunate in being able to recruit Trevor Pollock into a new position of mill engineer. Trevor had spent his entire working life with Pattons and, having spent much of the previous year exploring the options for a new mill in Monaghan, was fully conversant with the latest technology available to the feed-milling industry. He was thus a significant contributor to the discussions between William McAusland and Jim Wilson.

In the meantime, the W & C Scott directors were seeking the advice of Kevin MacAllister of PricewaterhouseCoopers in Belfast. Kevin had been seconded by his firm for six months in 1996 to McCorkell Holdings Ltd, where he was successful in turning the company around, eliminating considerable bank borrowings and bringing it back into profit. He had also advised Scotts in the previous discussions with Fane Valley regarding a possible joint venture. It was Kevin whom Fane Valley's professional advisers approached in November 1999, expressing an interest in acquiring Scotts Feeds Limited.

In response to this approach, an information memorandum was prepared and handed to Fane Valley in early December 1999. This provided a considerable amount of information to allow the prospective purchasers to evaluate the opportunity that was being offered them. It included a timetable suggesting the completion of a possible sale by 31 March 2000, as it would not be feasible to delay the decision regarding the proposal being worked-up by William much beyond then.

Fane Valley's response was positive. Additional information was requested and provided. Robert and Fred met David Graham again in February, and felt confident that Fane Valley's purchase of the company would result in minimal changes to the business. A further meeting took place in Kevin MacAllister's office on 21 March at which the sale price was agreed, subject to contract.

Thus, at the Spring 2000 meeting of the board of W & C Scott, the choice was either to commit to William's reinvestment proposal, or to sell to Fane Valley. At the Scotts Feeds board the previous day, the executive directors had agreed to give further consideration to, and approve if appropriate, the proposed expenditure, once planning permission for the tower had been received. The board of the holding company were comfortable with this, but also discussed at length the offer from Fane Valley. The conclusion was that both options were attractive, and the directors agreed that this 'twin-track' approach should continue, and that if the offer from Fane Valley could be converted into an agreement on acceptable terms, it should be accepted.

For the record, at April 2000 the board of W & C Scott Ltd, the holding company, was David Scott (chairman), Robert Scott (company secretary), Fred Charters (managing director), William McAusland and Charles Scott. The board of Scotts Feeds was Robert Scott (chairman), Fred Charters (managing director), David Scott, Siobhan Kelly (finance), Des Given (purchasing and transport), William McAusland (production), and David Garrett (sales).

Accordingly, W & C Scott appointed the Belfast firm of solicitors McKinty & Wright to advise on the terms of the proposed deal. Fane Valley was advised by L'Estrange & Brett. Detailed terms were agreed and signed on 18 April. Until then, by mutual consent, only the directors of W & C Scott knew of Fane Valley's interest, but it was now necessary for Siobhan Kelly to be brought into their confidence, as the 'due diligence' process began. Her contribution to this process proved quite outstanding, despite the fact that the timing of the deal was not at all convenient to Siobhan, who was due to depart for two months of maternity leave at the end of June.

While the negotiations in May were becoming increasingly detailed and time-consuming, particularly for Robert Scott on Scotts' side, the mill continued to trade profitably. The board of W & C Scott met again in the mill offices on 29 May to discuss the draft share purchase agreement, in considerable detail.

On the evening of Friday 2 June, a party was held at the Silverbirch Hotel to celebrate our 150 years a-milling, to which all employees and former employees and their spouses were invited. This was a memorable occasion, but tinged with sadness for some who knew that it could turn out to be the last gathering of the wider mill family before the Scott family handed over control of the business.

The negotiations were eventually completed on 23 June, and the moment of decision had finally arrived. The only document executed to date with Fane Valley was the Heads of Terms agreement, signed in April. This stated quite clearly that either party could walk away from the proposed deal at any time, without having to give any reasons for doing so.

Robert telephoned the four other W & C Scott directors, and also Richard

Scott, over the weekend of 24/25 June to discuss the detailed terms on which the negotiations had been concluded. The question addressed by all of them was 'Are we right in selling on these terms?' Since embarking on this exercise, the mill's trading position had become stronger. The management accounts to the end of March showed a profit in excess of £525,000 for the previous eight months; the company was clearly set for another record year-end result. The immediate outlook for Scotts looked bright. The directors also realised that W & C Scott would find it hard to maintain current earnings per share if Scotts Feeds left the group.

Against these positive factors, the company was in an industry going through a period of revolutionary change. To remain competitive, it would have no choice but to commit itself to a major capital investment project at a time of deepening economic crisis within the agricultural sector. The choice was either to get bigger or to merge with another feed-milling business. The board were satisfied that the proposed deal was the best available option for all concerned, whether employees or shareholders, and if they were to reject it, a similar opportunity would be unlikely to present itself for many years. After much debate, the five directors and Richard Scott agreed unanimously that the deal should proceed, and it was finally completed on 29 June, upon which 80 per cent of the shares changed hands for the agreed sum by way of financial consideration.

David and Robert Scott resigned from the board of Scotts Feeds Ltd on 29 June and 31 July respectively. Robert chaired the meeting on 14 July at which he thanked his colleagues on the Scotts Feeds board for their support over the previous four eventful years, and warmly welcomed three new non-executive directors, representing Fane Valley: David Graham, Shaun Milligan and Robin Irvine. David Graham was appointed chairman with effect from 1 August 2000.

The following press statement was released to the local and agricultural press:

> Fane Valley Co-operative Society Limited, one of Northern Ireland's largest agri-food companies, has confirmed the recent acquisition of a controlling interest in Scotts Feeds Limited, the animal feed milling business, located in Omagh.
>
> Scotts Feeds has a high reputation for its quality and service, and has been milling on its present site in Omagh since 1850, and is thus celebrating 150 years in business this year.
>
> Robert Scott, chairman of Scotts Feeds and a great-great-great-grandson of the founder of the business said, 'We are delighted to join with Fane Valley Co-operative Society Limited, a company with interests in many aspects of the agri-food business in Northern Ireland. Fane Valley has shown its commitment to the industry by the expansion of the organisation over recent years. We believe that this strategic move is in the best

interests of our respected customers and dedicated staff, and will secure the future of the business for the period ahead.'

David Graham, chief executive of Fane Valley, said, 'Following our recent investment through Linden Foods in Slaney Meats and Irish Country Meats we see our investment in Scotts Feeds Limited as a further expansion and consolidation of our core activities. Scotts Feeds has a reputation for supplying quality products and this will complement our range of supplies from the Fane Valley mill in Newry.'

Both mills were among the first to be passed under the UKASTA Feed Assurance Scheme, which is independently audited to ensure rigid standards throughout all stages of production.

Scotts Feeds team photo 2000

BACK ROW: Ian Managh, Seamus McGinn, Andy Robinson, Victor Donald, Stephen Robinson, Dessie Beattie, Richard Glass, Leo Flanagan

THIRD ROW: John Doherty, Raymond Martin, Willie Vaughan, Gerald McCollum, Raymond Flood, Richard Shortt, David Young, Gerald Beattie, Jimmy Dodds, Philip Dick

SECOND ROW: Alan Graham, Victor Anderson, Marcus Taggart, Rita Muldoon, Una McAnenly, Elaine Managh, Nicola Bailie, Sandra Cunningham, Audrey Millar, Beryl Doherty, Cahal Furey, Lindsay Dawson

FRONT ROW: David Dunn, Noel Anderson, Sam Bullock, Desmond Given, Fred Charters, Robert Scott, William McAusland, Siobhan Kelly, David Garrett, Herbie Bell, Noble Whittaker

Epilogue

TONY DEESON

IT IS POSSIBLE TO ARGUE THAT THIS BOOK should not have an epilogue. The word 'epilogue' is closely bound to 'conclusion', and there is every reason to believe that the story of the Scotts and their involvement in their long-running enterprise is very far from being at an end. But perhaps this is the place for a few reflections, given that what many would regard as the core of the business – the milling company – has passed into other hands.

Enterprises that have been in existence for 150 years are rare and the great majority of these have long ago lost sight of their origins. The names of the founders may still be preserved in their titles but their descendants have no connection with the businesses as they are today and have not been involved for many decades. Many have been bought and sold, sold and bought and sold again, and often the areas of business they are in today have little or no connection with those in which they were originally engaged.

The business that has been in the same family for 150 years is very rare indeed. Scotts, now in the hands of the sixth generation, is one of them. How has it achieved such longevity while so many have dropped by the wayside? As I was researching and writing this book I often asked myself that question.

There is probably no single answer, although a major factor in the success of the Scotts is the family's apparent absence of greed in all the generations that have succeeded the founder. All of them have been content to restrict their living from the business to the level that it could afford at any given time. The antithesis of this is well known. The founder of the business does well but one of the succeeding generations, children or grandchildren, decide that they can live it up on the proceeds of their father's or grandfather's success. Thus the Yorkshire saying, 'From clogs to clogs in three generations'.

Perhaps they have been saved from such temptation because it is hard to make a fortune a-milling in Northern Ireland; success does not come easily, and each year presented a new series of challenges and opportunities.

Then the Scotts seemed not to spawn any black sheep – or none that came into the business – and those that did come in had a fine sense of corporate discipline for the task in hand. In short, the leaders of the business were committed and have been so for six generations. Hand in hand with this commitment there was a great sense of balance, and a certain philosophical approach which is a fine guard against undue euphoria or unbalanced pessimism.

Another basic quality that is important in this story of success is 'integrity'. These days integrity is a much-defiled word, which often means a great deal less than it should, but the *Concise Oxford Dictionary* defines it as 'wholeness; soundness; uprightness; honesty'. The six generations of Scotts from William downwards have possessed these virtues and are well-known and respected for them by their customers, suppliers, business associates, managers and workers. Over the past 20 or so years, management expertise has grown considerably; appointments have been wise and the integrity of the Scotts has been rewarded by a high degree of loyalty and commitment.

A final guarantee of the business's stability has been particularly notable over the past 25 years, namely the willingness to invest for the future, rather than shovelling-up the fast buck. As the last chapter demonstrated, that commitment has remained in force and all the signs are that the new owners of the mill, Fane Valley, will continue with it, for the future strength of the milling business.

By writing this, I hope I do not cause the Scotts too much embarrassment. I know they are a modest family, but all that goes before is written in sincerity. For many years I have researched and written company histories. Sometimes, I am sorry to say, it is difficult to summon up much respect for the principles of business that the owners display on a day-to-day basis, and I am delighted that quite the reverse is true of the Scotts. One can only admire and respect them and their business.

As to the future activities of the family holding company, for the first time in its history during the past half-century at least, W & C Scott Ltd – having sold its milling business – now has 'money in the bank', while its directors search for an alternative investment strategy.

But the directors of the sixth generation continue to share a strong sense of responsible stewardship of family money, as well as a commitment to the county town of Tyrone and the province of Ulster. It is not difficult to imagine that these qualities may well result in investment decisions that will be of benefit both to the family shareholders and to the wider community, as the twenty-first century unfolds.

Appendix I

Jottings from a Miller's Notebook, 1916

LEWIS IRWIN SCOTT

R EPRODUCED BELOW IS AN EXTRACT from 'Jottings from a Miller's Notebook, 1916' by Lewis Irwin Scott, published in *A Hundred Years A-Milling*, which gives further insights into the mill of those times. The editor of that volume, when introducing the 'Jottings', wrote that they were produced to sum up for Lewis Scott the experience he had gained during 20 years in control of the mill and 'to leave a record which he hoped would be, and in fact has proved, of real and lasting value to his successors'.

It has often struck me that a few notes written by one who has for over 20 years been engaged in carrying on the business of an oatmeal miller and oat buyer and the various allied trades consequent on being connected with a country grain mill, would be of interest.

When I took over the mills we had here [in Omagh] a flour mill, a 2-sacks per hour rollermill plant, which was not operating, and another mill in which oatmeal and Indian meal were manufactured. Both mills were driven by breast water wheels, the oatmeal mill being driven during light water by a steam engine of the beam type. The first radical change I made was to replace the water wheels with McCormick Achilles* turbines, which I found more than doubled the power and were more effective in light water than the water wheels. The next step was to separate the oatmeal and Indian meal [maize meal] manufacture, as elevators working during the day on oat products and at night on Indian corn products were not satisfactory and the building was too much cramped to admit of both being carried on in the same place. I, therefore, dismantled the flour mill and fitted up to my own design an Indian corn plant and an oatflaking plant, the latter merely for flaking the groats [kernels of oats dried, shelled and polished] prepared in the other mill. For efficiency and economy I installed a No. 3 Greenhill disintegrator for grinding the Indian corn; giving a good sifting area for the meal with a Greenhill sieve and a large reel from the flour plant.

Up to this period and for some years later all Indian corn was stored in various stores in sacks; having been carried off the carts and piled up it was trucked into the feed hopper in the mill as required. This often involved

*Editor's note: as recorded elsewhere in the text, one of these turbines, installed in 1903, is still in operation and is producing elecricity for its owner, Hamilton Kee of Camowen Green, near Omagh.

several shiftings from store to store before reaching the hopper and led to a great loss while the grain was in the sacks, from vermin and damp walls and floors.

I later introduced [horse-drawn] lorries instead of two wheel carts and found a slightly heavier horse could draw 30 hundredweights against 20 hundredweights on the cart, and the horses lasted longer and were not troubled with sore backs and necks.

To get rid of the carrying off of Indian corn I erected a large store adjoining the Indian corn mill, where previously there had been a wooden hay shed and some old pig houses. I fitted a set of elevators to lift the corn from the lorries into this store or into the feed hopper in the mill ex shed or lorry as required. This gave me a large quantity of bulk storage adjacent to the mill and enabled the corn to be delivered ex lorries either into store or mill without any manual labour or loss. To give more room in the oatmeal mill I decided to do the flaking of oats in the new mill, so installed the steamer and rolls on the top loft, my own patent dryer on the second and the packing bench on the ground floor. This was a very great improvement on the cramped, badly lighted corner available previously. I found with this change I increased the capacity for grinding Indian corn very considerably.

I then turned my attention to improve the oatmeal mill. Up to this time to manufacture groats for flake, as there were only three stones for oatmeal (the others being for Indian meal) it was only possible to produce groats when the supply of oats was short, for when oats were coming in fast, the mill required to work on oatmeal to keep the oats cleared off; the milling of groats being too slow a process. In consequence we could only manufacture a limited quantity of groats and therefore of flake. Having removed the Indian meal plant from the oatmeal mill I had now the space, erecting in its stead a plant for preparing groats for flake, comprising three pairs of shelling stones on the stone loft, a pair of aspirators and brush machine on the second loft and a small duster on the top loft. This allowed me to have two shellers for the other ordinary cuts of oatmeal and a pair of stones for grinding very fine cuts; the other cuts we put over a cutter. We could now work continuously on oatmeal and groats at the same time. To facilitate the groat milling process I put in a grader on the top loft which would take off three different grades of oats; the first grade went over a cylinder to take out all foreign matter and was bagged off to go over the groat plant, the second grade went direct to the oatmeal mill to make the cut of meal required, the third grade was bagged off, this consisting of small oats was put aside till we had enough to run the mill for a couple of days; we then closed the grader up and milled these third grade oats by themselves. Anything the grader took off, which was too light for oatmeal, we used for making ground oats by running it through a stone for that purpose. It is at once clear that by working each grade of oats by itself the shelling stones can be set so as to work at greatest economy, as compared with ungraded oats with which if you are to catch the hull of the smaller grain you must pulverise the larger. I quite recognised that the installation of upright emery shellers would have been a further economy as against the old style of grey stones, but the speed of the heavy shafting was slow and I could not see how to do it without a great deal of expense which I did not care to undertake.

The result of all this was I had a roomy mill for Indian meal and for flaking the groats, and room to carry on the manufacture of oatmeal and groats in a continuous manner. The turbines gave ample power in average water enabling me to scrap the old steam engine, while for auxiliary power in summer, when the rush on Indian meal is on, I put in an 80hp National gas engine running under producer gas. [This replaced a 45hp engine which ran on town gas, after the family's interest in the Omagh Gas Company had been bought by the Urban Council.] Thus I had practically doubled the output with less cost for power and less man handling for the increased output.

Naturally, the old storage arrangements were inadequate, so opposite the oatmeal mill I erected a large iron store with three feet of stones and concrete in the floor, this turned out a good storage arrangement as the floor was bone dry. A similar store with elevators as previously mentioned, I put up beside the corn mill. I gutted out all the old low lofts, put in sound floors, let in light and air and in time had stores which protected our grain with little risk from damp and vermin. In 1903, when the kiln was burnt down, I re-erected it with a wire floor, put the fires in the centre instead of the end as before and arched it with brick to obviate the risk of a similar outbreak again. The kiln dried much better and more economically thereafter. I turned the old dark, damp stables and loft into a one-storey store and built new stables with air and light and a loft above. I tried to improve the old office, but this was not a success. I put up a decent upstairs office where there had been a couple of low lofts, but the lower office still left much to be desired.

When the turbines were installed I widened the water-course and strengthened the bank solidly where it had been weak and light. These are the main changes which I made during a period of 19 years [1897–1916], and all brought in a good return. A few years ago I installed electric light, driven direct off the turbines, this paid for itself in two years, the turbines and stores having paid for themselves many times over.

Taking into consideration our inland situation and that we have to pay high transport rates, I acted on this assumption: if we make just ordinary oatmeal, no better and no worse than our neighbours, we are, as against those on a port, just to the bad in price competition by the amount that we are penalised by our high freights. We had been doing a good deal of Scotch trade, which it struck me the port mills were in a better position to do. I found our meal had a good reliable reputation so I set out to grade it up and *make it the best*, and by merit command a price and see if it could not be distributed in our own Island. Having gone carefully into the question of patent drying kilns, I saw at once they were a great economy in every way as compared with the flat heads, but on working it out I came to the conclusion they reduced the cost of production by say 7s 6d [37^1/2p] per ton and the quality, 12s 6d [62^1/2p] – so I held on to the old style kiln and have not so far had any occasion to change my opinion.

For a couple of years before 1897 I had been working on *improvements* in methods of flaking oats and in early 1897 had patented a dryer which we are still using, this with various improvements we made in steaming, rolling, etc. had brought our flake into public notice. At this time the flaking of grain was a new thing and only being tried out. When the new wing of the mill for groat finishing was completed we were in a position to turn out a well cleaned article in sufficient quantity for our trade, and in the other mill we were in a position to turn out the flake well rolled and dried, and I am proud to say that for many years our flake has maintained a foremost place for flavour yield and quality, and I believe it to be the most economical meal to use in the market.

I aimed at turning out a decent, well cleaned pinhead at a moderate price, without any fancy touches such as rounding the ends by stones, etc. The meal has held a leading position in most of the public institutions as clean, well flavoured meal giving a good yield. We also managed to improve the quality of the other cuts – although since we graded off the largest oats for groats our coarse meal has not such a round look to it as it used to have. But any time we like to turn the first grade of oats in we can, of course, make the coarse cut more impressive. Owing to our using steel for cutting none of our cuts have any pulverised or dusty meal present; the fine cut is granular and has a definite cut, though fine.

It is obvious the better the oats coming to the mill the better the result; this district, till you come to Newtownstewart, is not one to produce a first class sample; the local tawny oats have gone back greatly in the last 20 years. And as a profitable oat its course, it seems to me, is run. A number of farmers here can produce a very decent sample of white oat, but none of them seem to clean their oats as well as they do in the Strabane or Derry districts. Since, owing to scarcity of labour, threshers have become so common we get more well cleaned oats than formerly, but if not properly set a thresher can turn out a very poor sample.

I found that by using a scourer we got rid of a lot of the light stuff that should never have been in the oats and that getting this away gave the machinery a better chance to do its work. I often think when the green oats are hoisted if they went over scourers before drying, it would save using coal etc. to dry this refuse that is taken out. Perhaps, however, the undried oats might not scour as well as they do when dried, so with this in mind I continued the old but more convenient methods of scouring them as they came on to the mill.

Now, as the buying of oats and the handling of them are two of the main points of our business, I shall put down just what I have been in the habit of doing. The ability to judge oats will only come with practice and keen observation; the judgement of market values is quite another matter but goes hand in hand with the judgement of the quality of the grain.

Tillage of oats in our district is declining and each year we have to go further afield in order to get the quantity of oats we require; owing to an extraordinary good yield in season 1915/16 we were able to draw the bulk of our supplies from more or less the immediate neighbourhood. When it takes 14 to 15 stones of oats to make 112 pounds of high dried oatmeal it is at once manifest that the question of freight on oats is a serious item if a large percentage of our supply is drawn from districts with a high freight on the raw oats. It is, therefore, obvious that it is advisable to secure all oats possible offered locally and at near points and only go to the further off districts for supplies essential to keep the mill going at full work; secondly, it is obvious that the nearer the port the oats are bought, the higher the price of the oats and as the oat growing districts, as far as we are concerned, all lie nearer the ports than Omagh, the result is we must pay higher prices for them as compared with local oats and the freight in addition. It would be, of course, very much better for us if we could get all our oats in what we may call the Omagh district, but of recent years, with the decrease in acreage under oats and the increase in consumption for stock feeding by the farmers themselves, we are gradually getting less and less from our home area ...

Both Fintona and Dromore markets which 15 to 20 years ago gave us good supplies are now almost worthless to us and the quality of the grain offered there is poor; the tawny oats, which are grown largely there, seem to have deteriorated very much. To both these markets we send our traveller who, with the assistance of an experienced buyer from Fintona, B. McCaffrey (who has brought oats for us for many years) buys and takes delivery of the oats. In the case of Dromore the market is held in the yard of a local merchant, who takes the oats for us into store in bulk, fills them into our sacks and delivers them to the railway store for a small charge.

The Fintona market is held beside the railway station where the oats are emptied in bulk into railway waggons for transit to Omagh.

Omagh market is only a shadow of what it was when I started to attend it – one cause is the growth of the steam threshing habit, owing to the scarcity of labour on the farms. In Omagh the oats are delivered from the scales into our oat bins, making this the best and handiest market I know, and if there is an experienced man examining the oats as he takes delivery of them one has a good check on the qualities of the various lots; which is essential as of course cases of heading the tops of bags or of variation of quality are not unknown and must be firmly checked.

Newtownstewart is a good oat growing district, but the market is inconvenient. We bring a man from Omagh to take delivery of the oats in waggon in bulk, as they are carted from the market. He, being half a mile away from the buyer, if anything turns up in the way of unfair delivery cannot leave the waggon to report, so the check is more apparent than real. A very large percentage of the oats from this district come up direct from the farmers by rail, being sold by sample on the market day ...

Oats of medium quality are now [October 1916] worth 15d to 15^{1}/2d

[7¹/2p] per stone, which is double the usual prices ruling here. Indian meal is worth £13 15s 0d [£13.75] per ton; oatmeal £20 per ton; oat dust £6 per ton; flour 56s 0d [£2.80] per sack; and oat hulls about 45s 0d [£2.25] per ton. These war prices compare with the average prices of pre-war years as follows: oats average here 7³/4d to 8¹/2d [3¹/2p] per 14 pounds; Indian meal £6 to £6 10s 0d [£6.50] per ton; oatmeal £10 to £11 per ton; oat dust which I sold 20 years ago with difficulty at 25s 0d [£1.25] per ton, has gradually, even before the war, been appreciating in price. For two or three seasons before 1914 we were making £3 10s 0d [£3.50] to £4 per ton for it while oat hulls varied, sometimes we could make only 7s 6d [37¹/2p] per ton on rail and always considered £1 per ton on rail a good price.

Hessian bags which I bought 20 years ago at 2d to 3d [1¹/2p] and indeed made a purchase a year or so before the war at 3d after they had been a long time in the vicinity of 4d to 4¹/2d [2p] are now quoted 8d [3¹/2p] each and a short time ago were 8¹/2d.

Indian meal has been for short periods higher than at present and up to £14 10s 0d [£14.50]. Indian corn which had been up to almost £14 at present is worth about £12 10s 0d [£12.50] at the port, so the farmer argues that his oats are worth more as a feed than £10 to £10 10 0d [£10.50] per ton ...

The price of malting coal is more than double the pre-war figure and is now 50s 0d [£2.50] at the port. Wages have advanced 50 per cent and the quality of labour has declined, the present staff during this wartime have not the keenness on their jobs that we used to see. With our best away serving we find the temporaries, not having been trained as mill hands, rather careless of the valuable food in their care. When we get our men back after the war we shall have specialists and craftsmen where we now have to do our best with many untrained hands. The old men spent a lifetime at one work, were properly trained and had to be careful; they knew there would be trouble if fault was found and another inside job might not be come by easily. Today, alas, the standard is by no means so high.

Here let me say, if you have cool oats in the dry loft, hot oats from the kilns should not be turned on to the mill, as the hot oats chip under the shelling stones and cause waste, whereas if they have cooled there is an element of toughness in the groat. But the man or boy on the dry loft does not mind. From his point of view it is easier to set the conveyor so as to discharge the hot oats as they come from the kiln into the feed hole for the mill; why should he shovel up the cold oats from behind over the feed hole and let the hot oats drop back to be in their turn shovelled forward when cold? This, he says, is no game for him, it means work whereas why not lie quietly on the oats and watch the hot oats dropping just where he wants them. Personally, I have found a cuff on the ear or a lift gently and properly applied behind better than remonstrance and the knowledge that when I come round I put my hands into the oats over the feedhole to see whether they are warm or not.

I am, thank God, the captain of a happy ship. She wouldn't be happy long if our head miller, Sam Cockburn, my mate, put the ship off course through the slackness of a lubberly cabin boy ...

With regard to flake in wooden cases we are at a great disadvantage as we must import the cases from Newry (which is our cheapest point) if we wish to supply 'free cases', i.e. the case included in our price per hundredweight. Before the war some of our competitors added on 1s 0d (5p) for the case, but our flake being higher dried is more bulky and our cases had to be larger and cost us wholesale from 1s 5^{1}/2d to 1s 7d each [a little less or a little more than 7^{1}/2p] so we could not do likewise. So we supply ourselves; our mill carpenter makes heavy cases or we buy them from Belfast. These are returnable; we charge them at 4s 0d [20p] each and credit same when they come back. It is, of course, a bother to the buyer to see that cases are returned, while it costs us on an average 6d [2^{1}/2p] in return freight on every case. And were it not for the fact that our flake is the *very* best on the market buyers would not touch it in cases. Another plan we have adopted as a war-time measure is to enclose the empty paper bags when required in the hundredweight bags, charging 1s 0d [5p] per hundredweight extra. It used to be 6d [2^{1}/2p] but paper has gone up owing to the war. This, of course, lends itself to abuse, as some unscrupulous dealers may use our paper bags to get rid of a flake inferior to ours but for some years before the war it was almost impossible to sell the ordinary trader anything but cases packed, as it saved them trouble. All the leading firms catered for this and some of them packed their whole output in cases. Owing to our inland situation and the lack of a box-making firm near us we are at a great disadvantage. Since the war began we have been able practically to eliminate the packed case trade. Owing to the price of wood and scarcity of labour we have refused to pack in under hundredweights and if customers like to pay 1s 0d [5p] extra per hundredweight they can have paper bags enclosed. The other firms must have adopted the same attitude, as at present we sell all our output in hundredweights.

A couple of years ago it really was absurd. It looked as if grocers would shortly expect to get our flake packed in sizes for a breakfast; they talked of 1lb packages being supplied by some firms and they were gradually coming to the point at which they expected it to be left in their shops and opened for them just when they wanted it. It has always struck me as being an absurd trade for a miller to pack a staple food like oatmeal up in fancy packages, and doing everything possible to raise the price on the consumer just because the retailer is slack and wants to be saved trouble. Imagine Tate's people sending out sugar packed in pounds in cases to save the grocer's apprentices trouble of weighing it.

[Nevertheless, while this may have seemed absurd in 1916 it eventually came to pass, for both sugar and oats and many other commodities. Scotts packed in 1lb, 1^{1}/2lb and 2lb cartons as well as the standard 3^{1}/2lb. The 7lb size in paper bags, once so popular, vanished before that. The Editor of *A Hundred Years A-Milling* adds: 'The modern miller, packing under his own brand in hygienic conditions and buying his packing materials in bulk quantities can obviously supply a better packed product more economically than was provided in the old days of bulk supply.']

... Of course there is more flake used now than there used to be. Our present agent in Belfast, although not well up in oatmeal trade, has been drilled by me to confine himself to the larger buyers, bakers etc. and to sell them on a close cut basis rather than cater for the smaller buyer who must have packages. In the end there is more nett money in the wholesale trade for us and we leave the re-packers and the mills who live by advertising to cater for the package trade.

The season 1915–16 was a good Irish wheat season and we sold a big lot of wheatmeal from Irish wheat in Belfast but we had a good deal of trouble from it going fusty with those who kept it too long, and I do not think it is worth following up. The native wheat has a bit too much moisture to keep long on hand and although we warned our buyers we would not be responsible for its keeping qualities that made no difference. If it went musty we had to take it back. Foreign wheat had been so dear we could sell Irish wheat and wholemeal about 50s 0d [£2.50] to 60s 0d [£3] per ton cheaper – hence the attraction to the buyer.

One very important thing to watch with all agents is that if the oatmarket is advancing or looking that way you must advance your price at once to them. Do not hesitate an instant. You must remember these city traders are being called upon by numerous sellers' representatives at the rate of several per day and if there is the least sign of an advance they are on to it. If your agent comes along and is cheap they at once clip him for a line to be booked for forward delivery. Consequently, if this is not closely watched, some morning you have a pile of orders booking all your buyers their requirements for perhaps six months, which may mean a loss on all the meal involved – this because you did not advance the agent at the first sign of a rise by 10s 0d [50p] or so per ton. Remember, this forward booking is a curse. Customers will take all they book if the market advances right along. But if it comes back they buy it in cheaper from someone else and tell your man they are not ready for more yet or have no demand etc., etc. Consequently you lose their current trade and are left with meal on your hands at the end of the season, but which you thought you had sold. I have reduced the forward selling amongst the smaller traders as much as possible. Some years ago in oatmeal, during the winter months, I would sell for delivery to 31st March only. I found this worked well and have kept to it. The oat purchasing system is over in March. You see what stock you have, have a fair idea of what it cost you to make, and a fair idea whether it is wise to make further sales for forward delivery up till end of the selling season. Remember, your agent will sell all he can. It means more commission to him and if he gets a chance of running loose, through not being advised of an advance, he will book a whole district all he can place, as he is far keener on pleasing the buyer than his employer ...

We had an agent in Dublin for many years but when our old agent died after trying several, all of whom were unsatisfactory, I gave it up. However, we have some good buyers, so that if our price meets competition we are always sure of good lines. We can as a rule place a good deal there free of intermediate expenses and this is much more satisfactory than employing agents.

In Newry I tried a local agent for that district last season. This was not a success as the commission knocked us out of the big buyers' orders, so I gave him up and in future we will work direct. Consequently we are now selling all direct to customers in Ireland, except Belfast. Our present man there is a better sort than most. He does not exceed his instructions and keeps after the large wholesale buyers. I have no fault to find with him ... What affects us most is that the present day trader in the main will buy the cheapest article and they expect to get our oatmeal and flake at the same price as inferior dried and milled meal; we do not see it this way. There are others, to whom I must give credit, who will give us a preference in price and therefore we allow our meal to sell itself. Derry and along the GNR to Ballyshannon [where Scotts had an agent and stores for many years] we work with our office traveller and always have a regular stream of orders. In fact, taking one season with another it is wonderful how our meal sells itself. Not the least important part of our oatmeal trade is the large number of buyers who order direct, on whom neither agent or traveller of ours calls, but who from year to year get our meal. We never spend anything on advertising, going on the principle of turning out a good article and trusting to holding its connection by its own merit ...

The worse oats are usually in the hands of the smaller farmer, who makes a great outcry that he is being 'robbed'; that his oats are the 'very best', 'never saw rain', etc. etc. They never admit you could get anything better and often the worse the oats the more the seller lauds the quality. It is very seldom he will admit any inferiority, so you buy the rough with the smooth. Some lots you have to give too much for, some are good value. You get to know the sellers and their ways. Often I know I am giving too much, but we like to buy all we can get our hands on and look to our average, not to one or two individual lots. A considerable number are carted into the mill yard and, of course, these are well seen by the buyer as they are emptied.

When buying one must remember the farmers are watching your every bid and comparing one man's price with another's. They soon find out if the buyer is a reliable judge or not. As a rule a farmer tells his neighbour that he got ^{1}/2d [1/6p] per stone or so more than he did get. That leads to red hot trouble as the man told the price will never believe it was not right; they all compare notes. I have made it a practice to give them the precise value I thought their oats worth, but some sellers are hard and force you up over the value, while others leave it very much in your own hands. These we treat fairly, even generously. As I say, you must not stick for ^{1}/2d or so on a good lot; the thing is to take the best quality oats even if too dear and average on the worse ones. After all millers are the only people to take the soft oats – they are no use to feeders ...

Omagh market is handy. Oats are bought by ticket, weighed on the GNR weighbridge and then barrowed into our bins and emptied in bulk; the seller than comes to our office with the buying ticket and the weighbridge ticket. We deduct the weight of cloth, which is marked on the weight ticket by our man taking delivery in the bins, who initials the docket – *this initial is our receipt for receiving the oats.* No ticket must be paid for unless the weight ticket bears the receiver's initials. The weight deducted for cloth in all our markets is a rule of thumb method. Three corn sacks to the stone*, or six meal bags to the stone, four corn sacks 1^1/2 stones, five or six sacks, 2 stones etc. etc. The man taking delivery should have experience as on a wet day sacks may require more to be taken off. If the seller disputes the weight he pays for the weighing of them and gets a ticket and is paid on that weight. Care needs to be taken to supervise these weights deducted, as under deduction in a large market would mean a serious leakage. The farmers will always dispute the weight but I have found on weighing out several markets bought on wet days that we were short of oats we had paid for.

In the case of oats delivered in the mill yard, if in our bags or light bags, we put a similar bag against them when weighing. If in farmers' sacks we deduct as in the market; we weigh them to the nearest half stone. Oats from the steam thresher coming in large lots weighed there have to be closely watched. Whether it is the hurry and rush or that the weights are inaccurate, or the bridge not even, they often do not weigh out; of course the owner of the thresher, being paid for his work by the stone, has an interest in assessing as much weight as possible. As a rule they guess the total by weighing a few bags. Mostly now they take our own weights, but many farmers who load their oats on to us by rail direct from the thresher weigh them in say 16st, 15st or 14st and we often find they do not weigh out. This means trouble as the farmer says he saw them weighed good weight and they must be right. As a rule there is no intention to give short weight, but once the farmer thinks he has put the weight in the bags nothing will convince him to the contrary.

A very large percentage of oats from Newtownstewart district are bought by sample and come up from the thresher. Sometimes they may vary considerably from the sample; in some seasons different parts of the same field vary considerably and as a rule you see the best in the sample. With our regular suppliers we give a certain amount of latitude as we understand what the season leads us to expect, but if there is anything wide it must be dropped on and the price cut accordingly, as you must always show that oats are well examined on delivery. In some seasons, especially when the grub has been working in oats there will be a serious variation and no oats are worse for the miller than greenish grub eaten oats. There is no meal in them. Of course you meet a lot of reliable farmers who will tell you exactly what their oats are like, but on the other hand the man is common who says, 'There could be no difference, all grew in the same field. You saw the

*Editor's note: older readers may recall the former 'imperial' weights and measures – 16 ounces to the pound, 14 pounds comprised a stone, 8 stones made up a hundredweight, of which there were 20 to the ton.

sample and bid me the price and it is outrageous to say there was any difference; there could not be, and my neighbours know it.' It is extraordinary the amount of oats that *'never saw rain'.*

Newtownstewart market is rather inconvenient. To begin with the yard accommodation is poor and on a wet cold day it is a miserable job hanging about for 1/1^1/2 hours buying oats. The yard is so small it takes a long time to get the oats off the carts and weighed; only two or three carts can be in the yard at the same time. When oats are bought they are carted by farmers either on their own or hired carts to the station where we empty them in bulk into the waggons, or if our sacks we don't empty them but load them as they come ... I have always bought the Newtownstewart oats myself and brought down a man who stuffs up any holes in the waggon with old bagging he brings along for the purpose. He then signs the farmers' tickets as receipt for the oats. There is no regular weighman in this market, so it is well anytime one is about to keep an eye on the weighing. We have often found ourselves well short of what we paid for when we reweighed the market on taking delivery in our mill. Of course, Newtownstewart is a good oat district. There are usually a number of large lots in the market as compared with Omagh and the quality is better. A lot of steam threshed oats are sold to me by sample when I am down on Mondays. Farmers with large lots do not take them into the market but come to me with their samples and I buy them. One gets to know the district and the men one can rely for quality etc. All this takes time and experience. You get to know your men and act accordingly, but as the freight is a low one compared to bringing oats from Strabane, Castlefin or Derry it is better to secure all one can in what we consider our home district.

The former grain market, Newtownstewart, in 1950

To sum up. In a market go round and secure the *best oats first, they are always the cheapest in the end.* The poorer oats whether they are soft in condition, or perhaps poorly cleaned, the miller will have to take in any case, as feeders and buyers for storing will not take them. It is, therefore, time enough to fight over this price when you have swept up all the good lots – for the man with the good oats is usually the larger farmer who has a fair idea of their value and does not waste your time. Often the man with rough ill-cleaned grain is the small farmer who is asking 'too much' and is not ready to sell until the market is almost over.

By bidding at once what I believe to be the value I have got farmers to see that there is not much good in wasting my time. When I bid the value, if it is not taken I pass on. It takes all sorts to make a world and you find a great difference in men when selling oats, but you get to know them. Above all don't get riled or lose temper when sellers are unreasonable, as they are only trying to get all they can. It is when they are acting crookedly that one must light on them. Some of them fill the bags about three-quarters full and specially clean again some oats with which they top out the bags. An extra run through the fan makes a great difference in oats. In any case like this cut the man sharply in price. I had a case yesterday [4 January 1916] at Newtownstewart. The market was small and I sent all oats bought to our Newtownstewart mill. Our man, Alex, examines all oats very carefully and he sent for me about a six bag lot, three of which were fair and three bad. He saw I had given 20d [8^1/2p] for them which he knew indicated at present prices they were fair, good oats and I would not have given the price for the three bags he condemned. I told the man I would pay 18d [8p] or he could remove them. He took the money!

There is a difficulty when emptying at the waggon; you can't open and examine all the seller's lot when it is lying on the cart and if you see a bad bag he may say, if you say you will cut the price: 'No, give me my oats!'. Any cases I have had, if your man is stiff the other farmers will usually back us up if the oats do not empty right and you can reduce the price. But I must say in Newtownstewart I have little of this sort of thing. I know the men likely to do it and do not bid them the extreme value of their oats, as I know I will not get as good as I am shown. If you see a man careful about which bag he opens get him to open them all and see if they are alike.

On the other hand with some sellers you will find your oats better than the quality you have seen. In Omagh market on Saturday I bought 10 bags and when I saw them emptied they were better than I had thought so I gave the farmer ^{1}/2d per stone more. When you are constantly buying you know by the price what quality to expect ...

Appendix II

Oatmeal Recipes and Commentary

SINCE THERE IS SO MUCH about oatmeal in the early chapters of this book the reader may be interested in a little more. *A Hundred Years A-Milling* came about as a result of an idea put forward by Florence Irwin, who also supplied a number of recipes for cooking Scotts Excelsior Flaked Oatmeal. She was accordingly given a chapter in the book, 'Oatmeal Cookery', for which she wrote this introduction:

> It would be difficult to get far enough into the past to give a full history of oats and oatmeal in Ireland. This we do know, that oats were grown as far back as history and legend extend. Our Irish Museum shows reaping hooks from the bronze age, so that the use of oatmeal is bound up with the earliest traditions of our country. Joyce tells us in his *Social History of Ancient Ireland* that the staple food of a great mass of the people was porridge, or stirabout, made of oat or wheatmeal. In those ancient days it was eaten with honey, butter or milk.
>
> So well was it known in foreign countries that stirabout was the characteristic food of Ireland and its people that St Jerome, wishing to abuse his enemy Celestius who was a very corpulent man, refers to him as 'a great fool of a fellow swelled out with Irish stirabout'. Gruel is mentioned as the fasting fare of the children, and was laid down in the Brehon Laws as the necessary article of diet for children in fosterage, 'the quantity and condiment being regulated according to the rank of the parents'. Rich stirabout was made 'on' milk, if a special delicacy was required the milk was taken from a sheep. 'White' stirabout, as it was called, was designated by an ancient writer as the 'treasure that is smoothest and sweetest of all food.' Poorer people made their stirabout 'on' water or buttermilk and ate it with sour milk or butter.

Here is one of Florence Irwin's traditional Irish recipes, for Brotchan Roy. She specified Scotts Excelsior Ulster Oats among the ingredients, but as they are no longer in production the recipe has been updated to include Whites Speedicook Porridge Flake Oats. Florence Irwin introduced the recipe as follows:

Oatmeal continued to be the staple food of the Irish peasant until the introduction of potatoes as a common article of diet. Poor people for their dinner added to their porridge the tender tops of nettles, leeks, cabbages, and wild garlic; this was called 'Brotchan', which we may translate as 'broth'. Brotchan Roy (Brochan Ree) was a potage with leeks added, for instance.

INGREDIENTS
1 quart stock, vegetable stock or milk and water in equal parts, 2oz Whites Speedicook Porridge Flake Oats, $1/2$ pint chopped leeks, bunch herbs, 1 tablespoon chopped parsley, $1^1/2$oz fat, pinch powdered mace, $1/2$ teaspoon sugar, pepper and salt.

METHOD
Cut the leeks as for broth, wash and drain in a colander. In a saucepan make the fat very hot, sprinkle in the flaked meal and cook till a nice brown – don't burn it as the soup would be made bitter. Now add the leeks and cook slowly without frying till they absorb the fat. Stir in the liquid, add the herbs and seasonings – which must be adequate. Simmer about 30–45 minutes. Remove the herbs, add the parsley, cook a second or two. Serve at once. Bunch of herbs: includes a bay leaf, sprigs of thyme and parsley tied together with a thread.

We have taken further 'modern recipes', more or less at random, from the several dozen that are included in *A Hundred Years A-Milling*, many of which were devised by Florence Irwin for the housewife of the 1940s and 1950s, rather than for the hungry years of a previous century. Some of them may find favour with the cooks of the twenty-first century, provided that they are content to use imperial rather than today's metric measures.

GINGERBREAD

INGREDIENTS

8oz flour	4oz sultana raisins
4oz Speedicook Oatflakes	3oz syrup
2oz treacle	4oz lard or margarine
2oz sugar	$1/2$ teasp. ground allspice
1 teasp. baking soda	saltspoonful salt
2 teasp. ground ginger	2 eggs
buttermilk or sweetmilk to taste	

METHOD
Sieve the dry ingredients, add the oatmeal and mix well. In a saucepan melt the fat, treacle and syrup. Cool slightly. Beat the eggs. Add all to the flour, etc., to make a batter. Only beat until all is well mixed. Bake in one tin or in patty tins.

For gingerbread start in a moderate oven about 350 degrees F and at the last, if insufficiently brown, increase the heat a little. Store in an airtight tin. This cake will keep a week or two.

FLAKE OATMEAL SHORTBREAD
SADIE'S RECIPE

INGREDIENTS

4oz Speedicook Oatflakes
2oz sugar
pinch baking soda

4oz margarine
2^1/2oz flour
good pinch salt

METHOD

All the mixing is done in a saucepan. Into a saucepan put the margarine and sugar and stir till the sugar is melted. Stir in the flour, oatmeal, salt and soda and stir till all is moist. Have a tin about 11 by 7 inches greased. Spread this mixture on to it. Bake in a very moderate oven for 30 minutes till nicely brown. Remove from the oven and after it has cooled a little, while still in the tin, cut into fingers. When set, cool on a tray and keep in a tightly closed tin.

NOTE. I think this is one of the best recipes I know.

FLAKE OATMEAL BISCUITS
MRS ROWLAND HILL'S RECIPE

INGREDIENTS

1 breakfastcupful flour
4oz sugar
pinch salt
1^1/2 tablesp. golden syrup

^{1}/2 breakfastcupful Speedicook Oatflakes
4oz margarine
^{1}/2 teasp. baking soda

METHOD

Mix the dry ingredients. Melt syrup and margarine in a saucepan, add to the oatmeal and flour and mix well. Roll into small balls in the hand. Place on a greased baking sheet allowing room for spreading. Lightly press each out with the thumb and, if available, put half a blanched almond or a piece of lemon peel on each. Bake 40–45 minutes in a slow oven at 250–300 degrees F. They should be ready when brown. Allow to cool on the sheet till set then cool off on a wire-tray. When cold store in an airtight tin.

NOTE. If they are allowed to get soft, crisp up in a moderate oven.

THIN OAT CAKES

INGREDIENTS

1 teacupful fine oatmeal	1 teasp. lard or bacon fat
pinch salt	pinch baking soda
hot water	oatmeal for the bakeboard

METHOD

Have a hot griddle in readiness. Mix the dry ingredients, rub in the fat. Mix to a spongy mass with the hot water. The mistake most people make at this period is to try and make it of a consistency stiff enough to roll out. It is best to make it moister than this, then to thickly scatter oatmeal on the board, and to turn it out and roll all in the dry oatmeal, as it is still too moist to attempt to knead it. Now start pressing on it with the backs of the fingers, pressing so as to keep it round in shape, keeping it dry on top with oatmeal and having enough dry meal underneath to prevent its sticking to the board. Continue pressing out like this until it is thin enough and of a consistency to roll. You have by now about doubled the original teacupful of meal. While rolling, be sure there is enough meal to prevent its sticking, also rub meal on top occasionally to keep it white. Roll till it is almost knife thin. Before cutting finally, lightly rub some dry meal on the surface to whiten it, then brush off any that is loose. Cut in neat squares.

TO BAKE

Place on a hot griddle and bake over a moderate heat till it dries and curls. When cooked underneath, place on a baking-sheet and toast off in the oven, to cook the top, be careful not to burn it. Cool and store in tightly closed tin.

NOTE. In old farm-houses an iron semi-circular rail a few inches off the ground was placed round the peat fire, and the oat cake, as it was taken off the griddle, was propped against this and the top was toasted, this is the ideal way to finish it off.

Oat cakes can be cooked in the oven – the heat should be between 250 and 300 degrees F.

THE OSLO BREAKFAST

In between the wars [Florence Irwin wrote] there was an experiment made in Norway with the feeding of school children. One section of the children was given daily, over a space of time, the 'Oslo Breakfast' while their opposite numbers had ordinary breakfast.

There was a marked superiority, when testing time came, both in the physique and growth of the children fed on the new plan, which incorporated the idea that each meal should have some raw fruits, salad or uncooked vegetable – that it should be well masticated.

The basis of this breakfast is flake oatmeal – to it is added any fruit in season, sweetened with condensed milk. In the summer, raspberries, strawberries, gooseberries, blackberries and currants. In the winter, grated apples – with only core and blossom removed, bananas, oranges, etc.

Here is a sample breakfast for two persons:

INGREDIENTS

1 tablesp. Speedicook Oat Flakes	1 tablesp. sweet condensed milk
$1^1/2$ apples	or runny honey
little lemon juice	1 tablesp. crushed nuts

METHOD

Wash the apples. Soak the meal in 3 tablespoons cold water overnight, until no water is visible. Add to it the honey or condensed milk and lemon juice. Mix well. Using a grater with a square mesh, grate the unpeeled apple over the oats, rejecting only the core, sprinkle with the nuts. Serve at once.

NOTE. The nuts are a valuable source of fat – but to make the dish look nice, failing nuts, sprinkle over it some shredded wheat, broken up, or other breakfast cereal. With this should be served wholemeal bread and butter.

If using raspberries or blackberries, crush most of them and mix with the condensed milk or honey and oatmeal and decorate the top with the whole berries remaining. If using plums, remove the stones.

SPINACH AND OATMEAL SOUP

INGREDIENTS

2oz Speedicook Oatflakes, 1oz margarine or dripping, $1/2$lb spinach, 1 tablespoonful chopped chives, 1 quart meat or vegetable stock – or 1 pint milk, 1 pint potato boilings (peeled potatoes), 1 tablespoonful cream, pinch powdered mace, pepper and salt.

METHOD. Wash the spinach and lift from the water to the saucepan – stems and all, put on the lid, and cook till tender turning the spinach over as it comes to the boil. Pass it through a coarse sieve. Into a saucepan put the liquid from the spinach and stock or milk and stock. Add the meal and seasonings and boil 20 minutes. Stir in the cream and serve with fried croutons.

NOTES

To save sieving, the spinach may be finely chopped after cooking and added to the cooked oatmeal. A coarser but no less appetising soup is the result.

A chopped onion may be cooked with the oatmeal if liked.

A good lettuce may be cooked and chopped with the spinach.

Glossary

This glossary of words that were in fairly common use in Tyrone half a century ago was originally published in *A Hundred Years A-Milling* with acknowledgements to W.F. Marshall, R.L. Marshall, Wilson Guy (Mat Mulcaghey) and W.K. Ellis. In some cases the English equivalents are only approximate and in some cases the various shades of meaning require illustrations. Much of the Tyrone dialect survives from Elizabethan days in Scotland or England.

It is sad to record that W.F. Marshall himself, in his later years, produced a dictionary of Ulster country expressions and had it in its final draft, ready for publication, when it was mischievously attacked by a spaniel puppy. The dog survived the experience, but the manuscript was destroyed and Marshall had tidied his house by disposing of his earlier drafts and working papers. He no longer had the energy to take up the task of re-creation, and thus this work of scholarship was lost forever.

Maddin Scott was heard to ascribe this loss, with a wry smile, to 'W.F.'s besetting sin of tidiness'.

* denotes words of Irish origin.

allow: guess, prescribe (medical)
apt: likely
ashy-pet: chilly mortal, fond of the fire
ax: ask

back-en: latter end (e.g. of harvest time)
bad scranta: bad luck to
bap: small round loaf with depression in the centre
barrin: excepting or unless
be to: have to
be to be: inevitable
birl: bowl, spin round
black-avised: having a very dark complexion
boast: hollow
bottle straw (or battle): tie with a short straw rope in a bundle
boxty: bread made from raw potatoes, grated, mixed with flour and baked on a griddle or pan
brattle: peal (of thunder)
brock: kitchen refuse
*broghan: porridge
*broo: extreme edge of a river bank or 'shugh'; usually of a stream
bruckle: brittle
*bruitin: bruised or mashed potatoes
buckled: married

caddy (or cuddy): boy
*canavaun: bog cotton
*carry: weir
champ: peeled potatoes, freshly boiled and drained, then pounded with a beetle
chimley: chimney

*clabber: soft mud
clamp: about 80 turf sods built up to
    dry. Second stage in winning the turf
clockin: sitting, broody (of a hen)
*coilidhe or kaley: informal visit
*crack: talk
crook: hook over fire holding kettle etc.
cub: boy
cutty: girl

dayligone: dusk (daylight going)
dilsey: light female character
*donsey: in delicate health
dish-a-bells: dishabille, in ordinary
    working clothes
dishorder: disease in poultry
*droit: small one of a litter
dulse: an edible sea-weed
dunder (dundher): throbbing noise
dunt: to knock against

fernenst: in front of, opposite
footery: insignificant
foot-stick: plank bridge
forbye: as well as
fums: inferior peats, 'white turf'

gallases: braces
gapes: choking disease in poultry
gazebo: an overlarge rather useless
    structure of any kind
ginneld: tickled
*glam: grab
goamey: fool
gowl: yell
gowpin: full of two hands cupped
*grieshig: hot ashes

halliday: hallowday (i.e. holiday or holy
    day); 1 November
hirple: walk lame
hooley: informal party
howl futt ta: keep up with
howlin: beholden

jeuk: to dodge or bypass

join: begin

kernapshious: irritable, cross
keep straight: look after, watch interests
*kesh: short bridge over a sheugh or
    drain

lap: small circular wrapped pile of hay
    about a foot high. The third stage in
    haymaking
lashins: abundance
lee (as): as lief, as soon
let on: pretend
loanen: lane
lock: a small quantity
lossingers: lozenges
lump of a caddy: boy about 12

make a poor mouth: plead poverty
meal-a-crushy: oatmeal and sometimes
    onions fried in bacon gravy
melder: a quantity of meal ground at
    one time for a farmer; a vague
    expression meaning the meal
    produced by one milling of corn
mines: reminds
more: although

nabbed: caught hold of
nadger: small boy or man
near-be-gone: miserly
nirls: chicken pox
no odds: makes no difference

oat scoudher: scorched oaten bread
oul-fashioned: knowing
out of the need of: require badly
oxther-cogged: supported under the
    arm

pack: intimate
*piggin: small milking pail
pirta-flither: potato bread or cake
praties or pritties: potatoes
put on the long finger: to procrastinate
    or delay

redd: tidied, cleared up (verb also)

*rickle: about 30 turf sods built up loosely to dry on the 'spreading ground'. First stage in 'winning the turf'

runt: small one of the litter

scarred: scared

*scraws: thin grassy sods

scunner: disgust

scutcher: worker in a scutch mill (flax)

*shanaghin: chatting together

shap: shop

sheugh or shugh: hollow or ditch

sib: related

skilagolee: thin gruel

shillen: light seeds

slap: gap in a hedge

*sloke: an edible seaweed

smittle: infectious

*smur: drizzle of rain

sned: to lop off

*sonsy: respectable/virile/healthy looking or fat

*sowins: dish made from meal seeds

sooley-mandhir: often used for a heavy blow

souple: supple, quick-footed

spricklybags: sticklebacks

stirabout: porridge

stirk: heifer or yearling ox

stoor: dust

street: yard or space outside house door

strippings: the last milk drawn from a cow

sweel: to wrap round

swither: hesitate

smitagiv: conscientious, effective

tare: drinking bout

the more: although

thinking long: longing for, homesick

thole: to bear or endure

thran: perverse

thrinnel: to roll or trundle

troth: in truth

throughother: careless; muddled

tidey: in calf

turmits: turnips

turf: peat

vale: veal

wakely: weakly

wake: watch by corpse before burial

way: with

wean: a child (wee one)

whammel: cover with something, e.g. an upturned box, creel or basket, and so keep confined

whangs: leather boot laces

wheesht: be silent

wheen: few

whitterit: stoat (white throat)

yokked: yoked

Index

Note: Page references followed by 'p' represent a photograph and 'n' a footnote.